CHISEL POINTS in the GROUND

CHISEL POINTS in the GROUND

The Memoir of Carl Drost

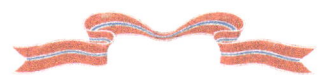

PUBLISHING + DESIGN

Chisel Points in the Ground. Copyright © 2024 by Carl Drost. All rights reserved. No part of this book may be used or reproduced in any manner whatsoever without written permission from the author, except in the case of brief quotations embodied in critical articles or reviews.

Paperback ISBN: 979-8-9854746-6-4
Hardcover ISBN: 979-8-9854746-7-1
Library of Congress Control Number: 2023922626

Published in the United States of America by the Write Place, Inc. For more information, please contact:

the Write Place, Inc.
809 W. 8th Street, Suite 2
Pella, Iowa 50219
www.thewriteplace.biz

Cover and interior design by Michelle Stam, the Write Place, Inc.
Cover tractor and field image provided as courtesy of John Deere.
Back cover flag image by the Write Place, Inc.
Author portrait by Nicholas Drost.

All Scripture quotations, unless otherwise indicated, are taken from the Holy Bible, New International Version®, NIV®. Copyright © 1973, 1978, 1984, 2011 by Biblica, Inc.™ Used by permission of Zondervan. All rights reserved worldwide. www.zondervan.com. The "NIV" and "New International Version" are trademarks registered in the United States Patent and Trademark Office by Biblica, Inc.™

I have tried to recreate events, locales, and conversations from my memories of them. In order to maintain their anonymity, in some instances I have changed the names of individuals and places. I may have changed some identifying characteristics and details, such as physical properties, occupations, and places of residence. Writing for this memoir was completed in March 2022; editing was completed in July 2024.

View other Write Place titles at thewriteplace.biz.

Dedication

Dedicated to Martha, my helpmate for years.

1. All the activities in this book from the moment I met Martha onward would not have been possible without her as the better two-thirds. Martha stayed home and raised our children, and she took care of me in spite of what society said about the role of a woman. She supported me even when it had to be difficult.

2. Martha has been the spiritual leader of our home. She has shown me how to serve and worship the Lord our God. She is the one who encouraged us to tithe and test God, proving that tithing works.

3. Martha allowed me to be the head of the house, and she loved me in spite of some of the things I did or said. Martha was always supportive of my decisions.

4. Martha trusted me with all the financial decisions I made, though she has taken care of the checkbook since May 1970 (when I got drafted). Early in our business career, Martha would tell me when she was out of money, and my part was to put money in the account to pay the bills. Martha trusted my decisions enough that she signed banknotes (loans) without reading them or asking a question. It was "sign by my finger," and she did (and some of the notes were for over a million dollars). Martha always believed in the providence of God—that when we put our trust in God and honor Him, things will always work out.

Thank you, Martha!

Table of Contents

Introduction ix

Chapter 1:	My Boyhood	1
Chapter 2:	My Junior and Senior High Years	15
Chapter 3:	My College Years at William Penn	23
Chapter 4:	Finding My Wife	31
Chapter 5:	Our Engagement	37
Chapter 6:	Our Wedding and Honeymoon	43
Chapter 7:	Our Marriage	47
Chapter 8:	Our First Year and a Half of Marriage	53
Chapter 9:	My First Job With a Time Clock	61
Chapter 10:	My Time in Basic Training	65
Chapter 11:	Advanced Individual Training at Fort Bliss	69
Chapter 12:	Shake and Bake School	75
Chapter 13:	My Trip to Vietnam	87
Chapter 14:	R&R Trip	99
Chapter 15:	My Last Month in Vietnam	105
Chapter 16:	My Flight Home From Nam	113
Chapter 17:	Working at Van Gorp Implement	117
Chapter 18:	Martha and Carl's Family	123
Chapter 19:	My Spiritual Journey	127
Chapter 20:	Ford Tractor	135
Chapter 21:	Public Service: Mahaska Rural Water	153
Chapter 22:	Public Service: My First Twenty Years on the School Board	157

Chapter 23:	Live Drive-Through Nativity	165
Chapter 24:	A Huge Transition	169
Chapter 25:	Thirty Years as a John Deere Dealer	175
Chapter 26:	The Sell-Out	191
Chapter 27:	Being NICE to Others	199
Chapter 28:	Coffee Time With Friends	207
Chapter 29:	Real Estate and a New House	217
Chapter 30:	One of Three: Joe Crookham	223
Chapter 31:	MCRF and the Multipurpose Recreation Trail	235
Chapter 32:	George Daily Auditorium	247
Chapter 33:	Trail Trams	251
Chapter 34:	Lacey Recreation Complex	255
Chapter 35:	William Penn Activity Center	263
Chapter 36:	Public Service: Second School Board Term	267
Chapter 37:	Dozer Day and Picnic Area	275
Chapter 38:	Brent Voss: A Lifetime of Memories	279
Chapter 39:	Our Travels	285
Chapter 40:	A Reward in Our Travels	297
Chapter 41:	Our First Fifty Years	303
Chapter 42:	Troubled Young People	325
Chapter 43:	Sunday Scholars	331
Chapter 44:	Momma Margaret White	339
Chapter 45:	Public Service: Bringing the Vietnam Wall to Oskaloosa	345

Conclusion 349

Introduction

As you will read in this memoir, there are a bunch of happenings in life that could defeat a person. But as I found out, God honors those who are faithful to Him. My wife, Martha, and I realized God was looking out for us when we were not smart enough to recognize that His wonderful hand of protection was upon us. God also gave me wisdom beyond my age.

Chisel Points in the Ground was written to explain that some lessons have an effect on our lives and make us who we are. I want you to learn from some of the lessons that were taught to me by the people I've known, as well as some lessons I've learned from the "classroom of hard knocks." After seventy-six years, memory fades, so don't be too critical of small errors.

I have lived my life and operated our business to honor and be a witness as a Christian to MY God and treat my family, our customers, our employees, and other people we came in contact with how I would want to be treated.

Chapter 1

My Boyhood

I came into this world at about 6:00 a.m. on July 17, 1947, which was also my parents' fourth wedding anniversary. My parents, Richard and Ada Drost, named me Carl. One might ask why? Before my mother died, I asked her how they came up with Carl. It was really quite easy—I was supposed to be a girl (the doctor had told them), and my name was supposed to be Cora. When I came out with a few extra parts, somebody decided to change the "O" to an "A" and the "A" at the end of Cora to an "L." Thus, they started with the same name, but it came out CARL. We lived on a farm northwest of Oskaloosa. The West Center Country School was just a mile east of us. I had a brother, Jim, who was three years older than me.

I was told that when I was two-and-a-half years old, I was helping my mother do the chores one day. She was breaking ear corn in a crank-powered machine, and I stuck my finger in a couple of exposed gears. Part of the finger was off. We were by the windmill, at the bottom of the hill from the house where the feedlot was. I think I can remember going up the hill with my mother on the run and me under her arm. I'm sure they took me to the doctor, but I have had a short finger with the nail covering the end ever since.

My brother, Dick, was born on June 10, 1950. Tom came along three years later, on July 1, 1953. Annie was a straggler on July 15, 1958. I think Mom was sure wanting a little girl.

The farm was a typical farm for those years, consisting of 112 acres, with some milk cows, chickens, and pigs. I only remember a threshing machine coming to our farm once. I just sat in the pickup and watched. I do remember farming in those days was hard work. Dad would go out early to work, and it would be late before he got done. I know that when Dad and Uncle Short rented some land, Mom and us boys would do the afternoon chores and the milking.

There was one thing that never changed: Every time we sat down to eat, we prayed at the beginning of the meal and Mom read the Bible. We prayed again when the meal was done. It was standard procedure that we went to church on Sunday morning. It was the First Christian Reformed Church. After the first years at the old church on Third Avenue East, the church moved to a new building on North Eleventh Street in 1958. It never entered my mind to tell my dad that I didn't want to go to church on Sunday morning. I don't even want to think about the consequences of that statement. (That's a real problem with homes today.) We went to catechism during the school year, then Sunday school in the summer after church.

For a long time, we would carry the milk to the house and pour it into an International Harvester cream separator. We would have cream in a can, then carry the skim milk back to the barn and feed the pigs. (Sometimes the milk was made into slop.)

I think every young boy will try to test his limits, and I had to test my dad! We always milked in the barn. Dad and Jim would each carry two buckets of milk to the porch, while I would only have to carry one bucket. One afternoon, it was my day to test my limits. I didn't carry my milk; I left it in the barn and went to the porch. My dad dumped one bucket of milk, two buckets of milk, three buckets of milk, four buckets of milk, and then . . .

"Where is the last bucket of milk?"

Not being very smart, I reported, "It is still in the barn, and I am not bringing it."

I really don't know what happened, but I do remember going through the screen door (which normally opened in), and out I

Chisel Points in the Ground

Left to right: Tom, my dad (Richard), me, my grandpa (James), Jim, and Dick.

went and got the bucket of milk. When I brought it to the porch, all I said was, "Here is the last bucket!" I don't think my dad said a word, but he didn't need to. That is the day I learned the meaning of *respect*, and I have never forgotten it. It seemed that quick justice was the way we were raised. I think I might have been seven years old.

The West Center Country School was a little over a mile east of our home on the T intersection by the railroad. In 1952, the school had kindergarten plus eight grades, all with one teacher. The only teacher I had in the country school was Mrs. Myrtle Maxted. I went there for seven years. Kindergarten was only one half-day all year. I started kindergarten with Lyle Stanley, Don Foster, and Daryl VandeGeest. We stayed together the whole time, but Daryl had to repeat third grade. We always were friends.

The country school was only one room, with a coal furnace with a stoker and two one-hole outhouses outside. We always had a Christmas program, and the whole neighborhood would come. I remember that one Christmas I had a speaking part, and I think it closed with: "I'm too young to preach, and I'm too young to teach, but I can make a little speech. Merry Christmas to all, and to all a good night."

In about fifth grade, the big kids were playing softball in the school yard at noon, and I was catching. Every time I missed a ball, an older girl named Gloria would grab the ball and throw it farther away. I told her a few times, "Quit that!" Then, "Quit that or you will be sorry." Well, she didn't quit throwing the ball, and I'd had it, so I grabbed this little older girl, took her over to the woven wire fence around the schoolyard, and put her hair in the fence. She really screamed when the hair tightened on her head. The teacher had to cut her out with scissors, and then the teacher came for me. Mrs. Maxted never got to me though, as the "big boys" (eighth graders) put me on their shoulders *and kept me from her*. And my dad didn't find out!

Chisel Points in the Ground

We always had fun at the country school, and the recesses and noontimes would sometimes get extended. When the snow was on the ground, the sledding hill was on Ray Franklin's farm, which was not too far away. One day, it was decided that we would go west to the next hill on the Else/Drost farm. I know we were having a very good time, and we didn't hear the bell to end noontime, so we just kept sledding. Eventually, we went back to school and found out we were not to go to that hill again for noontime.

Our parents always worked hard and gave all of us an example of hard work. I know our dad was a farmer and got up early every day to take care of the hogs, dairy cows, and chickens. He and Uncle Short farmed a few hundred acres together, but the big tractors were Uncle Short's WD Allis-Chalmers and Dad's B John Deere. Later, Dad bought an 8N Ford. I remember helping to load a ten-foot tandem disc on a hayrack to go from farm to farm. We'd also load a four-section harrow on a wagon to move it, and that was hard work. They planted corn with a two-row horse planter, which had the hitch timber cut off short to hook to the tractor. They picked all the corn with a two-row ear corn picker; then the ear corn would have to be ground for cattle feed or shelled to be sold. It was all hard work, and Dad would teach us all he could about farming.

The boys were always raised to help those in need. My dad set the example to his family that if some neighbor was sick and needed help, you'd go help them. If the neighbor was snowed in, you'd go scoop them out. If the neighbor or friend was in the hospital, you'd go visit them and see if you could help. (And just so you know, if you took any money for it, your hand would probably be broken before you could get it to your pocket.) I remember one winter in the late fifties when it had snowed a lot and nothing was moving, my dad and I hooked the old B John Deere to a little wagon, and we headed to town to get the groceries, coal, and supplies we needed.

The roads were all drifted closed. We were driving over the top of the snow and drifts. (The county would come several days later with a bulldozer to clear the road.) We had chains on the tractor, and we stopped on the way to town at a lot of places to see what our neighbors needed: Emmett and Carrie Franklin, Short and Mary Drost, Ray Franklin and Mabel, Virgil and Margaret Else, and the Hunts. Then to town we went. We went to the grocery store, then to Blackford's to get coal. Then we stopped at all those places on the way home to deliver the stuff. I really don't know why we didn't freeze to death, but I guess the heat houser on the tractor and the five-buckle boots made it bearable. The example was set for a lifetime of service, and how thankful I am for the example set by my dad.

My dad, and later us boys, would always trap fur-bearing animals (muskrats, raccoons, mink) in Painter Creek, which ran through our farm. I remember one year Carrie Franklin told my dad that if he caught a nice raccoon, she would like him to take the pelt and give her the carcass because she would like to cook it. He did catch a nice one, and he took it to Carrie as he was asked. The Drost family was invited to the Franklin home for supper one night, and we went (of course). When we went to the table to eat, Carrie uncovered the roast, and there was Mr. Raccoon on the table. Yes, we ate raccoon for dinner, but we also told Dad never to give people anything like that again.

We boys all trapped the creek for many years, and one year we decided that since we had a bathroom and a furnace in the house, it would be nice to have a full-size pool table. We decided to take all the fur money and buy a pool table for the basement. We took our furs at the end of the season to Bob Bernstein (the only fur buyer in town). It was an experience to hear Bob tell us all about how good or bad the furs were.

I think that was the year I got a surprise while checking the traps one morning before school. I went to one of the traps in a field tile outlet, and there was the largest mink anybody could imagine . . . alive! I took my club and clubbed him. Thinking he was dead, I put him in the gunny sack with the muskrats and headed home. In the middle of the cow pasture, I had to see that mink. I opened the bag, and out jumped Mr. Mink! He was making a getaway. I had to run him down, and he didn't survive that stop.

We bought the pool table and got it all set up. We were all so excited. We had worn the numbers off several sets of balls on the tabletop version. We racked the balls, and I lined up for the break. I hit the cue ball with the cue, and the ball split right down the middle—one half on each side of the rack of balls. Our dad loaded us boys up in the car and headed to Fuller and Ellis Pool Hall (a beer joint). We all walked in (which was probably illegal), and we told them we needed a cue ball. We got an ivory-colored ball, and I think it is still on the table in the basement of the house our folks built in 1968. (Though that table is probably the third pool table.) We spent many evenings in the basement. Then Mom would expect one of us to dry the dishes instead of playing, so the next year we bought Mom a portable dishwasher so we could play pool.

Our farm was always a good place for delivery people, veterinarians, and LP gas and fuel deliverymen to stop. Our mom always had cookies or coffee for them, and the boys were always ready to help them. The market hogs always got slopped or fed a mixture of buttermilk, ground oats, and skim milk from the cream separator. After a day, that mixture was bucketed out into a trough for the hogs to eat. In the summer, you had to get past a million flies around the slop barrel. Wake's always brought the feed to us, and one delivery driver named Doyle always liked to come to our farm. He taught us boys how to play mumblety-peg with a jackknife that had two blades, both hinged at the same end of the knife. The knife had to land in the dirt standing up. I don't think he got fired for taking too long on a delivery.

Wake's was the only business where my parents bought feed, and it was for a good reason: the loyalty of both the Drost and the Wake families. The Drost kids (the boys and later Annie) always went to Wake's to pay the bill for the feed. As far back as I can remember, there was Jim, who was the old man; Phil, his son; and Vivian Krizer, who was the bookkeeper. I know the Wakes knew they would get paid and that all the feed was coming from them. When the big chicken house was built, my parents went and talked to the Wakes about the feed, and they told my folks to build the chicken house because they knew they would get paid. The Drost family was always early for appointments or meetings like that. The family motto was: "If you are not fifteen minutes early, you are late!"

One early summer day, a big Lincoln car pulled onto the farmyard where we lived. It was Homer Doggett. He lived just northwest of our home, and he needed a couple of boys to help him build some fence and do odd jobs. He had heard there were some boys at the Drost farm. He wondered if he could hire some help, and our dad thought that would be okay. We went to Homer's farm at the arranged time, and Jim and I helped Homer build fencing for his hogs (which he let run loose in the pastures). He had a lot of hogs for the time, and I think we built four pastures for the hogs to run in. We also had to build a pasture for his sheep. He had an International 400 narrow-front tractor and an H Farmall to use, and we soon learned how to operate them. Homer and Ruth were great people to work for, as they always had coffee time and water in the field when we worked. Ruth always fixed us a good dinner (and she wanted us to eat). I was working there one summer on my birthday, and Ruth made me a big dinner with warm apple dumplings and ice cream. It was quite the treat!

We also helped Homer castrate the male pigs, and we had to watch out that Homer didn't cut our hands with the scalpel he used. Homer was an "old man" when we started (probably fifty years old). We also helped vaccinate the pigs with the veterinarian, Dr. Nuckols. He was fast, and we would usually vaccinate six hundred or more pigs in a couple of hours. We would also help Homer dock lambs' tails and castrate the male lambs. We got paid after every job. Jim got 75 cents an hour because he was the big kid, and I got 50 cents an hour because I was the little kid.

Homer and Ruth usually went to Florida for a couple of weeks in the winter. One winter, Ruth asked me if I would water her African violets while she was gone, and I told her I would try. She easily had a hundred African violet plants, and I listened really good about how to mix the plant food in the water and how much water to give them (not too much). Bad deal—almost all the flowers died while they were gone. Yes, she was disappointed, and so was I. But the next year, Ruth still wanted me to water the violets . . . and they lived!

Homer offered us lots of advice. One year, several of the neighbor boys had to get married because their girlfriends mysteriously showed up pregnant. Homer told Jim and me one hot day while we were putting in posts: "Boys, just remember that girls don't get pregnant if you leave your pants zipped up while you are on a date." I have never forgotten his sage advice (and he believed in the virgin birth). We helped Homer and Ruth for many years, and they treated us like we were their grandchildren. They were guests at our weddings, and I got an occasional letter or card from them when I was in Vietnam. When I got a little older, Dick and Tom went to work there and did the same things.

I can remember going with the family one evening to the Vos Farm Equipment Store in Pella. Dad bought a New Holland square baler for $600.00, which he was going to pay for with custom baling. He pulled it with the B John Deere for a few years, then he went to Kenneth Whitis' farm auction and bought an Allis-Chalmers WD-45 tractor. The farming operation had grown, and a larger tractor was needed. For some reason, my older brother, Jim, wanted a female tractor (an Allis-Chalmers).

I was in seventh grade when Jim and I took over the regular and custom baling. We had the AC WD-45 on the New Holland baler. Jim had driven the tractor on the baler for several years, even when he was so small he couldn't pull the clutch back on the B John Deere. Dad would have to jump off the wagon behind the baler and go stop the tractor. In other words, Jim was the experienced "driver," and I knew how to load bales on the wagon. So Jim convinced me that he should drive and I should load, because we would get done quicker and we could go fishing. (Jim is three years older than me, and you wonder why I call Jim my "smart brother.") He convinced me all those years that we were more efficient if he drove.

In the spring, the family would go see Harold Witzenburg on Highway 163 west of Pella, where we would buy 100 bales of baler twine (each would do 475 square bales). The twine would be delivered to our farm by semitruck before haying season. Jim and I would bale square bales after the hay dried around noon until all the hay was baled. We went as far away as west of New Sharon to Uncle John's farm and many other places. We were pretty self-sufficient, so we would take our own water jug (a nice Igloo five-gallon galvanized container), and Mom would always make sure we had plenty of food. We would put the water jug under a windrow of hay in the middle of the field to keep it cool, and we would throw the last hay in the baler when we were finished.

One day, our water jug was under a pile of hay in the middle of a field we had already baled. A young man hauling hay wagons lined up with that clump of hay and smashed our water jug! It doesn't make for happy workers. Our dad was never too far away, but when the hay was all baled, I refused to go to the barn and help unload the last loads of bales. I told them I had handled every bale, and I was not going to touch them again . . . and I never did.

Chisel Points in the Ground

During oat straw baling, we would leave in the morning and make a circuit, so we baled straw when we got there. One particular day, we started fairly early in the morning. We baled all day, and we got to the last farm (a small place, with only a few acres of oats) at about 6:30 in the evening. The farmer lived just around the corner from our home. We pulled in, and as I was opening the gate to his field, the old man came up to us and pointed a real crooked finger in my face and said, "You can always tell a lazy man because he comes to work when the sun is going down!"

I really wanted to hurt him, but I just ignored him (though I have never forgotten). We baled his straw and went home. I have to admit that Jim was really good with his AC on that baler, and he could keep that baler running. The AC had an oil hand clutch, and he was good at easing into wads of hay or straw. Not once in all those years did I get thrown off the wagon because of an abrupt stop. He would listen to the baler, and once in a while when we changed wagons, he would jump off the seat and almost fly to the baler knotter. With his two 9/16 wrenches, he would adjust that knotter. He could tell by the sound when it was not "purring." It was very rare that the knotter would miss tying a knot. I really believe that at the ripe age of seventy-eight, my brother could still make a knotter tie with his two wrenches.

We would bale hay and straw until all one hundred bales of twine were gone from the twine room. Then we would go to Bob Lewis at the Purina feed store and buy twine in ten-bale lots until the season was over toward the end of September. We would usually get another forty bales of twine from Bob. All our twine had to be Holland twine because it was the best, with very few thin or thick places in the twine to mess up the knotter. If you did the math, you would figure out that Jim and I baled over 66,000 small square bales of hay a summer from the time I was in seventh grade until after I was a junior in college. (Then I got married!)

I had the reputation of knowing how to load bales behind a baler. One day, the neighbor called and wanted to hire me to load bales for him, and my mother told him yes (for me) because she knew we had no baling to do. I went and he put me on the wagon behind an old man who couldn't turn his head backward. Their baler threw loose bales regularly, and it was a mess. All I could do was kick the loose hay off the wagon because the old man wouldn't look, and we baled over 1,200 bales that afternoon. It was an awful experience. I was happy being on the wagon by myself, but when we got done, I found out he had six people working around the barn, and we all got paid the same amount per hour. That was fine because we hadn't talked about wages, but I went home and told Mom to never hire me out to work for somebody loading bales again because I wasn't treated fairly. And my mom never did hire me out again. (We all have to learn by experience).

As far as school, I went to West Center for kindergarten through sixth grade, and then I went to the reorganized Oskaloosa School for seventh grade. It was at the new junior high school (which was the old high school).

I must have left an impression on Mrs. Maxted. Around corn harvest in the early 2000s, I saw an announcement in the *Shopper* that there was going to be a ninetieth birthday party for Myrtle Maxted on a Sunday afternoon at the Methodist Church in Oskaloosa. I told my mom that I wouldn't be over to drink tea because we were going to the party, and she said, "I want to go too!" I got a dozen roses in a nice vase, and we went to the party. Mrs. Maxted was sitting by a table when we walked in. I asked, "Do you remember who I am?" She replied, "I'm not sure which one, but you are one of the Drost boys. I think it is Carl." I told her that she was right, and that was close to fifty years after leaving West Center!

In the middle of December of the same year, I got a call from an obvious Easterner (I could tell because of his accent). He knew

Chisel Points in the Ground

I was about to hang up, and he asked me to please stay on the line. He went on to tell me that his grandma, Myrtle Maxted, had a stroke and had died. He was calling because his grandma had listed Carl Drost as a pallbearer for her funeral. (I did leave a memory.) When we got to Forest Cemetery in Oskaloosa, we carried Mrs. Maxted's coffin from the street to the grave. I remember it as if it was yesterday, that day God welcomed Mrs. Maxted to Heaven. The snow had been scooped back, and the grass was as green as it is in May. We found out later that when her husband had died in 1960, she'd put her funeral plans in place. She left a legacy for us all: Every morning, school started with everyone reciting the Lord's Prayer and the Pledge of Allegiance.

Chapter 2

My Junior and Senior High Years

I started going to the newly reorganized Oskaloosa Community Schools in the fall of 1958. I was part of the first seventh-grade class in the junior high building. It was on the lot just north of Jaarsma Bakery, and it was formerly the high school for Oskaloosa. It really was quite a shock to go from a school with twenty-eight students to a school with over six hundred students. I got on a yellow school bus at 7:10 in the morning, and I got home after 4:15 in the afternoon.

We always took our lunch to the country school. Now we were moving up to the "hot lunch" program, but the food really wasn't very good. After about ten or twelve weeks, the lunch program was changed, and they made a hamburger line. Instead of the regular food, they would give two loose meat burgers, milk, and Jell-O (or whatever). I thought that was great! I ate two hamburgers every lunch until I graduated from high school in May 1965.

I had some very good teachers, like Mrs. Arlene Fox, who was my homeroom and reading teacher. Miss Phillips was the geography teacher, Miss Dulin was the typing instructor, and Cappy McCormick was the physical education teacher. Our PE at the country school was playing some ball, sledding, or a good snowball fight. Now they told us we needed shorts, a tee shirt, and a jock strap, and we would take a shower after class. We never had a shower at home (only a tub for one). I for sure had never been naked in front of twenty-five other boys, but I made it.

The junior high was a new thing for Oskaloosa, and Mr. Richard Manatt was the principal. There were naughty kids, so to have more eyes and ears, he wanted to start having hall monitors. I volunteered and got the job. That was my first experience as a "cop," and I had a little button/pin that said "monitor." I think the program lasted for one year and then went away.

The big school offered all these activities, and I thought I would like to be part of one. They announced the all-school dance, and I told my folks I wanted to go. They tried to discourage me, but they didn't say no. They took me to a gym on a Friday night, dropped me off, and told me what time they would pick me up. They were so smart because I had a horrible time. I remember the food was not good, but I was really afraid of the girls, so I sat on the bench the entire time and watched. I never asked to go to another dance, nor have I gone to a dance since.

I also thought it would be really fun to play football. The coach made it sound like so much fun and like there were all kinds of advantages. I thought my dad would be in favor of it. He never got the opportunity to go to high school, and I thought he would want me to have all these wonderful opportunities. So at supper, I brought up the idea that I would like to play football at school. I asked if they would come and get me after practice every night. My dad didn't think about it very long at all.

He simply said, "So you are not getting enough exercise?" (He knew English really well.) "Tomorrow night when you get off the bus, the manure spreader will be in the barn. You use the manure fork and load it up, take it to the field, dump it, and then fill it again."

The spreader was in the barn when I got home, and the manure fork was close by. I never asked about football or any sport ever again.

My brothers were quicker studies than me, and they never asked about sports when they were in school. It seems I was the "slow" one of the family, and it just took me longer to learn. But I was a very nice, well-behaved young man in school, and I only got detention once.

I had an industrial arts class with a guy who I didn't think was a very good teacher. He left the room one class period and said everybody had to be quiet while he was gone. Well, the people in the office called and asked a question. There was dead silence, so finally I said, "The teacher is not here right now." Well, when he came back, the rest of the class said I had talked, so he gave me detention. I went to the office and tried to explain the situation (to NO avail). I was to stay the next night because I was a bus student. I went home and told my mother. She went to the school and explained to them in no uncertain terms that it was wrong and that her son was never going to stay for a detention for doing what was right. I don't think they ever wanted her to come back and see them again!

When I was in eighth grade, I told my folks I was done with school and didn't need to go anymore. I said I would be quitting at the end of the year. I think my dad would have let me quit (Jim was already in high school), but my mother had a real fit. She told me she and dad never had the opportunity to go to high school and I sure should at least give it a try. It would be a help to me for the rest of my life. I reluctantly agreed to give it a try.

On June 28, 1958, life changed on the Drost farm forever. My dad was cultivating the field of corn on the east side of the crick in the afternoon. He came home about twenty minutes past 4:00. He got the whole family to come to the house because the sky was green and looked very ugly. Our parents herded us all toward the basement. As we were passing the freezer at the top of the stairs, a hail ball came through the window and put us on notice that a bad storm had arrived. We all got safely to the basement, and we rode out the storm. When it had quieted down, we came out of the basement to devastation. All the windows on the north and west sides of our house were knocked out, the siding on the north and west sides was shot, and (of course) the Ruberoid roof was full of holes and leaking badly. The trees were totally stripped of leaves, and there were limbs everywhere. We looked at the crick flooding over most of the crops. The field of corn that had been hip-high at 4:00 in the afternoon was now just stubs, and the water was washing anything left over to the river. When I went upstairs that night, there was a piece of ice in my bed that was still the size of a bread pan (it had to have been a lot larger when the storm hit). The next day, my dad told us that in order to take care of his family and pay the bills, he was going to get his hammer and his ladders and go out to do carpentry work like repairing and shingling roofs. Mom and us kids would have to do the farm chores. All the boys went to work on the carpentry crew when we were old enough to carry shingles or help out in some way on the job.

The first shingling job I went on was when I was in eighth grade, and I was to paint the cupola on Lester Hoyt's barn south of the Des Moines River past Beacon. The barn had to be a hundred feet tall (or so it looked to a little kid). It was a hip roof barn. Thank goodness the top sections of the roof were flatter, so I could walk on it. I know I made it white. One of our older neighbor kids was Bert Bandstra, and he was working for my dad. We have been friends ever since. When I got the painting done, I carried shingles to the "big guys," who were nailing them on the roof. This business happens to be how all four Drost sons graduated from college with no debt. It was all thanks to a sixteen-ounce Estwing or Plumb hammer and a lot of sweat.

One of the jobs we got was shingling the big pavilion at the Southern Iowa Fairgrounds (which is still there today). It was a very tall, two-layered building. One layer was the bleacher section, which went all the way around it. Then there was a higher section where the show ring was at. I know it took over one hundred squares of shingles.

Paul Van Zee was the head of the Fair Board. About every afternoon, Paul would show up with his little Jeep and a bag of pop to treat us. I thought we were working too cheap! He introduced me to Dr. Pepper, which was a mixture of lots of fruit juices. I still like it today.

We worked in the evenings when it would cool off. The stock car races were held on Wednesday evenings, and we would work race nights. When the races would start, we would all sit (our dad and at least three of us boys) on the roof peak, where you could see the whole racetrack. One night, a policeman saw us sitting up there. He drove around the building a few times, so we knew what he was up to. Finally, he got out of his squad car and yelled, "Get down from there!" Our dad told him we had permission, and the cop still yelled, "Get down from there!" Dad hollered at him, "Just come on up and get us!" (We always pulled the ladder up.) After a while, he left.

The other interesting job our dad took on was shingling the new Methodist church in Fremont. We were laying a lot of shingles from Farmer's Cashway Lumber on the west side of Oskaloosa (which was owned by James McCurdy of McCurdy Seed in Fremont). McCurdy was also the head man in the church in Fremont. He asked our dad if we would be interested in shingling his new church. Dad told him we would be, and the agreed price was $6.00 per square.

We got there to put on the shingles; the bottom part was really easy and fairly flat. As we went farther up, the roof got steeper. For toe holds, we used two-inch-by-four-inch boards lying on their edges in hooks. Toward the top, the roof went straight up, and we were all trying to act like we had duct tape on our clothes to stick us to the side. I was getting paid $1.50 per hour, and I asked my dad if I could get a 25-cent-per-hour raise. I will never forget his response: "Boy, if I paid you what you were worth, you would be paying me!"

My Junior and Senior High Years

James McCurdy would bring us pop in the middle of the morning, then again in the middle of the afternoon. It didn't make sense to us because he had a reputation for being really tight. One afternoon, when James was there for our pop break, Dad asked him what the closest bid price was to put the roof on because he wanted to stay competitive. James replied, "$15.00 per square." Believe me, I never got the raise, and all we got was the $6.00 per square.

The high school had grades ten to twelve, and I started going there in the fall of 1961. I liked it because I could take a lot of shop classes. In fact, I took them all, though all the time I was thinking I was going be a farmer. I took all the drafting classes, wood classes, and metal classes. I had two of these classes every semester I was in high school. I spent close to half my day in the industrial arts department.

When I was a senior, Mr. Bob Bishop was a new industrial arts teacher at Oskaloosa. He was really a nice guy . . . too nice. He had a very hard time keeping order in his classes. But I really liked him, and he had a lot of knowledge of the subject. He told his classes about the Iowa Industrial Arts Fair in the spring at the University of Northern Iowa. I wasn't planning on going to college, but I thought, *Oh, why not enter just for kicks?* I filled out the application, and I entered a set of plans for a house. I also built a model of the house, which was made with scale model pieces of wood and other materials. My mother took me to UNI one day in April 1965 for the fair, where we got to show our projects and get interviewed about what we knew. That was on a Friday, and then we had to go back on Saturday for the results. I don't remember very much about it, but I do know I won first place in the Iowa Industrial Arts Fair at the University of Northern Iowa in Cedar Falls in April 1965. The prize was a full ride to UNI for four years, but I didn't go there.

My homeroom teacher was Mrs. Lisk, and I did pretty well with my grades (above a B average). Mrs. Lisk wanted me to get into the National Honor Society. I met all the other requirements for membership, but I was not in any activities (I remembered the manure spreader). She told me I needed to join an activity, so I joined the chair crew that set up chairs in the gymnasium for school assemblies. It was all during school time, and Mrs. Lisk got me admitted to the National Honor Society.

I graduated from Oskaloosa High School in May 1965. We were the largest class ever to graduate from Oskaloosa. I think there were 228 graduates, and I had class rank of 25. It didn't mean anything to me because I was not going on to college. I didn't know what I was going to do, but I thought I'd probably farm.

Chapter 3

My College Years at William Penn

I graduated from Oskaloosa High School in May 1965 with no intention of ever going to college. One of the big mysteries in our family is why our mother thought it was so important for her kids to get a college education. I sure didn't see the need for going on, and I would have been content being a farmer like most others in our church. My mother almost begged me to go to Penn like my brother Jim (who was a senior) was doing and just try it. She wanted me to do what he was doing: study to become an industrial arts teacher. I was pretty good with my hands. I think our dad was content with whatever we wanted to do, but with our mom, there was no letting up. So, I finally agreed to give it a try. I had to take the ACT test during orientation, and I think I only scored a 21, but I had to have a number in that slot.

If I was going to go to college, I needed a car (my parents and I agreed). I had been saving money to buy a car. Before college started, we went to my dad's friend, Mose Van Zee (you will hear more of him later), who was the Nash Rambler dealer in Oskaloosa. Mose had a 1962 Ford Falcon four-door car with a small engine in it and a stick transmission—really sexy to drive to college, but he would take $1,000.00 for it. We all agreed on the price, so my dad took me to the Farmer's Savings Bank in Leighton, Iowa, where I had my money in a savings account. We got there, and the bank president asked Dad if he could help him. My dad told him I needed to do some business, so he asked what he could do for me. It is as plain today as it was in August 1965.

"I want $1,000.00 to buy a car."

"You don't need a car," the bank president replied.

"I'm going to college, and I need a car and the money to get it."

"Your parents have a car and a truck, your brother has a car, and you don't need one."

Me being the mild-mannered person I was back then, I said, "I need $1,000.00 to go get the car, and I want it in cash."

To which the bank president responded, "You don't need a car, and you are not big enough to carry that much cash!"

I never did understand his comments. I had worked my tail off to get and save the money, and my dad was standing there with me. I responded in a very calm way, "Just give me all the money in my account now—and make that in cash."

The bank president looked at my dad and only said, "Rich?"

My dad told him to do what I had said, and then he added, "IN CASH." That was the last time I was in the Leighton bank. He gave me the money in cash, and we left. I went and paid Mose for the Falcon, and then I went to Mahaska State Bank. Somebody there opened me a checking account, which is the same account Martha and I use today at the same bank (though now it's called Midwest One Bank). It was a plain, light-green car, but it ran well.

I remember going to freshman orientation at Penn, where Dean Donald Schultze got up in front of the freshman class of about four hundred and told us to, "Look to the left, and look to the right. When this semester is over, one of you will be gone. By the time this class graduates, another one of you will be gone." Well, I don't know as I really cared because I didn't want to be there. Vietnam was starting to take young men, and I think my mother worried about her boys having to go the Army like her husband. A deferment for college would take care of that, and then the war would be over.

I went to class as much as I could in the morning, and then I worked on the farm or helped Dad with the carpentry business to make enough money so I could go to college. We were the only ones in our church from a farm who went on with school (other than those who wanted to be preachers). The first year was very miserable. It had all the basic stuff that was required for a liberal arts education. Then my mother thought I was Jim, so I had to take the same stuff he did. Well, Jim and I are very different; he would stay up all night to study, and he has always been very brilliant. Here are some examples of the classes I took.

I had to take a required basic communications class as a freshman. The class was at 8:00 in the morning. I think we had to read one of the Greek stories and then write a paper. My topic was "Women, Women, Women," and it must have been pretty good because I remember I got an A and a note that said I would not have any trouble in the class. My camaraderie with the professor did not last, and it became a very difficult class for me. I did pass.

We had to be on time for that class (the prof was nasty to latecomers). There was a girl who sat next to me, and girls were still a distant thing to me. One morning, she came in with a raincoat on, and she kept it on. I glanced over during the class, and the coat was open a little; all she had on was the raincoat and maybe panties, but I am not sure. I thought a lot of things about what I saw. (Remember, this was pre-Martha.)

I also had to take college algebra and trigonometry (because Jim had taken those classes and he advised me). The young professor was new, and I had not had any math in high school beyond geometry, so you know how tough this class was. And the professor didn't care if I got it. I got a D in the class and was glad it wasn't an F.

I was helping my dad on the farm when I went to college. During the early part of 1966, it was decided that a new tractor might be purchased. My dad and I went tractor shopping, and we looked at

John Deere, Minneapolis Moline, Oliver, and International. The decision was finally made to buy a new John Deere 3020 diesel tractor with a used four-bottom, semi-mounted plow and a four-row, front-mount cultivator. We also decided to get a used mounted 227 corn picker. The Allis-Chalmers WD45 was traded in, along with the three-bottom, pull-type John Deere plow and the two-row front cultivator. The new tractor did not get delivered until late June, so Van Gorp Implement provided the farm with a John Deere 3010 diesel to use until the new tractor arrived. The new tractor has never left the Drost family and is presently at the Jackson Drost farm.

As I've said, my mother was intent that I take the same classes as Jim, my brilliant brother. We were and are not in the same category of intelligence or study habits. About halfway through my freshman year, I was going to flunk out unless something changed. What needed to change was the courses I was taking, like advanced math, sciences, and stuff Jim excelled in and I didn't. My mom would get after me about my grades (yes, parents got them then), and they were never as good as Jim's. I told her one day, "If you don't get off my ***, I am gonna drop out or flunk out and I will be heading straight to Vietnam." I started taking some stuff I wanted to, and my grades picked up.

We were required to go to chapel service twice a week, on Tuesday and Thursday mornings at 10:00. Our seats were assigned. My sophomore through junior years, a young lady would walk up the east aisle, checking off the empty seats I suppose. She had a really cute walk to her, but there was no bribing this one. Her name was Martha Vernooy.

Now, some more stories. I did manage to get an industrial arts professor for drafting my freshman year, and he was just fresh out of teaching at a high school. His name was Allen Rodemeyer. He was an interesting character and a hard-liner, but you could tell he really cared. I never did get him figured out in the four years I had him for all kinds of classes. He was a very good instructor, and he knew his stuff. I had him for all the drafting classes, the woodworking classes, and the crafty classes.

In the late 1990s, I read in the *Oskaloosa Herald* that Allen Rodemeyer had gone back to Europe with his son to retrace the route he'd taken with General Patton during World War II, all the way into Germany. In about 2005, we went to the Oskaloosa Presbyterian Church for a visit. And there sat Allen and Julia Rodemeyer, who were members. A year or so later, I read in the church bulletin that Allen was recovering at home from a stomach aneurysm. So one Wednesday night, while Martha was at choir and bell practice at church, I went to visit the Rodemeyers in their home. They were of course glad to see me, and we had a nice visit. I noticed that on the wall behind their TV was a little piece of wood. Hanging on it were military medals that I recognized. Among them were the National Defense Service Medal, the Good Conduct Medal, the World War II Campaign Medal, a Bronze Star, and a Purple Heart. Before I left, I said I couldn't help but notice the medals behind the TV (since I had also been in the service). I had noticed the Bronze Star, and I knew that in World War II this medal was only given out for valor. I asked if Allen would tell me about it.

Allen broke down in tears and told me that in 1995 an Iowa senator had gotten him his medals. Then he told me about his experiences in Germany. His best buddy had been shot and killed before his eyes by a German prisoner in April 1945. The next day, Allen had been shot. He spent the rest of the war in military hospitals until he was finally sent to a hospital in Springfield, Missouri, which was close to his home. He told me I was one of the few he knew who seemed to care. A few days later, I got a letter in the mail from Allen Rodemeyer. It simply said, "I thought you cared about my Army experiences. I wrote them down for you, and if you don't care, throw it away."

It was an awesome letter that told the whole story. It started a friendship that lasted until Allen's death and continues today with his widow. The camaraderie of veterans is something non-vets can't and never will understand. We felt it, even though our experiences were forty years and three wars apart. Allen told me some time before he died that I was the only friend he had. I need to tell you that only then did I understand the real Allen Rodemeyer.

I also had my smart brother Jim as a professor at Penn. He had his PhD by the time he turned twenty-six. He has been a professor at Penn since he graduated from there with a Bachelor of Arts in 1966. I had him for metals, electricity, welding, and electronics. The department chair was Dr. Harold Case. Together, they conspired against me to force me to take college physics. They did it by telling me it was in the catalog, but it wasn't (until you read the fine print, which said the head of the department could change anything).

I took the college physics class, and I really did enjoy it. It was taught by Dr. Donald Robertus (better known as "the Surfer" because he had size sixteen shoes). I remember the first day of class when he came in and stood in front of us and held up a slide rule (that is what he called it, and I had never seen one). He told us this was how we would do all the calculations. I told you I wasn't very smart, so I raised my hand and said, "I have never seen one of those." The prof replied, "You are going to have a hard time." Then he went right on.

Well, I did enjoy that class, and I did pretty well (I managed to get a B). I liked running the little cars down the ramps with the wax paper and seeing the sparks and doing all the calculations. We also did a section in electronics with volts, amps, watts, capacitance, resistance, impedance, and lots of other stuff. I really learned a lot, and I have used this knowledge greatly since then.

I told you that my smart brother Jim was my professor. It was a requirement that I had to take electronics to graduate with a degree in industrial arts. I asked for a waiver to take something else because I had taken college physics and we had covered electronics. I was denied and forced to take the industrial arts electronics class. Jim still lived at home with us, so I told him at the supper table how stupid I thought that decision was. I said, "I have bought the electronics book and taped it shut. I am not going to open it, but I am going to pass your class!"

I showed the whole family the taped-up book. I think Jim planned to make an example of me because I told a lot of people what I was doing. The first test came in electronics. Ye gads, it was so long! We had two hours to take it, but I finished. The next two-hour class, we went over the test. The professor couldn't read the whole test with the answers in those two hours. I remember that the test was worth 415 points, and I had over 400 correct. I set the curve for the class! I never did open the book, and everybody knew it.

I also took an advanced woods class where I built a solid cedar chest using three-quarter-inch thick cedar. In the front, I embedded the initials MLD in white birch. (Those would be the initials of my future wife, Martha Lou Drost.) I made it in the class at Penn while Martha was working in the registrar's office. I threatened everybody that she had better not find out—I had not asked her to marry me yet! (My Plan B was to give it to my aunt, Mary Louise Drost, who was married to my Uncle Shirley.) My threats paid off. Nobody told her, and she said yes at Christmas of that same semester. (More of that story later.)

I also had to student teach, and the supervising teacher was Martha's boss, Dr. Conrad White. I got the assignment to student teach in the fall of 1968 at Montezuma Community Schools. I would be in the junior-senior high school with Mr. Dave Beck. It is hard to describe what student teaching is like. I was only four years older than the seniors in high school. Dave Beck was an excellent mentor and teacher for me. He kept good discipline and expected the kids to learn something. We got along very well, and he gave me a class to teach very early on. The lesson plans had to be done and checked over, and the demonstrations had to be done and done correctly. My student teaching ended on December 20, 1968, which was the last day before Christmas break. We got out of school a little early, but I told all the classes that day that I was getting married that night. What a way to end student teaching! (But again, there will be more of that story later.) I finished up my four years in the spring of 1969, taking classes in my major and some electives that were a lot of fun.

A lot of people have wondered why someone would get a liberal arts education. The answer is simple: We don't know what curveballs we will get in life or where we might end up. At that point in my life, the Army, Vietnam, the implement business, the school board, and a lot of other things had never entered my mind. I can tell you in hindsight that with a liberal arts education, one should be able to talk and speak to anybody because common ground can be found to carry on a quality conversation. I graduated from William Penn College close to Memorial Day 1969 with a contract in my pocket to teach industrial arts at Montezuma Community Schools, where I had student taught. Dave Beck had recommended me for his position.

Martha got a PHT degree—Putting Hubby Through.

Chapter 4

Finding My Wife

I grew up with a sister, Annie, and she was enough girl for me. I didn't need any others. I never had any interest in girls in junior or senior high, or even in college for that matter. Our family always spent a lot of time together, and I was trying to work my way through William Penn while helping on the farm, so I was too busy for girls. I think my mother thought it was time for both Jim and me to find a girl, but that was of no interest to me.

I went to Young People's Group at First Christian Reformed Church, and I always helped at the fundraisers. We usually had a pancake supper. I knew nothing about cooking, but I got to help with grilling pancakes. The group had a party one night, and I was never so embarrassed in my life as I was during one game we played. We all sat in a circle, then a guy had to carry a young lady around the circle on piggyback. The last guy got to pick the next pair. After Keith had his turn, he said he wanted Carl to carry Martha. Well, at least she was as embarrassed as I was. She got on my back, and I made sure she didn't fall off. We got done, and that was that.

I continued to go to Young People's, and so did Martha. She was working in the registrar's office at Penn, and I was registering for every evening class I could that would allow me to work in the afternoons. I registered for an education class in the evening and went to the class at the assigned time. The professor told me I was not allowed to take the class at night because it was reserved for "old biddies." The professor made me leave, and I was told to see the dean the next day. So I went to see Dr. Donald Schultze, and he told me I had to register for an afternoon class. I argued to no avail. He told me to take the paper to the registrar's office, which I did. Yes, right up to Martha Vernooy. She told me, "That will be five dollars payable in the business office." I argued and got no place; I kept arguing, but it was futile, so I went and paid the five dollars to change my registration. That five dollars then was like a thousand dollars today.

Martha and her friends went about every morning to Embers (the college café in the student union). They would walk down the sidewalk across campus, and I don't know what caught my eye about Martha's walk, but it got my attention. I got to thinking about this, and I finally got up enough nerve to ask her for a date. I caught her on campus by herself one day and asked her if she would go to church with me on Sunday night. She said yes. I don't know what I would have done if she had answered any other way.

Sunday evening came. I don't remember the exact date, but it was the last Sunday in February 1967. She had an apartment on North Market in Oskaloosa, but I had to pick her up on her family's farm west of town on Highway 92, then a little ways south. I knew where the place was, but it was so foggy I missed the turn off the highway and had to turn around. But I finally got to her house.

We went to church at First Christian Reformed, and I had never had a date with a young lady before. I sure had no idea what to do with her. I knew all the other kids rode around the square in Oskaloosa. We had just gotten 1,400 little chicks at our farm, and I thought she might like to see them. So on our first date, I took Martha to see the chicks. I also didn't know that you didn't take your date to meet your family the first time you went out, but my mother had some stuff for us to eat and my family treated Martha very nice. There had not been any other young single girls in our home. The only lady who came off and on was Annette Eustas, the wife of one of our friends, and we always got along well with her. After we ate the food my mother had prepared, it was probably 9:00. I took Martha to her apartment and asked her about going to church the following week. She agreed, and I said good night and went home.

I didn't know other couples were staying out until midnight; I had to get up and go to school and work. The next day, as my dad and I were working together, he said, "That Martha is a KEEPER!" I was just happy to have another date with her.

My car then was a 1962 Ford Falcon four-door with a six-cylinder engine. It sure was not a fancy car, and the rubber bushings in the suspension squeaked when you drove it. There really was quite a sound when we went driving around the square with the windows down after it got warm. But it didn't seem to bother Martha.

I think we went to church every Sunday night for a long time. On Easter Sunday in 1967, Martha told me she had to sing special music at the Good News Chapel in town. I told her that would be fine—we would go there. Martha sang "He Could Have Called 10,000 Angels," and it was unforgettably beautiful. I think it was there that I decided she was going to be mine.

The preacher there was Alvern Boetsma. He had just started there a year or so before. He didn't preach long, so we went there quite often, which started a lifelong relationship with him. Martha would play her accordion on special occasions, and other times she would sing for the chapel. Overall, we went to church every Sunday evening, and we went to the stock car races on Wednesday nights during the summer. I don't know if we liked them, but it was a place to go together and it was cheap.

After we had gone on a date, Martha and I would land upstairs in her apartment. She usually shared it with another young lady or two. An elderly woman named Anna lived in the back apartment, but we very rarely saw her (even though they shared the same stairs). Martha was and still is a very good cook, so most of the time on Sunday evenings, she made some good stuff to eat. What I remember most are her apple turnovers. I think they were out of a can, but they were really good. And I didn't need to fight with my brothers to have two!

Martha came along with us on Drost family picnics and fishing trips. She was always a lot of fun for our family, and Annie enjoyed having another lady around. One of the most memorable fishing trips was to Diamond Lake, just west of Montezuma. My brother, Tom, was always running around with his camera. Martha caught a little sunfish that was maybe three inches long, and she held the fish out on her pole toward the camera, so it looked like a five-pound bass in the photo. Mom always packed a big supper when we went. We fished a lot at Diamond Lake.

Sometime during our first year of dating, my brother, Jim, asked Faye DeRonde out on a date. It turns out Faye and Martha went to the Christian school together and were very good friends. Their families visited back and forth, and Martha and Faye would spend Sunday afternoons at each other's homes. We rarely did anything together.

Martha would come over to our home just to spend the evening. We would have supper and play pool in the basement. Brother Jim made a pool hall sign that we hung above the door. It had a red Plexiglass face behind the "pool hall" cutout and a lightbulb behind it so it would light up. I didn't know until much later that Martha about quit seeing me because she saw that sign and just knew it was a "den of iniquity!" She later found out that our family did a lot of things together and that our dad was just as big a player as anybody. And he even talked! (Martha's dad was very quiet and hardly spoke. When he did say something, he was very soft and hard to hear.) Martha found out what a real family was and that we could enjoy each other.

On Thanksgiving, we always went to church and celebrated all the blessings God had bestowed upon us. The Drost Thanksgiving offerings always went to Pine Rest up in Michigan, which was a home for folks with disabilities. Then we would go back home for a big feast. Ma Drost always cooked a big tom turkey that she had raised from a little baby. Each year, she raised ten turkeys, and we would butcher them just before Thanksgiving. We'd also have fresh rolls, mashed potatoes, vegetables, and cranberries (which I hated). Then we would finish off with homemade pies. Martha was shocked at how the Drost family ate and threw the rolls, but the family had a great time.

Our first Christmas together was in 1967. I had made that cedar chest in woods class for Martha. (Remember, the one with MLD inlaid in white birch that I made everyone swear to keep a secret?) It is obvious now that I'd planned to ask Martha to marry me, and I had to go get a diamond for her finger.

I took my mom along to pick out the ring at Reiley's Jewelry on the north side of Main Street in Oskaloosa. I didn't have any money, so the diamond was a very beautiful speck. I put the wedding band on layaway until we set the date. I don't know what day of the week it was that I proposed, but Martha and I had been on a date. We went to her apartment, but I was a real chicken. After a while, I asked, "If I were to ask you to marry me, what would you say?" She immediately said, "YES!"

So, then I did it right and got down on my knee and asked her if she would marry me. And she said yes again, so I gave her the ring. She really liked it, and then for some reason, I asked her if she wanted to keep it or whether I should take it and give it to her at Christmas. She gave it to me, and I took it home. I did find time to go talk to her father and ask him if I could marry his baby daughter. All he said was, "I reckon." Her mother asked Martha why she would want to marry me, as I was still in school. But Martha still wanted that ring. We went to her home after church on Christmas. When we opened the gifts, I gave Martha her diamond. Then when we went to my house, and the whole family was happy Martha was going be mine.

I gave her the cedar chest I had built with all that love.

Chapter 5

Our Engagement

When people started seeing Martha fixing her hair with the finger with the ring on it, they immediately wanted to know the wedding date. I was just starting my second semester as a junior in the industrial arts teacher education program at Penn, and Martha was a secretary in the registrar's office. I had to student teach in the fall and had three semesters of classes to go.

I had always felt that the "man of the house" should support his wife. How can you do that while also being in school? We talked about expenses and college fees and tuition. NO, not once did we ever talk about moving in together until we were married. After looking at the calendar, we saw my student teaching would end on the Friday afternoon before Christmas. The college basically closed down over the Christmas holidays, so we decided on Friday, December 20, 1968. All Dutch weddings in the Christian Reformed Church were held on Friday evenings with the reception following in the church basement.

We continued going out on dates. Our fancy restaurant was the Lil' Duffer, where you could get a 29-cent burger. I don't think we ever went for a nice dinner out in a full-service restaurant. I continued my studies in industrial arts, and it got down to where I only had my major courses left, which were all just easy to me. Martha continued to work at the college in the registrar's office. Life was really good. We went to the races at the Oskaloosa Racetrack, but there was getting to be so much beer there that we

Our Engagement

didn't like to go as much. (The person behind you could throw his beer on your back!)

I know a lot of discussion takes place today among couples who are going to get married. I don't think Martha and I discussed many "life issues," like where we were going to live, how many kids we were going to have, how much money it would take, would we have two cars, what was our retirement plan, what church would we go to, how would we celebrate holidays . . . and the list goes on. All I know is that I LOVED Martha and she LOVED me. Nothing else mattered.

I worked my way through college on the farm for room and board. Our dad still had his carpentry business too. All the boys helped him, and we shingled a lot of homes, barns, and a church. We also built machine sheds, hog sheds, and cattle sheds. We built a hog shed for a farmer just north of the Eddyville Drag Strip. He was quite the character and full of energy when he worked with us. He gave me marital counseling one day when he and I were working together, saying, "Now I need to tell you to have sex with Martha every chance you get. I have with my wife, and I haven't worn it out yet!" He also told me, "Never miss a chance to have sex with Martha because one episode that you miss is one you never get! There is no making them up!" He was at least twenty years older than me, and I sure didn't know what he meant. That was the most "birds and bees" talk I had before we were married. It was really good advice.

When we got around to planning the wedding, we had one bridesmaid: Martha's sister, Clara. The best man was my brother, Jim. We had ushers, a ring bearer, and a flower girl. We needed a preacher, and our church was without a minister at the time. We both liked a religion professor at Penn named Dr. Lloyd Cressman. We decided to ask him, but first we had to get approval from the First Christian Reformed Church's consistory. Dr. Cressman was a

Quaker, but they agreed; so, we asked Dr. Cressman, and he was honored. For flowers, we went to Mabel DeJong, who was my family's friend and had a flower shop. Mrs. Dale Roorda from west of Leighton was a Drost family friend who made our cake. We went to Dunsmoor Photography Studio for the photos. None of this was very expensive because we were on a tight budget. All I knew was that I loved Martha and none of the small stuff mattered.

I went and helped her dad square-bale hay one afternoon. Martha was home, so that made it fun! She always wore jeans that were cut off just above her knees with a fold in them. (I dreamed of what she was hiding in them, but I would have to wait until our wedding to find out.) She was always so cute. I couldn't wait to make her my wife. On that day, Martha was sitting on the fender of the 2520 John Deere tractor. I don't know what happened, but she tumbled off the fender to the rear and landed on some rock. Her really pretty knees weren't so pretty after she fell. I helped her get up, but I have always wished for a redo on that because I could have been more concerned. She limped around for several weeks after the accident, but she recovered.

Martha would come out to the Drost farm, and we would do some farm stuff. In the fall of 1968, my father went big-time on the farm. He bought a Cozy Cab for our 3020 John Deere diesel tractor. When I drove it home with the cab, I stopped and took Martha to our home for supper. It was a small cab, so we were close in there. She sat on the arm of the seat, which could not have been very comfortable.

My mother's oldest sister, Waultrina, worked in a Younker's clothing department store in Des Moines for years. She and her husband, Leland Covey, always liked the Drost boys. She wanted me to bring Martha to her store to get her some clothes, so we went to Des Moines for some shopping. I don't know what all we bought, but Martha got a short plaid dress that looked Scottish. It was really

Our Engagement

cute on the cute young lady! When Martha wore that plaid dress, it was beautiful (though I'm sure her father thought it hardly covered her behind). It was above the knees a few inches, and I really liked it. I'm sure we got a deal, as we had very little money.

We started looking around for a place to live, specifically furnished apartments. We would look at ads in the paper, then go look at the apartment. We couldn't afford most of them. We looked at one on the intersection of A Avenue East and South Seventh Street, and it was beautiful. It had a kitchen and a living room downstairs with a fireplace. There was an open stairway to the upstairs bathroom and bedroom. But we could never have afforded it. Martha's friends were getting married and moving into nice farm homes or other places, but we couldn't. She was making $1.75 an hour at forty hours a week, which didn't add up to big money. Then we went to look at an apartment on Fourth Avenue East. It was upstairs on the western half of the floor. The electricity was turned off, so we looked at it with a flashlight. It looked okay to us, and it was $65.00 per month and furnished. It had cupboards in the kitchen, which we could fill with all the kitchen stuff she already had. So, we rented the place and paid the first month's rent. We got a shock when we got the electricity turned on because the couch and chair in the living room were not fit to sit on. We had to go buy covers for them, but Martha made it a home. She moved in on the first of December 1968.

Martha and I had gone to several of her friends' weddings in the church; a lot got married to stay out of the Army, and a lot happened in a big hurry. The church had steps up both sides to the platform, but no steps in the middle. I decided it would be really nice to come down the aisle and go directly up on the platform, so my dad and I built a very solid set of steps to go in the center. We covered them with carpet. After we used them for our wedding, we left the steps at the church. I think every couple who got married there after we did used them. I know all my brothers and my sister used them. When they remodeled the church later, they put steps all the way across the front.

As the day of the wedding got closer, Dr. Cressman saw Martha at the college and told her we had to come over for counseling before he would marry us. The date was set, and we went to his home. He and his wife met us at the door of their porch. When he opened the door, we walked in and Dr. Cressman said to his wife, "Won't this make a wonderful couple!" And that was our marriage counseling! His wife got some tea and cookies, and we visited about the ceremony. We wrote our own vows there and were all set for our wedding.

Chapter 6

Our Wedding and Honeymoon

We had our rehearsal at the First Christian Reformed Church on North 11th Street in Oskaloosa on the evening of December 19, 1968. It was uneventful; Mildred DeJong and Dr. Cressman led us through the schedule of the wedding, how we were to march, and where we were to stand. We practiced the "lines" we were supposed to say.

On Friday, December 20, Martha took the day off work to finish up the final details, check with the ladies about coffee time, and get her hair done. I went to Montezuma Junior/Senior High School for my final day of student teaching. I told all the classes I was going to get married that night. My supervising teacher, Mr. Dave Beck, and his wife were coming to the wedding. (Until the day of, I had made him swear to keep the wedding secret from the students.) We got out early at 1:00 that day, so I headed home to get ready to go to a wedding. I drove to Ottumwa and checked into the Gaslight Motel on the north side of town and got the key so I would not have to do that when we got there later that night. I had never checked into a motel before. (I don't believe I had ever stayed in a motel in my life.) But I got it done without a credit card. I used cash, but try to do that today . . .

I got to the church early. (I wasn't going to be late for my wedding!) Then I went to the basement, where we were keeping the reclining rocking chair my parents were giving us as a wedding gift. I sat in it until it was time. We are old enough that the bride and groom were not to see each other on the wedding day until she started coming down the aisle, so there were no pictures taken before the wedding; they would all be taken after the reception. My aunt, Waultrina Covey, was looking out for Martha and making sure everything was okay with her. But she didn't know Martha's watch had stopped! They discovered this around 7:20. Martha hadn't started getting dressed yet, so they really had to hurry. I have always been on time, and Martha sure did not want us to start out late.

Brant Bruxvoort was our organist, and he played all the music while people were being seated. I think we had around 125 guests. The seating never did make a lot of sense to me—my friends and relatives were seated on one side of the church, while her friends and family were seated on the other side. Neither one of us had many friends, so that was not a problem. My friends from college had all gone home for Christmas.

When I saw Martha start down the aisle holding her father's arm, wearing her wedding dress and a veil over her face, I thought I had never seen anything so beautiful. I had not seen the dress or Martha on our wedding day. I don't remember much of the wedding, but I do know my uncle, Jim Lillie, sang a song or two, and we repeated the vows we had written with the help of Dr. Cressman. Then I placed that "huge" diamond ring on Martha's finger and the gold band she had purchased was put on my finger. Then came the words, "I now pronounce you man and wife. You may kiss the bride!" Wow, she was mine! Then Dr. Cressman said, "I introduce to you, Mr. and Mrs. Carl Drost." And down the stairs we went.

We had the greeting line in the foyer of the church. After the greetings, we went to the basement, where we cut the wedding cake and had our ham buns, mints, and a dip of ice cream and punch (a Dutch tradition). We walked through the room where all the gifts had been opened. On display was a Kodak Instamatic camera from my brother, Tom, that we were going to take on our honeymoon. Then, it was back to the sanctuary to take the rest of the pictures. I had other things on my mind then. Martha gave me a gold Bulova wristwatch as our wedding gift, with the date engraved on the back. I still wear it for church and other very special occasions, though it has to be shaken to wind the watch to keep time.

After we got the pictures taken, Martha went to change out of her wedding dress. Then we were ready to go out of the church and down the steps, where we were greeted by rice and camera flashes. The Ford Falcon—which I had repainted in our farm shop and equipped with a white roof—was parked just outside the church. It was all covered with shaving cream; there were cans on the bumper, and there was a note that said, "Just married!"

We got into the next car, which was a new blue Nash Rambler that my parents had just purchased. Nobody followed us when we left because they all knew the Falcon wouldn't run. (Martha's brother, Henry, had taken the rotor out of the Falcon's distributor and was keeping it in his pocket.) We headed straight down Highway 63 toward Ottumwa. Two miles east of Oskaloosa, we realized the Kodak camera was still at the church. It was the only camera we had, so we turned around and went back to the church. I went inside, ran to the room, grabbed the camera, and was back in the car before most people realized I had been there. Then we were on the road again to Ottumwa!

We got to the Gaslight, and I had never been to a motel before (let alone with a woman who was now my wife). To say I was nervous would be an understatement. All I knew was that I had waited nearly two years for this time. (I had never even looked at a *Playboy*!) Then we turned the lights out.

I woke up the next morning before Martha. I looked over and there was this woman in bed with me; all the time before it had always been my older brother. As I looked, I said to myself, *Now I got her, what am I gonna do with her?* When she got up, she put on that short little plaid dress . . . and oh was she beautiful in it! We were going to Cape Girardeau, Missouri, to spend a few days. I had never driven outside of Iowa, and there were no interstate highways or four-lane roads, so it took quite a while. When we got into southern Missouri, all the roads were very winding and crooked. The Cape is on the Mississippi River, down near the boot. It took all day to get there, and we checked into a motel on a little hill along the main highway.

We went to the Meramec Caverns, which was an hour away. We had never seen a cave before, let alone a big cavern. We were like kids in a candy store in amazement, and the operators used colored lights to make the rocks look all different colors. Then when they shut the lights off, it really got dark.

The last night that we were in the Cape, I wanted to take Martha out for a nice dinner, so we found a pretty nice-looking restaurant. When we got inside, it was really expensive. I was used to a 29-cent burger at the Lil' Duffer. Brother Jim had given us a frame with 50-cent pieces in it for a wedding gift, and we had grabbed it on our way out. We used the money to pay for our last meal. It took all of our money, and we had no charge card.

The next morning (Tuesday, December 24), we drove home. I know we crossed the Mississippi River into Illinois, then turned north so we could see other scenery. We only had enough money to buy us a tank of gas and very little food. But what did it matter? We were in love. We got back to Oskaloosa and our apartment late on Christmas Eve.

The tradition at the Drost house was to open gifts early on Christmas morning, so we got up early and went to the farmhouse. Later in the morning, we went to Christmas church, and then dinner was at the Vernooy house. After we ate noon dinner, we were allowed to go into the front living room (which was off-limits for anything but big days like Christmas).

Chapter 7

Our Marriage

From the day we were married on December 20, 1968, until I left for the Army in May 1970, we were in love and that about expressed it all. We were living the life of ease with two incomes and very little responsibility, except to each other. And then I left (not my choice). We had only been married a year and a half, so we knew what marriage was, but not what marriage really meant or what marriage could be. I had heard the phrase, "Absence makes the heart grow fonder." I have come to believe there are several things that make a great relationship in a marriage. Some of them are: (1) unconditional love, (2) respect, (3) trust, and (4) God at the center.

Unconditional love is exactly what it says. It means that no matter what is done or said, one must forgive and forget. A lot of times, when one partner is tired, beat, has had a bad day, or one of many other reasons, things can be said or done that were unintended. Both partners must realize that is not what was meant; the best way out is to admit that we screwed this one up and ask for forgiveness. My dad was not a good example of how to treat a wife, but not once did my parents ever shout and scream at each other. We all know that perfection is hard to achieve.

When I came home from Vietnam, I was a different person, but Martha accepted me as I was and loved me. For example, one day, Martha reached for the hanky out of my back pocket without saying anything, and her arm about got broken. There were other changes she had to adjust to. Martha tried to help by asking questions and praying for me. In the Bible, 1 Peter 3:1–2 says,

Our Marriage

"Wives, in the same way submit yourselves to your own husbands so that, if any of them do not believe the word, they may be won over without words by the behavior of their wives, when they see the purity and reverence of your lives."

Respect for each other is a key component in any marriage. Respect is really shown in how we listen and talk to our marriage partner. The way we speak about our partner in front of others and how we pay attention to our partner in a group really shows if we respect them or not. Communication is a key part of a marriage relationship, and it is displayed in front of other people and demonstrates respect. Making fun of a spouse in front of others is very disrespectful. Words like "dumb" or "stupid" or comments about their dress are sure signs trouble is on the way.

The third important part of a relationship is trust. Trust must never be broken, and that means that what we say is true to the best of our knowledge and not stretched or made less. Martha has taken care of the family checkbook since May 1970, and there has been no reason to question how the money was spent. I trust Martha all the way and all the time, with everything we have (including our love and her fidelity). When I was in Vietnam, the boys would sneak a young Vietnamese lady through the wire and get her in bed. The boys would line up, but Martha could be assured I never so much as went for a look. I never had to be concerned about Martha stepping out either. A lot of relationships have a real problem with trusting and being trusted.

Having God in a relationship makes getting along lots easier. We have a plaque in our bedroom that says: "Marriage takes three: You and me and God, with God at the center." We must really believe what the Bible says in several places. For example, Genesis 2:24 says: "That is why a man leaves his father and mother and is united to his wife, and they become one flesh."

If God gets up with us in the morning, we spend the day with Him at work or play, and then we spend the evening with Him in all that we do, the relationship gets easier. The Bible also says: "Husbands, love your wives, just as Christ loved the church and gave himself up for her . . ." (Ephesians 5:25). And Martha doesn't get off easy, because the Bible says in Ephesians 5:22–23: "Wives, submit yourselves to your own husbands as you do to the Lord. For the husband is the head of the wife as Christ is the head of the church, his body, of which he is the Savior."

Martha and I both wanted our marriage to be the best it could be, and we both read books on the subject. We watched how other couples lived together, and we attended marriage enrichment seminars. We learned that we needed to spend time away by ourselves, with the kids (when we had them) at their grandparents' house. This worked out well for us because we earned many weeklong trips when we were in business (that's a story for another chapter).

The Bible says in Leviticus 21:13, "The woman he marries must be a virgin." And he should celebrate her for the prize. It also says in Proverbs 5:18–19: "May your fountain be blessed, and may you rejoice in the wife of your youth. A loving doe, a graceful deer—may her breasts satisfy you always, may you ever be intoxicated with her love." We've learned to celebrate special events in our lives. We have gone away for a night for our wedding anniversary ever since our tenth anniversary. We spent the night of our tenth at the Live Drive-Through Nativity at the Nazarene Church, but then we went to the Traveler's Motel in Oskaloosa for the night and haven't missed going away since (even though some years we've had to adjust the date). We also celebrate every twentieth day of each month as our anniversary, and we have a contest to see who can tell the other "happy anniversary" first in the morning. We also celebrate full moons and other days when it seems fit.

Somebody once asked, "What you do in a motel room?" Let me tell you: Get a nice room with a jacuzzi and a basket of fruit. Do that first and see where that leads (bed, I hope). Then, go for a nice dinner at the place that is the best you can afford. (That was

McDonald's for us for several years.) Go find Christmas lights and then go back to the motel. We play games sometimes, like rummy with cards and Mexican train dominoes, but my favorite game is checkers. Every time she moves, I jump her. Enjoy being together and alone!

The Bible has lots to say about marriages and relationships:

- **Proverbs 18:22:** "He who finds a wife finds what is good and receives favor from the Lord."

- **Proverbs 19:14:** "Houses and wealth are inherited from parents, but a prudent wife is from the Lord."

- **Proverbs 31:10:** "A wife of noble character who can find? She is worth far more than rubies."

- **Mark 10: 7–9:** "'For this reason a man will leave his father and mother and be united to his wife, and the two will become one flesh.' So they are no longer two, but one flesh. Therefore what God has joined together, let no one separate."

- **Deuteronomy 24:5:** "If a man has recently married, he must not be sent to war or have any other duty laid on him. For one year he is to be free to stay at home and bring happiness to the wife he has married." (I really like this one.)

- **1 Corinthians 7:3–5:** "The husband should fulfill his marital duty to his wife, and likewise the wife to her husband. The wife does not have authority over her own body but yields it to her husband. In the same way, the husband does not have authority over his own body but yields it to his wife. Do not deprive each other except perhaps by mutual consent and for a time, so that you may devote yourselves to prayer. Then come together again so that Satan will not tempt you because of your lack of self-control."

- **Ecclesiastes 9:9:** "Enjoy life with your wife, whom you love, all the days of this meaningless life that God has given you under the sun—all your meaningless days. For this is your lot in life and in your toilsome labor under the sun."

Martha learned from a book and study guide that lots of people say a marriage should be 50/50 for both and equal. Martha has taught me that 50/50 is not correct; it should be 100/100 for both parties. If we both give 100% to the relationship and are not selfish, it will work well. All parties will be happy. Nobody believes us, but Martha and I have never in over fifty years had a serious argument or disagreement. Everybody must remember that when a word is spoken (in love or anger), it can never be taken back. This is what is meant in the Bible about the two shall be one flesh; the goals and outcomes desired are the same.

Chapter 8

Our First Year and a Half of Marriage

We got back from our honeymoon and enjoyed the Christmas and New Year's holidays. Then it was back to reality. Martha and I made our home in the upstairs apartment on Fourth Avenue East in Oskaloosa. Martha had to go back to the registrar's office, and I had to finish up my senior year. The good part was that I had planned my class schedule correctly. All I had left to complete were classes in my major, so it was an easy year.

In the first semester, I took a teaching methods class. Dr. White, the professor, would not accept a tardy because teachers were supposed to be prompt and on time. Class was at 8:00 a.m., and one morning Martha and I woke up at 7:35. We realized we would have to hurry! We got out of the house, and I made it to class just a second before 8:00. I sure didn't want to have to hear about being a newlywed, and I knew I would have heard it from Dr. White (and so would Martha, since she worked in his office).

I wanted to get a part-time job to help pay our bills, so I went to Van Gorp Implement and got employed. More on that later. I had to make sure I put in my time, as we sure could have used a little extra money. Remember, Martha was making a grand total of $1.75 per hour. At forty hours per week, her gross pay was $70.00 per week. Then there were the deductions, and the apartment was $65.00 per month. I think I might have made $1.50 an hour for no more than twenty-eight hours a week at the most. We did not have

Our First Year and a Half of Marriage

The outside of our first apartment on Fourth Avenue East.

a budget, nor did we do any talking before we were married about how we were going to make money. We also didn't talk about how we were going to spend the money. We were in love, and that is all that mattered. We got a joint checking account just before we were married in December 1968 at Mahaska State Bank, and we still have that account today.

The guy always gets all kinds of comments about how to treat his wife, and I was no exception. My father was not a very good example to his sons of how to treat wives (I found this out later), but he was a good husband and a GREAT father. I was told to make sure my wife knew her place in the house and that she needed to be told who was "boss." I got ready to go to bed one night, and I took off my Fruit of the Loom undershorts and threw them at Martha. I told her to, "Put 'em on!"

She looked at me and said, "Now, honey, you know I can't wear your pants."

And I told her, "That's right, I wear the pants in this house!"

Then Martha very carefully pulled her dainty little panties down her great legs and tossed them to me and told me, "Try to get in those."

Now how does a guy who is six-foot and five inches get into little panties from a 125-pound girl? I said, "You know I can't get in those."

She simply responded, "You are right, and you ain't gonna get in them until you change your attitude!" (THIS IS A JOKE!)

I quit listening to all the guidance about family life and proper husband-wife relationships and tried to learn on my own.

It was twenty-two steps to the top of our building and our apartment. I was so excited about leaving to go to school or work one morning that I must have bounded down the steps. When I got to the bottom, both doors of the two ground-floor apartments opened, and the two little old ladies living down there gave me the word that I sure was disturbing them coming down that way. I told them I was sorry, and I tried to be much more careful. I don't know what they thought one night when Martha and I were in bed and the bed collapsed completely and dropped the box spring right on the floor. It really surprised us, and it made a lot of noise. We vowed then that if we could afford it, we would live in the country and not have neighbors that close again.

There was no washer and dryer close, so we had to find a laundromat to wash our dirty clothes. We found one only about a block and a half away, down by the overall factory (where the post office is on South Market in Oskaloosa). It was pretty rundown; I didn't think it was safe for Martha to go by herself, so we would do it together.

In about mid-March, the teacher jobs in Iowa open up. I needed to get a job that paid more money, so I looked in the *Des Moines Register* at all the teacher openings in Iowa. The *Register* was the place where all the openings were advertised, so the search was on. We thought it would be good to get a job in the area, so we wouldn't have to move a long distance. I interviewed at Tri-County Schools in Thornburg, which is just northeast of What Cheer and would have been forty miles away. They offered me the job teaching industrial arts in the junior-senior high school. I was about to accept the job when Jim Carroll, the superintendent of Montezuma Schools, called and told me that Dave Beck had resigned and they wanted to offer me a contract to teach industrial arts in their district. Montezuma Junior-Senior High School was where I had student taught in the fall. We set up a time to talk (it was not an interview, but a meeting to decide the terms of the contract). The salary for a beginning teacher was $6,500.00 per year. I asked them to give me an extra $100.00 per year in materials so I could make some projects to show the kids, and he agreed.

Martha and I continued working as I finished up my schooling, but having one vehicle was not working out very well. We went to

White's Bicycle Shop and purchased a Schwinn three-speed for me to ride to work at Van Gorp. I rode that bike until we moved to Montezuma. Graduation day came, and I got a piece of paper called a diploma. Nobody has ever asked to see it. I continued to work full-time for the summer at Van Gorp Implement, doing whatever Lee and Ray wanted me to do. My theory of work was, and still is, that if the boss wants the floor swept, all I need to know is which broom they want me to use; it doesn't matter to me whether they want me to use a huge broom or a toothbrush. I am theirs from the time I punch the clock in the morning until I punch out to go home.

We went to church at First Christian Reformed Church by Forest Cemetery, where we were raised and where we'd gotten married. We went on Sunday mornings and Sunday nights. (But now after church on Sunday night, we went home instead of "scooping the loop" like the kids did.) We went there for many years.

During the summer, we had to find a place to live in Montezuma. Dave Beck and his wife were moving out of their home, and they were more than willing to rent us their house in Montezuma. It was diagonal across the street from the water tower and close to downtown. We had no furniture, so we went to Mr. Reynold Watts at the Western Auto Store on High Avenue West in Oskaloosa. We looked through his store and his catalogs, and we purchased a sofa and chair for the living room, a bedroom suite (no king), and a dinette set for the kitchen. It was all under $1,000.00. We paid cash, using part of Martha's savings. (She was rich, with $3,000.00 in a savings account. All I had was a debt-free education and an old car.) Our furnishings were not the fanciest, but they were good enough for us.

Reynold delivered the furniture to Montezuma for us. We were all moved in when the 1969–1970 school year started in late August. I taught industrial arts to seventh graders all the way through seniors. We got involved with the kids at school, and I was the junior class sponsor. We videotaped the football and basketball games (both home and away). We also had an HO-scale slot race car set in an upstairs room, and some of the boys would come over to race cars and eat snacks. Sandy Van Cleave was a junior at the time, and she was the star forward of the six-on-six girls' Bravettes basketball team. They played in the state tournament, and Sandy still holds the record for the most points scored in a state tournament game.

I got an after-school job working for Lowell Ferguson, a farmer who lived south of Montezuma on Highway 63 on Moon Creek. Lowell wanted me to plant corn one evening, and I told him I had never planted corn before. Lowell's response was simple: "You will never learn any younger!"

We were living a near-perfect life in Montezuma, as we both had jobs and the community was friendly. I went to Van Gorp's on Saturdays, and we drove to church in Oskaloosa on Sunday mornings. We would spend the day visiting our families after church, then maybe stay for Sunday night church or just go home.

Martha thought she was a pretty good checkers player, so we would play that occasionally. My parents came to visit one night, and Martha wanted to show them how she could beat me at checkers. She set the game up on a little stand in the living room in front of my mom and dad, and we proceeded to play. It was not her night, and I beat her pretty handily. I made a smart comment, and my sweet wife reached across the table and swatted me on the face. That night, I learned another important lesson about relationships that I will never forget. I guess it hurt enough to get beat.

On December 17, 1969, the National Draft Lottery was held in Washington, D.C. It was on national television and would determine how they were going to get troops to send to Vietnam. The Defense Department had put small pieces of paper with all the dates of the year in a fishbowl. Someone would draw the dates out. If the date of your birthday was called, you would be the first to be drafted and so on. That's how they made the order of the draft.

Chisel Points in the Ground

We watched intently for when my birthday, July 17, would be drawn. To us it was no big deal because we were naive enough to think that even if I got drafted, a smart farm kid from Iowa with an education and a teaching degree would get good duty in the Army. We kept watching, and July 17 was number ninety-eight in the draft order. From what the announcers were saying, it probably meant I would get drafted or else I could get a deferment to keep teaching. No worries on our part, but neither of us claimed to be very smart.

We celebrated our first wedding anniversary while living in Montezuma. I had so much to learn about taking good care of a wife, but I thought it would be a good thing to take Martha out for dinner. We went to Dickey's Prairie Home, a truck stop at the intersection of Interstate 80 and Highway 63 north of Montezuma. I couldn't begin to tell you what we ate, but I can still point out the area we sat in when we drive by the closed truck stop. It sure was fancier than the Lil' Duffer! I at least knew not to forget the anniversary.

We also decided that maybe it was the proper time to start a family. About mid-March, Martha knew she was pregnant, and I got a letter in the mail from the Mahaska County Draft Board. It said in part, "Your friends and neighbors have selected YOU to serve ... and you are to report in mid-April."

I still had a school year to complete. I sent a letter to the Draft Board asking for an extension, and they gave me one until May 20, but no longer. We went and told my parents about the baby coming and the draft notice, and my mother immediately said, "Martha can move in here. We will finish the upstairs, and she can have the whole basement." They had built a new home in 1968 and were living in the basement until they got funds to finish the upstairs. Mom, along with her new baby, had lived with her parents when Dad was in Europe during World War II. Martha willingly agreed to move in with my parents and my two younger brothers and little sister. I also told Montezuma Schools that I had been drafted and would resign because we didn't think I was going to be a teacher for my career. We all agreed that I would close up the school year early and do the grades, and the students would finish up the year in study hall.

We made friends with Ron Wilrich, who was the senior high math teacher. We did some things with him and his wife, Lola. For example, Lowell Ferguson had a lot on the new Lake Ponderosa west of Montezuma, and in the spring after school, Ron and I would go out and get in Lowell's boat and do a little fishing. Martha and Lola might come out later, and it was fun. I remember rowing the boat across what is now West Lake to a cow pasture and going mushroom hunting. We caught fish on the way back, and then all four of us grilled and ate our catch on the lot.

As the middle of May approached, we rented a space in a warehouse in Oskaloosa for part of our belongings and planned our move. My dad and brothers came one day with the Chevy ton truck with the livestock rack folded up. We put all our belongings in it and drove to Oskaloosa. We went to the warehouse across the road from Edmundson Park and deposited some of the stuff there, then we unloaded what Martha was going to keep in the basement of Mom and Dad's home. The living room furniture was given to my folks for their living room. Martha kept the bed and dresser and some personal stuff, and we lived there together for two or three days before I went to Fort Des Moines.

Chapter 9

My First Job With a Time Clock

After Martha and I got married (and before I graduated and started teaching), I decided that with one semester left at Penn, I should see if I could find a part-time job. I went to Van Gorp Implement, the John Deere dealer in the southeast corner of Oskaloosa, which was where my family did our business. I saw Leland Van Gorp and told him I had gotten married and was needing to make a little money to support us. I told him I only had classes in the morning, so I could work every afternoon and all the time he could use me on Saturdays. He told me he could use an extra employee, but I would have to do any job they needed done, which was not a problem for me. I started on January 2.

I told my dad about it, and he said I needed to get some basic tools to take to my job. So, he and I went to the Big Bear Store. Vern Stout, the manager, helped us get a toolbox and some tools. I know I got a toolbox with a hip roof on it; the top opened up both ways. We put in a half-inch socket set, along with a set of combination wrenches, some screwdrivers, pliers, wire cutters, an adjustable crescent wrench, a set of punches and chisels, and a ball-peen hammer. I don't remember for sure, but I think the total cost was $79.00.

I went to Van Gorp Implement the afternoon of January 2, 1969. Raymond VerSteegh, the partner and shop foreman, had a burnt John Deere 2010 utility tractor with a loader on it that needed to be cleaned up, reconditioned, and painted. All this would be my job. There was no indoor wash bay, so all the washing was done outside on the south side of the building. The power washer hose was brought outside through an open window. The pressure was two hundred pounds.

Burnt equipment is the dirtiest equipment that can be found, but I had a job. I was working for Lee and Ray, and I would work hard, do my best, and never complain. I worked on that outfit for a long time, and I even got to overhaul the engine with Ray's help. The only experience I had up to this time was with a one-cylinder Briggs engine in college, so this was big time. A 2010 was a four-cylinder gas engine, but all the basics were the same: fuel, air, and ignition. When I got the mechanical part of the reconditioning done and all the hydraulic hoses had been remade and replaced, I put gasoline in the fuel tank and turned the key. The engine started the first time we cranked it over. Everybody was surprised by that, but none was more surprised than me. Harlan Groenenboom, Dwight Morrow, and Dennis Dursky were working that day, and they all gave me advice about my work and how to take care of a wife. (Some of their wisdom about wives was not very accurate.)

Van Gorp Implement sold Van Dale silage equipment along with John Deere farm equipment. I helped anybody Ray or Lee told me to help. I have told people that when I punched the clock in to work, I was theirs until I punched the clock out to go home.

Ed was a salesman at Van Gorp who a few years earlier had really upset my dad. Our Kelly Ryan elevator had blown off the big Behlen twenty-foot-tall ear corn cribs on the river bottom farm. The Kelly Ryan elevator was bent really bad and ruined, which I was happy about because it was little and narrow. I thought maybe we could get a new wide John Deere elevator. First, we had to stop at Carmichael's and get a price on a new narrow Kelly Ryan forty-four-foot elevator. Then we went to Van Gorp to get a price on a

John Deere elevator. When we got to Van Gorp, there sat the most beautiful and wide John Deere forty-four-foot elevator, with a folding hopper and spouts for ear corn. We went in and got the price from Ed. It was a good price, and I knew I had a new elevator coming!

And then my dad asked what his damaged Kelly Ryan was worth on trade, knowing it would be very little. Ed said, "NOTHING, that elevator wasn't worth anything when it was new!"

We went out the door and directly to Carmichael's, and my dad bought that new NARROW Kelly Ryan forty-four-foot elevator. To the corn crib it went.

Now I was working at Van Gorp, and I was to help that same Ed put in a bunk feeder on a Saturday morning, which could take all day. He asked if I could be at work by 7:00 on Saturday morning, and I told him I could. Then he had to question me if I would be there, and he just carried on. Ed showed up on Saturday morning at 7:20, and I gave him a hard time and told him my time started at 7:00 and it was not discussable. We went to the farm southeast of Martinsburg and put in the feed system off the silo. Overall, we got along very well, though Ed had a personality that clashed with mine sometimes.

Van Gorp asked me to work the summer after my college graduation, and I told them I would like to do that. That's when we went and bought that Schwinn bike, on which I would ride the two miles from work to our apartment. Martha drove me to work on inclement days.

I worked at Van Gorp all summer on regular hours (five full days, then Saturdays until noon). I had a great time and experience. My dad had taught his boys pretty good about the care and maintenance of equipment.

As you know, I accepted the job teaching industrial arts in Montezuma, and we were moving once the summer was over. Van Gorp asked me if I wanted to work on Saturdays, as they needed me.

I told them, "Of course!" In the fall, I worked most Saturdays all day until 4:00 in the afternoon; I only occasionally did so in the spring. I got my draft notice, and then things of importance had to be taken care of. But Van Gorp told me they would really like to have me come back.

Chapter 10

My Time in Basic Training

As the government started drafting young men, it became clear that I would either have to get a deferment or I would have to go to the Army. I chose the Army for a couple of reasons: (1) I was doing a good job of teaching and could have continued, but being inside all the time and putting up with kids that were like me (or worse) every day was not exactly what I wanted to do; (2) we were convinced (wrongly) that if I did get drafted I would get good duty and we would still be together; (3) I felt something in me that said I didn't want to get a deferment and have to live with that the rest of my life.

My dad had been in Europe in World War II, so I knew I could go if called upon. Sure enough, in March, I got my draft letter. Martha was pregnant, and I had a teaching contract until the end of May, so we had to make some decisions. I tried to be a good husband and make plans that would take care of her until we could get together after my training. I got an extension until May 20, and we set up Martha to live with my parents.

A recruiter contacted me and told me to enlist for two years instead of getting drafted because that would improve my chances of better duty. I did that, but it was not approved, so I followed my draft notice and orders by reporting to Fort Des Moines. My folks drove Martha and me to the fort on the south side of Des Moines, where I started my military career.

My Time in Basic Training

I am intrigued by the fact that throughout my time in the Army, my parents would take Martha and me to the fort or the airport, and they would bring Martha to pick me up, but they always stood in the background. Not once did they ever get in our way—they always waited until Martha and I had met or they left us alone to say our goodbyes.

The next day was just a bunch of tests. I didn't need or get a physical because my preinduction physical was only 364 days old, and it was good for a year. At about 2:00 in the afternoon, we all went to a big room and took the oath to protect and defend our country and the Constitution of the United States of America. From there, a group of us were taken to the Des Moines airport and put on an airplane to Kansas City. This was my first airplane ride. After we got up in the air a little ways, the pilot came on the speaker and told us we were making an emergency landing back in Des Moines because the windshield had blown out. After a couple of hours, we were back in the air. When we got to Kansas City, we were put on a bus to Fort Leonard Wood in the Ozark Mountains of Missouri, south of Jefferson City. All I know is it was late at night, and they took us to a barracks and told us good night. All I had was a little duffle bag with a toothbrush, a razor, and a pair of clean underwear. I spent the next ten days in the reception area because they were not starting a new basic training class until after Memorial Day. It would have been just as well for me to be back teaching my kids in Montezuma. This was my first experience with the Army way. It was pretty nice there, except they were the old World War II barracks and Martha wasn't there.

After Memorial Day, they moved us to the basic training area, where the barracks were almost new. Then the torment started. The drill sergeants with their brown hats did their best to intimidate everybody. If they came down the hall, everybody had to scream, "Make a hole." Then we'd act like a spider against the wall. It was

Chisel Points in the Ground

only to teach everybody they were the boss. Out of the 250 men, I got picked to be a squad leader. (I guess it was because I was a pretty big guy ... and being ugly helped.) That meant I would be in charge of sixteen recruits, leading them where we needed to be, helping with their training, praising them for doing good, and kicking their ***** for doing bad. It also got me a private room and out of KP (kitchen patrol) and guard duty.

I had it pretty good. My dad had told me before I left to keep my nose clean, do what I was told, and get out as soon as I could. Basic training was very interesting to me and not hard because I was in pretty good shape. The push-ups and calisthenics didn't bother me, getting up early was normal, and quickly eating everything on your plate was the way we were raised. The brigade chapel was close, and they would always let us off to go to chapel on Sunday (but the rest of the day we were theirs).

I really enjoyed the military tactics training, the rifle range, tearing apart and putting together weapons, and first aid. I could walk ten miles with the best of them. I also really enjoyed leading men and showing them that I would go first, so all they had to do was, "FOLLOW ME!"

Sometimes the drill sergeants would use somebody as an example in pugil stick training. I think I had upset this one sergeant because after our lessons, he pulled me out to fight this big kid with pugil sticks. This guy made me look like a midget! They had told us in the class that when we were going against our enemy, we should scream as loud as we could to startle him, then give him an uppercut directly to his groin, hitting him hard enough in the nuts to incapacitate him. This guy was big enough to kill me, so I screamed at him, swinging up on the pugil stick. He went down in a heap. The sergeant didn't like that, so he grabbed the pugil stick and was going teach me. Thank God the class time was over, and I got a reprieve! We never went back.

My Time in Basic Training

I remember my folks and Martha coming and getting me over the Fourth of July. I spent a few days at home, then they took me back. Another weekend, Martha's sister, Clara, and her husband, Don, brought Martha down. We went to Jefferson City for a night, which was nice. For graduation, my parents brought Martha down to see me march in the parade. Then we got to spend a few hours together. My younger siblings—Tom, Dick, and Annie—always came along.

Just a few days before graduation, I got my orders for AIT (advanced individual training). I was told that I was a very lucky draftee because I was going to Fort Bliss Texas for radar and missile control training. They said my family and I would be in Germany in ninety days. What a great way to tell my wife that life and the Army were good! They took me back to the fort so I could be back in time to ship out.

Chapter 11

Advanced Individual Training at Fort Bliss

When it was time for me and others to head to Texas, we got on a big jet at the St. Louis airport. We dropped off guys at a couple of places. (I know one was San Antonio.) Then we went to El Paso, where we were met by a man and a bus and taken to Fort Bliss.

I know it was about 2:00 in the morning when we got there. The big, ugly sergeant had these words for us: "WELCOME CONG BAIT!"

I asked him what he was talking about, because I was told I got radar and missile control duty and would be going to Germany. He simply said, "You are a Foxtrot 40. That's here—the other is across the street."

It turns out, the guy in Fort Leonard Wood I'd talked to thought all of Fort Bliss was radar and missile control training, but that wasn't the case. I was assigned to F40, which I found out was convoy protection only used in Vietnam. After the initial shock, we got taken to the barracks to sleep. All the earthly possessions I had with me were in my duffel bag, which was a canvas bag about twelve inches in diameter and maybe thirty inches tall. It had a strap for a handle, and when folded shut, there was a place for a padlock. We were in a fairly new barracks, and about half of us were National Guard or Army Reservists.

We were introduced early to the weapons we would be trained on. That included a "Duster," or a twenty-five-ton armored track vehicle with an open turret. The driver was under armor but could open the hatch and be exposed. The turret had twin 40mm automatic cannons that were fed with four-round clips of ammunition. It was manned by a driver, a gunner, two ammo loaders, and a crew chief or "squad leader." The other weapon was a "Quad 50," which was a small turret that would electrically turn 360 degrees and elevate from 30 degrees to 120 degrees. It had a steel plate in front of the gunner's seat. It was armed with two 50-caliber machine guns on each side of the plate; they were fed by a loader on each side, with the gunner in a center seat with the sights. This weapon was mounted on a five-ton tandem truck stateside, but it was on a ten-ton tandem truck in Vietnam. Its crew also consisted of a driver, a gunner, two ammo loaders, and a "squad leader." I think the 50-caliber ammo came in boxes that held 500 rounds each.

We had physical training every morning, then we went to class to learn about these weapon systems. I decided that if I was going to Nam to serve in a protection vehicle tucked in convoys, I would probably be the target of the enemy and had better learn everything I could so I could stay alive. I decided that if God was allowing me to go to the Army—to go to Vietnam—that He wanted me to return to my family. But my part was to learn what I could, so I didn't do anything stupid.

It wasn't very long until we were working and learning hands-on about these weapon systems. In the classroom, we studied how the guns were put together and the operation of each. We tore apart 50-caliber machine guns and put them back together. Each 50 will shoot 750 rounds per minute, so the four of them would be shooting 3,000 rounds per minute. All four guns would be aimed to hit the target 3,000 yards away—and nobody would want to be that target. It was devastating firepower.

The 40-milimeter barrels were so large that we could only work on them on top of the track. The barrels were heavy, and it took several men to handle them. We had to know how the firing mechanisms of each worked and be able to make them work. I think the 40mm cannons fired thirty rounds per minute each, so a total of sixty rounds per minute.

Our training also included more first aid, field sanitation, and how to survive in the jungle. They gave us driving lessons in the motor pool parking lot and let us feel the controls. The track vehicle was powered by a V12 gasoline engine (a Korean War vintage), and it skidded a lot in the gravel. But it was easy to drive a tandem-axle truck in the motor pool area. They took us to the desert one day and told us it was time to get the track driver's license. We got a little hands-on training, then they turned us loose to drive. Our license would be issued when we came back with a jack rabbit we had run down (squashed). Would you believe that on the desert roads, a jack rabbit can get going up to forty-five miles per hour? And they can turn a lot faster than a small tank! I got along pretty well, and I had the rabbit in my grasp (or so I thought). But then I saw a big washout in the road in front of me. It was six feet deep and maybe thirty feet wide. I can tell you that a twenty-five-ton tank only stays airborne for a short period of time, and then it drops. My body came out of the hatch and then down and my elbows hit the one-inch-thick deck. It hurt like ****. Then I had to get myself out of that washout. Nobody saw it that I know of, but I am sure the rabbit was laughing!

Advanced individual training (AIT) was more relaxed than basic training; they didn't work us all hours of the night, unless we were doing nighttime maneuvers or night fire. The night fire was really pretty, as every third round out of the 50-calibers was a red tracer round. The four guns were targeted to come together at 3,000 yards. At 3,000 rounds per minute, there were 1,000 red rounds per minute.

One of the very interesting parts of this training was map reading, target locating, and navigation techniques. The Army wanted us to be able to figure out where we were with a map and use a compass to get back to a friendly area if ever required. I thought that would be a good idea too. I did have KP (kitchen patrol) and guard duty while in AIT. I remember one night for guard duty, I got picked to be the guard at the finance building. I think that was the only place on base that had money, and it was the only guard post where the guards were given live ammo—for an M16 (or today an AR-15). At about 2:00 in the morning, a guy came walking up. I did what I was told, shouting, "Who goes there?"

Well, he thought he was too good to respond, so I pulled back on the charging rod and told him to get in the front-leaning rest position. He knew he had better do it because he'd heard the M16 load. He got down really quick. I found out he was the officer of the Guard, the man in charge of all base security and he had come to do a check. I guess I passed. The National Guard troops all had some experience with the military and knew how to shine their boots... and their noses. (They'd brown-nose the officers for special treatment and did really well in the inspections.)

We got several trips to the dentist to have our teeth in top shape (I assume because if we got killed, they wanted us to die with good teeth). I studied my stuff really hard, and I was mechanical enough when it came to field-stripping weapons and taking care of the vehicles that I was near the top of the class.

The Army had an NCO Academy there, which was called a "Shake and Bake School." In five months, they would take a private or PFC and turn them into a squad leader (sergeant) for Vietnam. We had some of those guys in our AIT class; they had all enlisted for three years to go to that school. About halfway through AIT, I was doing really well, and I was big enough to take charge. So, the lifers started talking to me about extending a year (making it a three-year hitch) and going to Nam as a sergeant instead of a PFC. I told them every time that I was in no longer than I had to be, but every time the rank of the person talking to me got higher. Finally, the battery commander (captain) had his go at me to get me to extend for another year, and I told him what my dad had told me: "Keep your nose clean and get out as soon as you can."

A week before graduation, we all got orders for a thirty-day leave. Then we were to report to Oakland, California, for assignment to the Republic of Vietnam. It was not a good feeling to have those orders. I would be going to Nam in the mid-part of October, and our first child would be born in late November.

Graduation day came, and I was the number-one graduate and was supposed to be recognized in the ceremony, but instead I got assigned KP duty. I worked all day in the kitchen and never got to graduation, but I was done when the time on my orders came, so I could leave to be on the flight home. I went to the orderly room to check out with my gear, and they asked where I thought I was going. I told them, "HOME. That is what my orders say."

They had changed my orders, and I had to stay at Fort Bliss another two weeks, go home for two weeks, and then report back to Bliss for the NCO Academy. I spent the two weeks there doing busy work and odd jobs around our area, and then I went home for two weeks. That was my first independent experience with airports, airlines, and airplanes. We always had to fly in dress uniforms, either the fully pressed khakis or the full-dress green uniform. I had never checked in for a flight, gotten a seat assignment, or had to get around an airport. The good news is that El Paso International Airport was small, so it was easy to get around in. Denver was a different story.

I made the transfer, and then I was in Des Moines. My parents always brought Martha to pick me up, and when I got off the airplane, she was just inside the gate (this was before all the security). We kissed and greeted each other, and then my dad and mom came over and said hi. Martha was 90% pregnant by then, and I don't remember what we did, but I know it was nice to be away from the Army.

Chapter 12

Shake and Bake School

I went back to Fort Bliss on the required date to attend NCOCS (Non-Commissioned Officer Candidate School), which was in the same area as my advanced individual training. It was about the same weapon systems, except that it was designed for more advanced training and LEADERSHIP.

I got to the barracks, and the lifers were ready for us. I knew they were going to harass us, but I was not prepared to be the target of all the harassment. We were all promoted to corporal when we got to the school. I never made PFC, so I went right from private to corporal. I found out that out of the class of sixty-five, I was the only draftee and the lifers wanted me gone and gone quick. They gave us spit-shined fiber helmets. Mine was number eleven, and that was how we were identified. It seemed I did nothing right (in their eyes) for the first seven or eight weeks. We also had to wear spit-shined combat boots and pressed and starched uniforms with bloused pants, and that helmet had to shine. Our beds and our areas had to shine too—the bed had to be made so tight that a quarter would bounce on it . . . and mine had to be better than everybody else's stuff.

Needless to say, I never did pass an inspection. I always had a thread out of place on my uniform, my bed was never right, they found dust on the blinds, my locker wasn't organized right, and once they placed a penny in my area and gave me demerits for defacing Lincoln. (Brass not polished, beard not trimmed. It was a "real hoot.")

I was there from mid-October until Christmas break. Since I was always in the barracks, I had to get a pass to go get a haircut. I was allowed to go to chapel, which I did almost every Sunday. Otherwise, I just studied the books, and I was number one in the class as far as academics go. I had the weapon systems down, along with the map reading and target acquisition, military traditions and flag etiquette, and first aid stuff. When we went to labs, I was the top because I knew that when I got to Nam, not only would my life depend on my training, but also the lives of my troops. The drill sergeants took real pride in putting it right to me every chance they got.

I got an intercom call on Veterans Day, November 11, 1970. This is a holiday in the military; nothing goes on, and everybody has a break (except I hadn't passed any inspection yet, so I was restricted to the barracks). I went to the orderly room, and the person in charge told me that my mother had called to say Martha had a baby girl. I asked if I could call home and was told, "NO!" So, all I could do was go back to the barracks and think about a baby girl. I went down and asked if I could go to the post exchange (PX) and buy cigars for the rest of the class. Again . . . "NO!" It was a nice thought.

Late in the day, with a new person in the office, I was allowed to make a call home and talk to Martha. I remember how excited I was. In a few days, I made a request to go back to Iowa over Thanksgiving to be able to see my baby daughter. Again, I was told, "NO!"

I'd finally had enough, and I told the head dog one day that I was really a pretty nice guy. I said that if they would give me a chance, they would see that, and if they were trying to break me emotionally, they needed to find another guy. I told him that a day putting up with them was better than spending a day in Nam. Nothing changed. In the whole course of school, inspections, tests, and evaluations, I was tied at the top of the class with another guy who had the top in all the inspections. His name was John. He really didn't like me a bit (well, very few did as I was a draftee and they had all signed up for three years, so I guess I understand). By Christmas, they had eliminated two of our candidates, so the class was down to sixty-three.

I found out in late November that Martha and I could get a little house on the base if she wanted to come down with our daughter, Judy, after Christmas and spend three months there. About the first of December, they started to lighten up on me and give me a few freedoms. I did get a little house on Hope Street by the main PX. I was allowed to go to the PX, where I got some material off the bolts to pin up curtains. I also called a place on Dyer Street and rented us the basics of furniture.

Still, I never did get a very good score on any inspection. I was allowed to go home for Christmas, the only reason being that no lifer wanted to have to stay around to keep track of me. I got to the Des Moines airport, where I saw Judy for the first time and even got to hold her. I know my folks were there, but true to form, they gave Martha, Judy, and me time to get reacquainted before they stepped up. It was great to be HOME again, and Martha had the basement all ready for us, so we had some private time. We had Judy baptized in the First Christian Reformed Church (our church), with me in my Army dress greens and corporal stripes. It seemed nobody in the church really cared about what was ahead for Martha and me. A few days before the first of the year, I loaded down our Mercury Comet with the little stuff we had, and the three of us got in and headed to our new home in Fort Bliss, Texas. We got there and settled in, and I told Martha I didn't know if I would ever see her, but I loved her and we would see how the lifers reacted.

I had to report every morning at 4:40, which was okay. I normally had class until at least 7:00 in the evening, but I made it home most nights. They also had a little Vietnamese village set up in the desert, and we would go out there for training on how to clear a village, never knowing whether it was friendly or hostile.

The Army was concerned about our mental welfare, so while in NCOCS, we had a group meeting with a chaplain every week to go over our fears and feelings about going to Vietnam. We talked about being leaders and being responsible for our soldiers and our actions. Lieutenant William Calley and the My Lai Massacre had just hit the news when I was in training. One day, the brigade chaplain was in charge of a group of ten of us, and we were talking about getting killed, wounded, or maimed. It was really a downer. I hadn't said anything, and finally the colonel said, "Drost, what are your fears?"

And I told him: "The first son of a bitch who fires on my convoy had better be prepared to meet his maker, because I'm gonna scream 'fire' and we are gonna take that Quad in a 360-degree turn. Then I will ask who did it. If God is allowing me to go, then He is giving me the sense and the means to bring me home along with my troops. And they can call me Sergeant Calley Drost."

He was taken aback, but class ended shortly after that.

One of the most exciting parts of the NCOCS experience was that we went to the Army War College at Fort Bliss. It was a great lesson in the psychology of troops and what makes them tick and how they will respond. I remember them showing us on a map that if a plane load of paratroopers jumped out of an airplane, I could go to a spot selected on the map and wait for them all to show up. I could find them by simply knowing the terrain and how humans will react. The class also included military history, more about flags and flag etiquette, negotiations, leadership traits, and what troops expected of their leaders. Much of what I learned still holds true today for employees. Everybody wants to follow a person who has their best interests at heart. They told us to lead, which meant we needed to be out ahead.

The final two weeks of school was the last part of February 1971. We did a field exercise, where we would be divided into squads of five and would be evaluated on everything from leadership skills

Chisel Points in the Ground

to mission operations, map reading, warfare techniques, and even how we ate and disposed of the waste. The lifers picked our crews; I got candidates with class ranks of sixty-three, sixty-two, sixty-one, and sixty. Of course, John got class ranks of three, four, five, and six.

Each crew was given a vehicle to drive into the desert. We had to get to the bivouac shelter. On the way out, we had a little talk at break time. I told my crew that the lifers sure didn't want us to succeed because they wanted me out. But just to be clear, they didn't want *any* of us losers to succeed. We all agreed that when we were being watched, we would let the leader lead, but all other times we would work together and make the best of the situation. We all knew it was best to go to Nam as a sergeant instead of a private, if only for the extra pay.

The lifers gave us terrible tasks to do during that field exercise. I will give a few examples. First, they blindfolded us and took us out into the desert a long way from base camp. Then they gave us a map and a compass and told us to find our way back. They were hoping we would all die out there and the buzzards would eat us. But a little after dark, we came rolling in (to their dismay). The sergeant who was evaluating us told us that when we were in the middle of the desert the track had come off our vehicle. We told him that it looked pretty good, but he had words for us. He sat on the sand dune and watched us loosen the track, take it off with a couple of monkey wrenches and a long pry bar, and then put it back on, put it together, and re-tension it. The evaluator sat on the dune eating and drinking water the whole time.

They brought drone jet aircraft out one afternoon (these weapons were used for anti-aircraft fire in Korea). We were supposed to shoot the banner being towed behind the drone. I think there were six Dusters with twin 40mm cannons and six Quads with 50-caliber machine guns lined up on the firing line ready to go. We had anti-aircraft sights, and here came drone

79

number one. He went down in smoke. They got us all together and told us we just shot down a $2 million drone, and we shouldn't do that again because we might have to pay for it. Drone number two made it a little farther. Then came the puff of smoke. We got a good chewing, and I asked under my breath, "What are they going to do? Send me to Nam?" Besides, if we had to pay for it, how many lifetimes would it take to pay off $2 million at $180.00 per month? After drone number three went down in smoke, they decided we were incorrigible, and we left.

Another time, we were out on "patrol" with the evaluator on board. They had the enemy hide in a pile of desert brush in a narrow spot between the sand dunes. He started firing at us. That meant the driver of the track had to put his foot down. You don't stop until you are clear or immobilized. I don't know who was in charge or who was driving, but we did GREAT! We roared out of there and blasted the enemy as we were leaving.

One evening they told us they were bringing all our wives and girlfriends out on a bus to watch our firepower display in the dark. (It was impressive!) We drew a Quad for the night, and we found out that a 50-caliber will fire about 1,200 rounds per minute instead of 750 if you put a quarter under the buffer spring under the back plate. Our squad figured out that the lifers were going be ogling our girls instead of watching us. We were told that each Quad was getting 3,000 rounds for the opening display. We all agreed that we would hook all the ammo belts together, one for each gun. When they said "fire," the gunner would squeeze the electronic trigger and the other four of us would feed the belts in our gun. We also agreed that each gun would have a quarter under the plate behind the buffer spring. When we were empty, the plates would come off, the quarters would be flung into the desert, and the plates would be put back on because we would have them all over us in minutes. We were all set, and when we got the command to fire, we executed our plan flawlessly. We were correct. The radio started blaring "fire," and we told them we were empty and that we'd ruined four barrels. In a few minutes, lifers were all over that truck, but nobody found the quarters because they went a long ways out in the desert.

Finally, the last night we were out on the field exercise, all the lifers wanted to get a nice night's sleep in the bunkers. We had been sleeping on the ground in sleeping bags, and we would have ice in our canteens in the mornings. We had a huge supply of blank ammunition for our M16s, and our squad decided that the lifers shouldn't have a good night's sleep. So, we loaded our magazines full of blanks and snuck around in the dark to the stairs to the bunker. All five of us emptied our M16s and disappeared into the dark. A couple of hours later, we went and did the same thing. We didn't get caught, but we didn't want a fun thing to go bad, so we crawled into our bags and slept the rest of the night.

When we got back to the base, we found out that they actually scored us the best squad of the field exercise. My buddy, John, was in charge of his squad. When they hit the ambush, he screwed up and commanded them to halt because he wanted to fight it out. He was nearly put out of the school, but his brown nose kept him in.

The next thing was graduation day. It was a big deal at Fort Bliss when another class graduated; the ceremony took place in the base auditorium, and the commanding general of the fort was in charge. After all the speeches and formalities, Sergeant Carl G. Drost was announced as the distinguished graduate of the class. They read a pretty nice citation about me. I was the only draftee in the class, and they all watched as the general shook my hand. The distinguished graduate had always been given the rank of sergeant E-6, which was really good. But the draftee only got sergeant E-5, which I believe God knew would be better for me in Nam according to His plan. Following the graduation, they had a reception for us back in the brigade area. The colonel, Martha, and

Shake and Bake School

This family photo was also taken before I was deployed to Vietnam. Judy was four months old.

Photo courtesy of Alan Adams Photography.

I cut the cake, and it was all pretty nice. After graduation, I had thirty days of on-the-job training, helping with the new class of "Shake and Bakes" who were coming in.

It was almost miraculous how overnight I turned into a nice guy, and the lifers showed me some respect. Martha and I got to spend weekends together, and sometimes I had the day off but had to do a study hall in the evening. We went to Carlsbad Caverns in New Mexico, and we took the tram to the top of the mountain in El Paso. We had our family picture taken on post at the military place with my dress greens and the sergeant stripes. It is still one of my favorite pictures, with Judy being only four months old and Martha in her short dress. We always got paid in cash on the last day of the month, and we had a ritual: Go to the PX and buy diapers, resupply anything we needed, go to the commissary (or grocery store) and get baby food and anything else we needed, and then go to Der Wienerschnitzel on Dyer Street and have a hot dog and a Coke (we still have a collector glass from there). Then we had no money left until payday.

I had orders to report to the Oakland Transfer Station after a thirty-day leave at home. When the day came to leave Fort Bliss, we rented a U-Haul trailer and tied it behind the Comet. We went to the PX and got a baby crib, a buggy, a stroller, and some other stuff. Then went to the commissary and bought boxes of baby food that Judy liked. We also loaded a three-foot-tall Christmas tree with all the lights and ornaments that my group had bought for Christmas at $0.50 each. Nobody wanted the tree, so we took it home in the trailer. (We still have that special tree today—now it has all John Deere ornaments on it.) We headed to Iowa on Route 54. I was going to drive it straight through, but when we got into central Kansas, I was tired and Judy was screaming. So, we got a motel for a few hours, then we drove the rest of the way home the next day.

Shake and Bake School

DEPARTMENT OF THE ARMY
HEADQUARTERS, UNITED STATES ARMY AIR DEFENSE CENTER AND FORT BLISS

CERTIFICATE OF ACHIEVEMENT

AWARDED TO

CARL G. DROST

SGT, UNITED STATES ARMY

for exceptionally meritorious service during the period 26 October 1970 to 26 February 1971 and is designated as the Distinguished Graduate of Class 2-71, Air Defense Noncommissioned Officer Candidate School, 1st Air Defense Training Battalion (Automatic Weapons), 1st Advanced Individual Training Brigade (Air Defense), United States Army Air Defense Center and Fort Bliss, Fort Bliss, Texas. Sergeant Drost's sincere devotion to duty, display of professional competence, and outstanding military attitude served as an inspiration to be emulated by his fellow candidates. His unequaled desire to excel has provided an example of outstanding leadership for all the members of Class 2-71. Sergeant Drost's exemplary performance of duty, unswerving dedication, and outstanding professionalism are in keeping with the highest traditions of the United States Army and reflect great credit upon himself, the Air Defense Noncommissioned Officer Candidate School and the United States Army.

Given at Fort Bliss, Texas
this 26th day of February 1971

RICHARD T. CASSIDY
Major General, United States Army
Commanding

I was the distinguished NCOCS graduate.

Chisel Points in the Ground

My Shake and Bake diploma.

Chapter 13

My Trip to Vietnam

After spending three weeks at home in Oskaloosa, in the basement of Mom and Dad's house, it was time to head out. I had helped plant the corn because Dad was laid up with a very bad back. My ticket was out of the Des Moines airport, and I know my folks took Martha and me to the airport where we said our goodbyes. I kissed Martha and Judy, and under my breath I said, "I hope I will see you again."

It was the uncertainty of everything that caused all the anxiety. I know there is a photo that I assume my brother, Tom, took of me about to go up the rear stairs of a Boeing 727 aircraft. I had turned a little bit and waved goodbye. My mother had done the same thing in late 1944 with a little boy in her arms when my dad was sent to Europe in World War II. I flew to the San Francisco airport, saw the Golden Gate Bridge, and went to the USO club for a while. Why be early for a plane ride to Nam? The Army provided buses from the airport to the Oakland Transfer Station, and we went across the Oakland Bay Bridge and on to the center. There were a lot of soldiers there, waiting on orders for rides to some place. It was close to the Pacific Ocean; I could see the port with all the cranes, the cargo containers, and the ships being unloaded there.

I went to chapel there. I know it was Mother's Day 1971, and all I could think of was how Martha was a new mother by herself. We had to go out on the parade field two or three times a day, where they would read off the roster for the next plane load headed to Vietnam. Once, they announced they were going to take a hundred soldiers to Germany. They started reading off the names in this group. I knew my name would be next, until the hundredth name was read. Then reality set in that I was going to Vietnam.

My name was finally called, and I gathered up my personal belongings in my duffel bag. I was now dressed in green jungle fatigues and jungle boots with green underwear and green handkerchiefs. There were four more sets of jungle clothes in the duffel bag and one set of khakis and dress shoes. We went to the airport and got on a chartered commercial airplane. Of the three hundred people onboard, I only knew one person. There were for sure no ceremonies or speeches, and we lifted off.

We went to Anchorage, Alaska, and I remember looking out the window on the approach and seeing a moose just outside the chain link fence of the runway. We got off the airplane in a guarded, secure area, where we stayed for a couple of hours. Then we went to a military airport in Yokota, Japan, which is just outside Tokyo. We were there for a few hours. The next stop was Long Biên, Vietnam, which was the United States' large airbase just outside Saigon. The reality of war set in when the buses pulled up to take us away and all the windows had chain link fence over them to keep the rockets and grenades from coming in. I remember it was 2:00 in the morning their time, and we had been in transit for a lot of hours. We were taken to the transfer station, and before we got to find a bed, we got a big shot of hemoglobin in the butt. We also had to get fluoride treatment on our teeth. (Can't die without good teeth.) I finally found a bunk at some time, but I had hardly lain down when my name was called to report to the center. I was sent back to the Long Biên airport and put on a C-130 transport plane. I had been assigned to the 23rd Infantry Division at Chu Lai, then to the 3rd/82nd Field Artillery of the 196th Light Infantry Brigade at Da Nang. I got to the airport in Chu Lai (the 23rd Infantry's headquarters), and it was a short walk to the orderly room, where

I was checked in. I knew one soldier in the group: Sergeant Dross from NCOCS. I never saw him again during my whole tour.

I was finally allowed to sleep for a while and eat some, but the next day started three days of in-country orientation. It was miserably hot, and the air was full of water, but it was right on the coast of the South China Sea. As a farm kid from Iowa, I had never been close to a body of water like that, and we could go out in it; it was very beautiful. They had classes on what to expect in-country, including on the culture, language, religions, and other stuff. It was supposed to be a secure area, so when we had to go on drills into the jungle, they would issue us an M16 and ammo. The first night I was there, I was assigned guard duty with another guy along the beach of the South China Sea. They told us we could alternate sleeping, but that didn't look like a good deal to me. I couldn't sleep, and the water had small waves on it. It looked to me like there was a Viet Cong riding on every wave. I was so glad to see the sun come up and that I was still alive. I had never been so scared in my life.

They had real-life booby traps set up. They threw grenades at us and got us stinky with all the mud, crap, and water that was thrown on us. It was pretty realistic of what to expect in the jungle. I only prayed I would not go there and was thankful for the artillery assignment. After a few days, I was again given my orders to go to Da Nang, so I was off to the Chu Lai airport and another C-130 (the only airplane I know about that can reverse). We flew to the Da Nang airport, which was reputed to be the busiest airport in the world with all the bombers and fighters that took off twenty-four hours a day.

I was met at the airport by Staff Sergeant Richard White, who was the personnel sergeant of the 3rd/82nd Artillery. He took me to the headquarters, Battery on Freedom Hill and Camp Redhorse. Everybody wore helmets and flak jackets. We drove through a little village. The street was narrow, and I could imagine lots of stuff. They had told us little kids would run out and push a grenade into the fuel tank neck. If that happened, it was all over because that was a perfect spot. I was scared.

We got to Staff Sergeant White's office. My training was in convoy patrol. I had just ridden in the only vehicle they had with tires on it, since this was an air/mobile unit and everything (that is *everything*) was moved by helicopter. Staff Sergeant White asked me what I wanted to do because they had no Dusters or Quads. I asked what my choices were. He asked what I did in civilian life, and I told him I taught high school industrial arts. He told me he would give me a choice: "I can send you to a hill, and you can learn artillery, or you can help me. What is it?"

It didn't take me long to tell him I would help him. I just asked what I was to do, and his response was simple: "Do what the colonel, the captain, and I need done, and it will be good." He took me to a hootch that had a tin roof, four-foot plywood sides, three feet of netting, and a wooden floor with cots on it. There was a place to plug in a fan and a refrigerator. I got settled in, and then Staff Sergeant White introduced me to the group I would be working with: Lieutenant Colonel Martin, the battalion commander; Captain William J. Klus; Specialist 5 Willard Kinman; and Specialist 4 Larry Rascoe. There were a couple of other guys, but I was never well acquainted with them.

Camp Redhorse had been a U.S. Marine post (until a month earlier, when the Marines had been pulled out of Vietnam). Our responsibility was the security of the Da Nang airbase, so we had guns on the hills that stood on three sides of the base. The fourth side was the South China Sea. I found out we had batteries of 105mm, 155mm, and 175mm howitzers, as well as eight-inch howitzers, scattered on these hills. I got a desk and a typewriter in the Battalion S-1 office (personnel). My assigned task was to do what needed to be done, but I was also in charge of the public information releases about soldiers that went in hometown newspapers. I was to write news articles for various military publications. Then the colonel wanted to know if I knew how to take pictures. I told him I had taken a few with a Kodak Instamatic, but I would learn. So, he gave me the Army camera.

Before I left Oskaloosa, I had gone to the photo shop in town and asked Mary Jane which camera I should buy when I got to Vietnam. She told me to buy a Mamiya/Sekor 1000DTL camera. It was as good as it gets. So, I got a ride in our jeep to the post exchange (PX) down the road a piece, and they had that exact camera in there. It was just a little over a hundred dollars, and I got it. Now, I had my camera with a shutter speed of one-thousandth of a second and shooting color Kodachrome film, plus the Army camera (shooting black and white because the photos last a long time).

Lieutenant Colonel Martin told me he had a division meeting once a month, where he always got the award for having the least public information releases (though an artillery battalion is the smallest of the division). My goal was to change that, so I sent out a blank form to everybody in our battalion and had them fill in their name and important information. I kept those forms on file. When a new soldier came in, I got them to fill one out too. I would fill out a public information release on anything—if a soldier got moved to a different hill, got an in-country or out-of-country rest and recuperation (R&R), or got a medal or anything. They all needed a zip code, and I knew that if the first number was zero it was in the Northeast, one was the Southeast, and five was in the Midwest. The first month, the colonel came home with the award for the most releases in the division, and he was a happy camper. He really liked me!

The colonel had a little observation helicopter at his disposal that carried four people: the pilot and up to three others. I had the black-and-white Army camera and my camera with color slide film, and at least once a week the colonel would take me along to get pictures of the firebases that we had scattered around the hills surrounding the Da Nang airbase. When he asked if I was ready, my answer was always, "Yes, sir." And I would don the flak jacket, get a rifle, and off we would go. The pictures I took would get printed and published in the military papers, and the colonel would get awards for them as well.

 I was in charge of all the awards and decorations for our artillery battalion. The Army, especially the lifers, really valued those and their effect on the morale of the troops. I wrote up releases on all the awards, including Army Commendation Medals, Bronze Stars, and letters of commendation. I only wrote one for a Silver Star. When the awards came through, we would have to organize a ceremony to honor the recipients. Sometimes it would be in the rear area, and sometimes it would be on a firebase. Some of the others we would just give to them. But for lifers, any award had to be in their permanent record. During one ceremony we had on a firebase, they actually loaded up the division band on a Chinook helicopter. They took the tubas, trumpets, trombones, and all the instruments to a hilltop for the ceremony. I have often wondered what the Viet Cong had to have thought when they heard "The Star-Spangled Banner" being played from a hill in the midst of triple-canopy jungle.

 At other times, I would go to the helipad and catch a ride on a Huey "slick" to a firebase for the day to take pictures. These birds had no doors, and there was a gunner on each side with an M60 (7.62 caliber) machine gun ready at all times. The chopper was the only means of transportation that we had since it was an air-mobile unit. There were no roads to any of our firebases on the hills.

 Martha was very faithful in writing letters every day and sending me pictures of Judy. Martha and my mom would send packages with homemade cookies (which always ended up in small pieces from being bounced around for three weeks) and other goodies; boxes like that were always shared with my buddies, as well as some people I did not know or had never seen before. Martha and I got to talk to each other in person two times while I was gone using a ham radio operator in Illinois. It was difficult to make the connection because of the twelve-hour time difference. But a couple of times I was on guard on Sunday night, and I would go to the orderly room and try the ham connection, hoping it would go through to Iowa, where it was Sunday afternoon. The only cost was for the person-to-person collect call from Illinois to Oskaloosa. It was great to hear Martha's voice and Judy's whimpers, but the calls were limited to three minutes, and we had to say "over" at the end of each statement so the guy would know to change the transmitter. We'd say "out" at the end of the conversation. It wasn't much, but it was better than nothing. I always felt sorry for the guys who would go to mail call every day and go for months without a card or letter. Then on my birthday, I'd get a whole pack of cards from my relatives and friends.

One day, the weather report was that we had a typhoon heading our way out of the Pacific Ocean, then into the South China Sea. A hurricane, cyclone, and typhoon are all the same, but the name depends on which ocean they are in. This typhoon's name was Hester, and as it got closer, it kept getting stronger until it was a Category 5 hurricane (they don't get much bigger). It was heading straight for Da Nang and we were told to get prepared. (Yeah, right.) Where were we going with concertina wire around our perimeter and Viet Cong all around? Our little hootch was sure not going to stand the 165-mile-per-hour winds that were predicted for us. So, we made sure our underground bunkers had good drainage, and we put our valued earthly possessions underground. (We used the underground for shelter if and when we were attacked with aerial and artillery or rocket bombardment.) We also had a thick, galvanized, round roof covered with three layers of sandbags.

When Hester arrived, it was a very furious storm. It started as a strong wind. When we couldn't stay standing anymore, we went underground with our weapons and what else, and we let it blow. It blew for twelve hours straight and rained like I had never seen before. We could look out, and it was raining so hard nobody could see three feet in front of the opening. The danger during the storm was that the Viet Cong would come through the wire and be on top of our bunkers and shoot the American troops as we came out. They had done that on one of our firebases during a rocket attack.

After about twelve hours, it seemed to get perfectly calm (the eye of Hester). It was calm for twenty to twenty-five minutes, and we went out to see that we had nothing left above the ground except the really heavy stuff. And then the wind picked up again, turning in the opposite direction as before. It blew for another twelve hours before the typhoon got away from us. During the storm, when the winds were really blowing, I would look out the entry and see the most horrific sight: the palm trees were bent down parallel to the ground. Then there was the shrill whistle of the wind . . . I had heard that whistle in movies and thought it to be fake, but it was all real.

When the hurricane left, we put up our security again, and my carpentry skills came into play. We could wait and subsist, or we could do something. So, we scrounged around for what we could find from our camp, as well as what had blown in from other places. Then we made shelters.

It is after the storm that one can see the real power of Mother Nature. But we used little sixteen-gauge communication wire all over the place, in the air and on the ground. The Army used Strongbarn corrugated steel roofing, which is about three times heavier than what Iowa barns have on them. I saw a piece of steel cut nearly two-thirds of the way across with a piece of communication wire. The wire had been pulled off its anchor, not cut. Nobody should have been out in the storm. Our base was front-page news in the worldwide edition of the *Stars and Stripes* because it was so severely damaged. Experiencing one of those storms in one's life is enough.

The Army chaplains would come to the hills and do a church service for Protestants, Catholics, and Jews. There was a different chaplain for each. When we were on the hills, they would have a short message, then the Lord's Supper with juice and crackers (usually spread on a bunker of sandbags). The chaplains would have to catch a ride on a chopper to get to our firebases on the hills. We practiced social distancing to keep separated in case of incoming fire (no COVID-19 then).

My boss was Captain William J. Klus, who was in charge of the five sections of Battalion S-1 and was also the commander of the Guard. He was a math major in college and seemed to be a really nice person. He had been to ROTC and was really clean-cut. He was just a newlywed, and he missed his wife. Because of the Army rules, non-coms (like me) could not fraternize with officers like Captain Klus. The Air Force base had lot better food than us, so a couple of times, we put sergeant bars on the captain and took the jeep down to the base to eat together at the Non-Com Club. They had really good teriyaki and other stuff there.

One night, Staff Sergeant White, Specialist 5 Kinman, and I took Captain Klus' jeep and went to the Air Force base for dinner. It was raining, and the captain had planned on riding in the dry in his jeep. He was really mad when we came back. He made all kinds of threats about what he was going to do to us. The good news is he cooled off after his threats and told us the least we could have done was ask.

Captain Klus wrote Martha two of the nicest letters any wife would love to receive. One was about what a great guy I was and all my accomplishments. The second was sent just before I was to head home to give Martha a heads up that I would be a different person than when she put me on the plane to Nam.

My Trip to Vietnam

DEPARTMENT OF THE ARMY
Headquarters 3rd Battalion (105T) 82nd Artillery
APO San Francisco 96256

13 September 1971

Dear Mrs. Drost,

I am sure you will allow me a few minutes of your time to talk to you concerning a subject most important to you-------- Your Husband.

Carl has been doing an outstanding job as the Public Information and Awards Specialist in my section, the S-1 (Personnel and Administration) section of 3rd Battalion 82nd Artillery. More ambition than Carl has shown could not be expected from one individual.

Let me tell a few of the achievements resulting directly from Carl's efforts:

    a. Durin an Annual General Inspection in March, the Public Information and Awards portion of S-1 received a Satisfactory rating; during a reinspection in June, an Excellent rating was received.

    b. For the months of June, July, and August, 3rd Battalion 82nd Artillery had the most Hometown News Releases accepted for publication of the 6 battalions in the 23d Infantry Division Artillery. This has not been achieved by 3d Battalion 82nd Artillery in over a year and that was a single month, not three months in a row.

    c. 3d Battalion 82d Artillery has had at least five stories recently released for publication in both 23d Infantry Division and United States Army Vietnam publications, the latter newspapers and magazines are circulated throughout all of Vietnam. This also has not been accomplished by this battalion in over a year.

    d. Each battery firstsergeant (there are five batteries) is submitting a weekly story with enthusiasm for Carl's review and editing. Enthusiastic performance by a first sergeant in a matter of this regard is a remarkable achievement. Enthusiasm is a difficult thing to draw from a first sergeant.

    e. The most recent achievement of Carl's is that during the month of August, the 3rd Battalion 82nd Artillery submitted more Hometown News Releases that were accepted for publication than any other battalion in the entire 23rd Infantry Division, not just Division Artillery. This has never been accomplished in this battalion before.

I am truly proud to have Carl working in my section. Besides an outstanding worker in a job in which he has had no prior experience, he is an outstanding individual.

You can certainly be proud of Carl. You may rest assured that I will do all in my power to see that he safely returns home to you.

WILLIAM J KLUS
CPT, FA
Adjutant

My good Captain.

Chisel Points in the Ground

DEPARTMENT OF THE ARMY
Headquarters 3d Battalion (105T) 82d Artillery
APO San Francisco 96256

AVDF-ATMZ

11 September 1971

SUBJECT: Letter of Appreciation

SGT Carl G. Drost
HH&S Btry, 3d Bn, 82d Arty
APO San Francisco 96256

1. The purpose of this letter is to express my appreciation in behalf of all members of this battalion for your accomplishments in the field of public information. Since you assumed your duties as information specialist the battalion's public information program has steadily improved. Many fine newspaper articles that have been prepared or edited by you have appeared in the division newspaper or Stars and Stripes. Further, the battalion now leads the entire division in the number of home-town news releases accepted for publication highlighting the accomplishments of members of this battalion.

2. Your work has had a definite impact on the morale of the battalion because many individuals and their accomplishments have been recognized in print both here in RVN and back in the world. This is a fine way to express the appreciation of this battalion to its individual members for a hard and dangerous job well done.

RICHARD C. MARTIN
LTC, FA
Commanding

My Trip to Vietnam

My first Bronze Star.

Chapter 14

R&R Trip

It came time for me to get my R&R trip. I had the choice of going to Bangkok, Sydney, or Honolulu. Or, the Army had just come with a new program where a soldier in Vietnam could take a seven-day leave plus his seven-day R&R and fly home. I took the last option.

I selected my dates to correspond with Judy's first birthday. The Army was really good at getting things all organized. Martha and I had to pay for my ticket from Honolulu home and back to Honolulu. But Martha was "rich" when I married her, so I think she paid for it out of her (or our) savings account. I had to fly on a C-130 from Da Nang to Long Biên. (I just went to the airport and waited for a flight from Da Nang to Saigon. I got on, but of course they got my name down.) Then I had to wait a day for the Freedom Bird to come to take me to Honolulu. All four hundred of us were so excited, but the plane didn't come . . . and it didn't come. They told us it would be there in a couple of hours. Finally, they told us the plane would not be coming that day, but it would be there tomorrow at the same time. What a letdown! So, another night at the center with basically nothing to do.

The Army told us not to worry about our kin on the other end, because they would notify them that we would be one day late. The next day came, and right on time we heard the Bird taxiing, but we could see nothing. They started calling our names. When they said, "Sergeant Carl G. Drost," I made a beeline to the door. Sitting on the tarmac was the biggest airplane I had ever seen: a Pan Am 747. The military was chartering these airplanes to fly us to Honolulu. We finally got loaded, and I will never forget how long that plane went down the runway before the nose came off the ground. The pilot pulled the nose in the air in a steep climb, and we were out of there. The pilot came on and told us we were on our way to Manila in the Philippines. Now, I hadn't seen very many "round-eyed" women in six months, and we were all expecting to find really young, beautiful stewardesses on this plane. But they were "old" (maybe forty) and not very good-looking. And they were crabby!

We got to Manila. When I was in the gift shop, I bought Martha a short dress made out of banana leaf fibers. I hadn't had my arms around her since May, and this was November. I had to try to get the right size, so I found a clerk who I thought was Martha's size and bought the dress to fit the clerk. (It fit perfectly when I got home.)

We loaded back on the 747. Seat assignments didn't matter; any seat beat staying there. I like to be on time, and I knew we were behind time. After we'd been airborne a little while, the pilot came on the speaker and said, "Good afternoon, boys! I know we are two hours behind, and I know some of you have flights to catch in Honolulu. But there are only four hundred on board today, and we are 90,000 pounds under maximum gross weight. I am going upstairs where it is shorter, and we will be in Honolulu ahead of schedule." I remember that I started to watch a movie as the sun started going down, and the sun was coming up again before the movie ended. I was much too excited to sleep.

We did get to Honolulu ahead of schedule. When we pulled up to the customs terminal and the doors opened and the aroma of Hawaii came in, I knew Martha and I would come back sometime. We cleared customs, and I grabbed my little suitcase (a small Samsonite) and headed to United to catch the plane to San Francisco. When we got there, I had to change terminals and planes. We had to travel in khaki uniform, and I can tell you that a lot of people had a lot of nasty things to say to a person in a military uniform in the airport there. If I didn't want to get home so bad, I might have made a scene, but I went to the gate and got on my plane to Des Moines. When we landed, I went into the terminal. There was Martha, holding our baby Judy, nearly a year old. We hugged and kissed, and then my folks came over and welcomed me home. I got my little suitcase and headed to the car.

It was then I found out that they didn't know I was going to be a full day late. The Army had not contacted them, and the four of them had spent the entire previous day waiting for me to come off the airplane. They stayed until the United person told them the last flight was off the ground coming to Des Moines, and my name was not on the list. They went home and came back the next morning to wait for me to show up. They kept checking with the United Airlines people. Finally, my name showed up on a manifest from San Francisco, so they knew the wait was only hours. My folks were always with Martha, and I know they supported her through some difficult days.

We got to the Drost farm on top of "Chicken S***" Knob, and we'd just gotten in the house when the phone rang. "This is the Department of the Army, and we are calling to tell you Carl has been delayed." Thanks!

I don't remember much of what we did in those seven or eight days, but I know we celebrated Judy's first birthday. Martha, Judy, and I loaded up in the car, and we were gone for two or three days as we took a driving trip up across Northern Iowa. We stopped at the Little Brown Church in Nashua. We had some other making-up-for time as well, and I'm sure we did good.

During the time I was at home, President Richard "Tricky Dick" Nixon announced he was going to draw down the military forces in Vietnam. Anybody who had served eighteen months in the military and had been in Vietnam for six months would be home permanently for Christmas. I could not believe my ears, but I knew people who would get me orders if this was true. I told Martha not

R&R Trip

to tell anybody, but I should be home for Christmas. We didn't have a place to live yet, but I had given her power of attorney to do what needed to be done.

It was around November 17, before Thanksgiving, when they took me back to the Des Moines airport and I left for Honolulu again. I was going to travel halfway around the world to get my time in, pick up my few belongings, and fly back home before Christmas. I checked in at Honolulu for the reserved Pan Am 747 flight back to Long Biên. I found out our stop on this flight was going to be the Air Force base on Guam.

We got to Guam in the early morning hours. It was really dark, and they gave us two hours to look around a little and then get back to reload. We got back, and they had found a piece broken on the flap of the plane, which they would need to fix. They told us to come back in four hours. We all came back, and the part had not arrived, but it was coming from Hawaii. So, they fed us lunch in the mess hall and told us to be back at 6:00 in the evening. I remember roaming over Guam for the day and getting back on time. The plane still wasn't fixed, so they loaded us on buses and took us to various resorts on the coast to feed us supper. Some of the guys and gals should not have had so much free time, as they were quite inebriated. Our bus got to this resort, and we were escorted to the tables under the torchlit area. We ordered steaks and all the trimmings. (Pan Am was buying.) We had just got a good start on our meal when somebody came in and announced, "The plane is fixed. Everybody to the buses now!" What a disappointment. Out of the blue, a colonel stood up and simply said, "I'm the officer in charge of this flight. Boys, I'm gonna eat my steak, and then we will go to the plane. Sit down and enjoy it." We did, and when he was through eating, we followed him to the buses and the plane.

We all got on the airplane, and one guy was so plastered the crew was not going to let him fly. They were going to take him off the plane. Again, our colonel simply told them, "If you take him off, we are all getting off your airplane. Your plane broke down, and that caused this. We will take care of him, but he goes with us."

We left Guam late in the evening, and I can only tell you that a day on that island is better than any day in Vietnam. We arrived at Long Biên, and then I had to find another C-130 back to Da Nang. I made a call to get somebody in our jeep to come and get me. They came and got me, and we went up through the little village of Dogpatch and on to Camp Redhorse. I asked a question about going home in mid-December and Staff Sergeant White and Captain Klus told me my orders were already in progress and would come shortly.

I can only tell people that being in a war zone in any capacity will have an effect on any person. Martha will attest that I left for the military as a bashful little boy but came home changed.

Chapter 15

My Last Month in Vietnam

I got back to Da Nang around November 20, 1971. I had less than three weeks in-country before I was going home. My friends in high places (Captain Bill Klus and Staff Sergent Dick White) already had the papers in and were processing them. All I had to do was prove I would have a job when I got back, and I had gotten a letter from Lee Van Gorp at Van Gorp Implement in Oskaloosa saying he had a job waiting for me.

As I had always done, I went to the firebases with the major serving as battalion commander (the colonel had moved on). One of the times, we went to a firebase where a battery (or two) of the 105mm howitzers were firing a mission. It was all wrong; they are never to fire over the top of another gun because of the danger of tube explosion. It would kill an entire crew, but they were doing it anyway. I never asked if it was a "runover by the enemy" mission. I had tried my whole time there to get a photo where an artillery round was caught in the air coming out the end of the tube. A howitzer is fired single shot with a lanyard, meaning each gun is fired separately by a gunner by pulling the lanyard. My camera was set on one-thousandth of a second, and I was snapping shots. I got back on the helicopter not knowing what the black-and-white pictures were of, but I was satisfied I had done my job.

A couple of days later, I got to the darkroom and developed my pictures. I thought they looked pretty good, except for a few flyspecks. I was examining my photos when a "top" (a first sergeant) came by and asked if he could look at my pictures. Of course, I let him. He let out a yell and said, "Sarge, you got the Joes (bullet rounds) in mid-air!"

I looked and I had one photo with both Joes in mid-air flight and one picture with just one. News spread like wildfire about the picture I had with the two Joes. The division-commanding general's assistant called and asked if I was the one who had the picture. He wanted to know if the general could get a copy. I remember telling him, "The general can have anything he wants because I am going home." He was very pleased.

The Army called the photo "Two for the Road from an LZ" (landing zone or firebase). The Army had a copy, but I kept the negative and still have it. I finished up my work. Since I was a sergeant, the Army would ship my stuff home for free; all I had to do was get it ready to ship, so I took my little refrigerator, fan, and some other stuff down to the shipping area, where they sent it to Iowa. I showed the new person what I was doing, and I prepared to go to the Da Nang processing center. It was pretty neat because at 11:00 on the morning I was to leave, the big wigs had an awards ceremony on the helipad at Camp Redhorse to present me with my second Bronze Star. They read off a bunch of flowery stuff that meant nothing to me because I was going home.

I got in the jeep with my duffel bag, and we drove to the processing center at the airbase. We had to turn in all our jungle fatigues and green socks, underwear, and hankies (except what we had on—we could take them home). I had sent several pairs of clothes with my refrigerator. They said we were not allowed to take home our D-ring, which everybody had to hang on their belts to keep stuff with them. But I wanted to keep mine. I was at the base a short day when my name showed up on the manifest for a flight out. We all had to fly in khaki dress uniform, so I hid my

Chisel Points in the Ground

The dark spots in the upper left are artillery rounds.

D-ring in the stinky pair of fatigues I had been wearing when I was processed. If somebody wanted to search them, they could go for it. Then I shoved the stinky things in my green canvas duffel bag and went to the plane.

It was an American Airlines charter Boeing 707, and that Freedom Bird sure did look pretty. It was about 98 degrees when we got on the plane at 1:00 p.m. on December 15, 1971 (I think). The pilot went down the runway. When he came off the ground, it was like he was mad because that nose went in the air, and we went high quick. The stewardesses were old and ugly, but I knew Okinawa was coming and we would have young blood. I found out the flights on this trip were hazardous duty pay since they went into a war zone, so the senior gals took all those trips. I never heard of a Freedom Bird ever being fired upon. I also knew that in forty-eight hours I should be in the arms of Martha and Judy—they didn't even need to have stewardesses on board. We got to Okinawa, and it took a couple of hours to get full of fuel. Then we went back to Honolulu.

Customs in Hawaii was totally ridiculous because of the way they searched us. I think they knew we were a bunch of "dope heads," and they checked everything. I was glad to get back on the plane and head to McCord Air Force Base in Washington state, which was right next to Fort Lewis, where we would process out and home.

We landed at McCord at about 11:00 a.m. on the same day we left Vietnam. I have never figured out where that day went, but it was gone. It was 28 degrees when we got off the airplane, and I kissed the ground to be back on the mainland of the United States of America for good. A lot of others did too. We all had on our khaki short-sleeve shirts, and it took two hours before they brought us field jackets. They escorted us off to the steakhouse for a nice steak dinner. That was the first stop for all soldiers coming home from Vietnam. Then we started processing out.

We were all measured for the new dress green uniforms we would get at the end of processing. Our uniforms didn't smell too

Chisel Points in the Ground

good anymore, but who cared? We had to go for a medical exam. For some reason, they were checking for venereal disease. The exam area was like a herd of cattle going through the chute. I remember somebody taking a long, thin Q-tip, grabbing my penis, and shoving it all the way to the end of the tip. It felt a whole lot better when it was out. We had to go to finance and get the last pay figured out. Then they had a transportation office, where they arranged for my flight home. They must have paid for it because I got no money on leaving. I had used too much leave time, so I mustered out broke. The plane ticket I got was SeaTac (Seattle/Tacoma International Airport) to Denver. I would change planes in Kansas City, then finally get to Ottumwa, Iowa. I found time during the process to go to the huge line of phones and call Martha and tell her I was in Fort Lewis and would be in Ottumwa at the airport at 7:30 the next morning. We finished up the paperwork, and then we went and got our new dress green uniforms that had all the insignias on it—the rank and overseas bars, plus all the medals in place. I don't know how they got it done for everybody so quickly. I changed, and the stinky khakis went in the green canvas duffel bag. They loaded us on a bus and to the airport we went.

I have thought about how people tried to understand the changes in my personality and some of my actions, but until somebody has been in a war zone, there is no way to begin to understand. Martha knows there is a time to leave me alone, like when we're at the half-size Vietnam Wall, a military cemetery, a Memorial Day or Veterans Day program, a patriotic event, and some other times. Some say, "Thank you." Others try to ask questions because they think "gory" details of war are fun to hear. I can only tell you that most veterans who talk a lot were never there. I think the experience can best be summed up by a quote from my friend, Tommy Franks, who is a four-star general. His first duty as an officer was in Vietnam. This comes from his personal museum in Hobart, Oklahoma: "We went as boys—we came home as MEN!"

My Last Month in Vietnam

There is a special bond among veterans. It doesn't matter which war they were in. Veterans understand that war is ugly, and it changes a person. Veterans will understand the changes in people when nobody else does. I found this to be true with our customers who "had been there and done that." They would come in to talk, look at my photo on the wall of my office, and start the discussion. Being involved with bringing the half-size Vietnam Wall to Oskaloosa twice let people know I had been to Vietnam. Many people were surprised I had been there; they thought we had lived the "good life."

Citation

BY DIRECTION OF THE PRESIDENT

THE BRONZE STAR MEDAL
FIRST OAK LEAF CLUSTER
IS PRESENTED TO

SERGEANT CARL G. DROST, ▓▓▓▓▓▓▓,

UNITED STATES ARMY

who distinguished himself by meritorious service in connection with military operations against a hostile force in the Republic of Vietnam. During the period

11 MAY 1971 TO 13 DECEMBER 1971

he consistently manifested exemplary professionalism and initiative in obtaining outstanding results. His rapid assessment and solution of numerous problems inherent in a combat environment greatly enhanced the allied effectiveness against a determined and aggressive enemy. Despite many adversities, he invariably performed his duties in a resolute and efficient manner. Energetically applying sound judgement and extensive knowledge, he has contributed materially to the successful accomplishment of the United States mission in the Republic of Vietnam. His loyalty, diligence and devotion to duty were in keeping with the highest traditions of the military service and reflect great credit upon himself and the United States Army.

Bronze Star number two.

Chisel Points in the Ground

30 November 1971

Dear Civilians, Friends, Draft Dodgers, ETC.

In the very near future the undersigned will once more be in your midst, dehydrated and demoralized, to take his place again as a human being with the well-known forms of freedom and justice for all; engage in life, liberty, and the somewhat delayed pursuit of happiness. In taking your joyous preparations to welcome him back into organized society, you might take certain steps to make allowances for the crude environment which has been his miserable lot for the past period of time. In other words, he might be a little Asiatic from Vietnamesitis and Overseaitis and should be handled with care. Don't be alarmed if he is infected with all forms of rare tropical diseases. A little time in the "Land of the Big PX" will cure this malady.

Therefore, show no alarm if he insists on carrying a weapon to the dinner table, looks around for his steel pot when offered a chair, or wakes you up in the middle of the night for guard duty. Keep cool when he pours gravy on his dessert at dinner or mixes peaches with his Seagrams VO. Pretend not to notice if he eats with his fingers instead of silverware and prefers C-rations to steak. Take it with a smile when he insists on digging up the garden to fill sandbags for the bunker he is building. Be tolerant when he takes his blankets and sheet off the bed and puts them on the floor to sleep.

Abstain from saying anything about powdered eggs, dehydrated potatoes, fried rice, fresh milk or ice cream. Do not be alarmed if he should jump up from the dinner table and rush to the garbage can to wash his dish with the toilet brush. After all, this has been his standard. Also, if it should start raining, pay no attention to him if he pulls off his clothes, grabs a bar of soap and a towel, and runs outdoors for a shower.

When in his daily conversation he utters such things as "Xin loi" and "Choi hei", just be patient and simply leave quickly and calmly if by some chance he utters "DiDi" with the irritated look in his face because it means no less than "Get the Hell out of here!!!" Do not let it shake you if he picks up the phone and yells, "Lanyard Sir," or says "Roger out," for "Goodbye" or simply shouts "Working."

Never ask why the Jones' son had a higher rank than he had, and by no means mention the term "Extend." Pretend not to notice if at a restaurant he calls the waitress "Number 1 Girl" and uses his hat as an ashtray. He will probably keep listening for "Homeward Bound" to sound over AFRS. If he does, comfort him for he is still reminiscing. Be especially watchful when he is in the presence of a woman, especially a beautiful woman.

Above all, keep in mind that beneath the tanned and rugged exterior there is a heart of gold (the only thing he has left.) Treat him with kindness, tolerance, and an occasional fifth of good liquor, and you will be able to rehabilitate that which once was (and now is a hollow shell of) the happy-go-lucky guy you once knew and loved.

Last but by no means, send no more mail to the APO. Fill the icebox with Coke, get the civies out of mothballs, fill the car with gas, and get the women and children off the streets because.............

THE KID IS COMING HOME BY 20 DECEMBER!!!!!!!!!!!!!!!!!!!!!!!!!!!

My recreation of Army jargon saying the kids are coming home.

Chapter 16

My Flight Home From Nam

The Continental flight out of SeaTac was to leave at 1:10 a.m. Pacific Time (3:10 a.m. Central Time). It was on time out of there. I was all snazzed up in my green dress uniform on my way to Denver. I was going home, so time really didn't matter. Neither did food or anything else—just HOME and Martha and Judy.

When we were approaching Stapleton International Airport in Denver, the stewardess came and told me they knew I had a close connection, and they were holding the plane for me. When we started taxiing, she came and got me and told me to come with her. I was standing at the door with her when the plane stopped and the door opened. She took me by the arm and told me to come. She and I ran down the jetway to the waiting airplane, and she basically threw me on. The door closed immediately, and the plane was moving before I got to my seat. It was another Continental flight into the old downtown airport in Kansas City. It went fast—I was getting closer to HOME!

We landed at the Kansas City airport, and I got off and went into the terminal. I had to change to Ozark Air Lines to get to Ottumwa, which was an old World War II Navy base. I ran to the ticket counter and told them who I was and where I needed to go. They pointed to an airplane just outside, which had a ramp off the tarmac to the door. I ran out and found a seat and settled in; I was about home. The plane (with turbo propellers) took off. We got to altitude, and the front officer came over the speaker to say, "Good morning, we have nobody to get off in Ottumwa. Nobody to get on in Ottumwa either, so we are heading to Cedar Rapids." I waved my arms, and the stewardess came back. I told her I had my wife and family waiting in Ottumwa, so the officer made a correction that we were going to Ottumwa.

We landed in Ottumwa at about 7:30 a.m. in the morning on December 16, 1971. True to form, when I got off, there was Martha and Judy waiting for me. We all got reacquainted again. And of course, my mom and dad were there because they had brought Martha and Judy. The miracle of miracles was that the crew threw my green canvas duffel bag out of the airplane and brought it to me.

I came home from Vietnam the same way I went: alone. There were no bands, parades, mayors, or spectators—just me on the tarmac of the Ottumwa Regional Airport. And for that matter, nobody in the town, community, or church cared where I had been or that I had come home. It was really a short drive. Then I was HOME!

While I was back in Nam after R&R, Martha finalized the deal on the Alf Grandia Farmstead with Durant and Betty Barnard. We bought five acres and buildings for $21,000.00. She and my dad had gone to Oskaloosa Home Loan and talked to Mr. Robert DeCook, Sr., about a loan. Martha could get a VA loan guaranteed for a low rate, and we would not need as large a down payment because of that guarantee. They would loan the appraised value on the place. Dad knew the appraiser, Mr. Oren James. The appraised value came back at $21,000.00, so no money was required.

When Martha and my dad went to sign the papers, Mr. DeCook told Martha he would need one dollar to make the contract legal. As the story was told by my dad, Martha said, "I don't have a dollar." In shock, Mr. DeCook got up from his desk, not to throw Martha out of the office, but to take his wallet out of his pocket. He opened it, took out a dollar, and gave it to Martha. Then he took it from her to make the contract legal, and they did all the signatures. I had the adjutant general in Vietnam prepare a full power of attorney for Martha to sign everything for us. A letter took ten days to make it from Nam to home. When they got all the papers signed, Mr. DeCook took the dollar bill and handed it back to Martha. He said, "Take it! You need it more than I do!" We were a loyal customer until Bob DeCook, Jr., sold out the bank. I think our payments were around $150.00 per month for twenty years.

My folks dropped the three of us off at our new home on Kirby Avenue, which was then Rural Route 3. The house had been slightly remodeled by my dad and brothers; they had removed the old chimney and taken out a wall to make the kitchen larger. They put some paneling on the walls. They had also gone to the storage unit and moved our furniture into our new home. We were a family again.

I had given Martha the checkbook before I left in May 1970. She'd managed quite well with no money, so she just kept doing the bills, deposits, and banking (she still does it to this day). Dad was building the Stonehenge Restaurant a mile north of Oskaloosa on Highway 63. He needed some help putting on the roof, so I helped him do that for a few days. Then it was Christmas. Martha had her cedar chest in the living room, and our "huge" thirteen-inch television was sitting on it. Our little Christmas tree was in the playpen we had bought at the PX. (Remember, this was the Christmas tree the NCOCS class had in our barracks at Fort Bliss in 1970.)

It was good to be home, and we had some lost time to make up. On January 2, 1972, I went to work in the service department of Van Gorp Implement—the local John Deere dealer in Oskaloosa—for $1.75 per hour. We continued going to the First Christian Reformed Church. Nobody said a word about welcome back or anything—not even the minister. I was just there with a really nice tan at Christmastime.

My Flight Home From Nam

I even got a Good Conduct Medal.

Chapter 17

Working at Van Gorp Implement

In 1972, Leland Van Gorp and Raymond VerSteegh were partners in the John Deere business at Van Gorp Implement. They had hired me on the GI Bill as a service technician trainee, and I got $1.75 per hour (plus I think we got something from the Veterans Administration). The house payment was the only outstanding debt we had, but if we had been smart enough to complete a financial statement, we would have been bankrupt. Raymond was my boss and supervisor. He was a very nice man. His son, Keith, had also been in the Army when I was gone; he was soon to come back too. Harlan Groenenboom, Dennis Dursky, Cliff Morrow, and Earl Sopher were the other main employees besides the owners. None of them could understand why a college graduate would work in a dirty old shop and fix somebody else's worn-out equipment.

I went to Mose Van Zee's used pickup lot, and we bought an old, dark-green Ford half-ton pickup with a white utility box on it for $400.00. That was my transportation. It was only wheels. To buy the pickup, I used the money I had earned in the last two weeks of December helping my dad put the roof on the Stonehenge Restaurant just north of Oskaloosa on Highway 63. The Stonehenge was owned by Charles Springer. Later, it was sold and became The Peppertree.

I started out working on tractor engines, transmissions, hydraulic systems, and electrical systems, as well as combines, balers, grinder mixers, and anything a farmer would bring to town. I had a lot of book knowledge, but not a lot of experience, so Raymond and the other mechanics helped me a lot. It was a lot of fun, and it got us enough money to make our house payment and live.

We would go to Moline, Illinois, for technical training. Dennis Dursky and I would usually go together, and we would have to stay in a big hotel in downtown Moline. These were the days of 3020s and 4020s and an eight-speed power-shift transmission. John Deere had just changed from a twenty-four-volt electrical system to a twelve-volt system on their tractors, so we had to study and compare both systems. We had class on the plateless finger pickup system on corn planters. The combine training was on the 100 Series (yes, the 3300, 4400, 6600, and 7700 and the hydrostatic drive system on combines were all new). The John Deere hydraulic pumps were quite complicated in the flow-compensated system or the closed-center system, but they revolutionized the farm tractor business. An eight-piston radial pump was hooked to the front of the engine, and there was a valve mechanism on the front of the pump. You'd connect the hydraulics system to the steering system, which allowed tractors to be steered effortlessly. And then there were the planetary final drives. It became the industry leader—and all that connected to the marketing with the famous green and yellow paint.

I had some experience on the farm with John Deere equipment, as we had purchased a new John Deere 3020 diesel tractor in 1966. I knew how to adjust a moldboard plow, but Raymond was an expert and taught me a lot. I knew how a planter and disc worked. I had also loaded bales behind a square baler, so I knew a lot about making square balers work. We had used ear corn pickers on the farm, so combines were new to me, but I always liked new and big equipment. My dad told everybody his whole life that all you had to do was give me a key to a piece of equipment, and I would drive and operate it quickly.

Chisel Points in the Ground

A farmer who lived just east of the Belle Fountain Bridge over the Des Moines River by Tracy came in the store and bought a new John Deere 4620 diesel tractor with a roll bar and a new six-bottom plow. He'd only ever used horses and really old and small two-cylinder John Deere tractors. The farmer told Lee Van Gorp that the tractor had to be delivered and the plow had to be adjusted and scoured before he would accept it. It was bad duty, but they asked me if I could drive it out to his farm and get the plow scoured and adjusted. I jumped at the chance; I had never been around anything that large in my life, and I was so proud driving it to the farm and getting to plow. I got PAID for having fun. The farmer and I became friends that day, and we were friends until he died. I also got to know his nephew, and we have been friends ever since.

Dennis Dursky and I always had fun, but we tried to take the best care of our customers that we could. We worked together well, even though we could give each other a hard time. Leland "Lee" Hicks called one day to say the clutch was out of their 55 John Deere self-propelled combine. He and his father, Carl, were combining oats. In the same neighborhood, Tom Burris had called in to tell us that the beater behind the cylinder in his 40 John Deere self-propelled combine was badly cracked and needed to be repaired. Raymond decided Dennis and I should go together and get both customers going. We went to the 55 combine at the Hicks farm first, and we jacked the combine off the ground and loosened the belt on the clutch housing. You couldn't get the clutch housing off if the wheels were set narrow for a two-row corn head. Dennis and I were getting along really well replacing the clutch when I noticed the jack was sinking in the oat stubble and the combine was tipping. We worked really fast to get that clutch in, adjusted, and the belt back on. We jacked to the top of the jack, then rolled that wheel in. The combine had to go up a full inch to get the wheel bolts in! The jack wouldn't go up any farther, so I grabbed a screwdriver (no spade on hand) and dug a hole in the dirt deep enough to get the tire on the axle and the wheel bolts in. Leland was very happy when he heard he could harvest oats.

Then we went north a couple of miles and got to Tom Burris' farm, where his combine was sitting in the yard. Dennis and I took the covers off both sides and saw that the beater was cracked badly and would need to be welded and later replaced. The inspection hole in the side of the combine was so small it was impossible to get two arms through it. We had an oxyacetylene torch with us to weld it. Dennis and I thought about how we could do it without burning up the combine. We decided he would hold the torch through the left side inspection hole, I would put the brazing rod into the flame, and we would weld it cooperatively. It took us a little time to get the sequence down, but we accomplished it quite easily. If you think it is easy, try it with your friend sometime (and remember that it's dark inside a combine).

During planting season, Frank Coppersmith from Indianapolis called in with a steering leak on his John Deere 4020 diesel tractor. Raymond dispatched the tilt bed delivery truck to pick up the tractor, so we could get it fixed and back to Frank so he could continue planting. When the tractor got to the shop, we saw Frank had dual tires on it. Our overhead door to the shop was just wide enough for the tractor to get in if it rubbed on both sides. Dennis and I were going to work on it together. I was driving the tractor through the door, being very careful. I pushed down on the brakes and the tractor . . . completely stopped! We wondered how Frank could plant with the tractor that way, but we got the tractor in the shop and told Raymond to call Frank and tell him the clutch was out.

We worked on the steering leak while Raymond tried to get ahold of Frank (there were no cell phones then). Frank told Raymond there was nothing wrong with his clutch, so we should fix the steering leak and bring it back. We questioned that, but at Frank's insistence, the truck driver winched the tractor up on the truck, and Dennis and I bet on how long it would be before the truck was back with Frank's tractor. In the end, we decided to work on Frank's clutch anyway and found the clutch disc facing thrown against the inside of the flywheel. It was very difficult to understand, but we put a new clutch disc in and sent it home that same afternoon. It took a long time to figure out what had happened, but we finally learned that when the tractor came off the truck the first time, the clutch was held down with the transmission in third gear. That caused the clutch disc to spin at approximately 9,000 RPMs, which literally spun the clutch facing off. Frank and I always kidded about his clutch and who was going to pay whom for the repair. As late as February 2020, when both Martha and Frank were being cared for at Northern Mahaska Rehabilitation, we talked about his clutch. I never got any money out of Frank, and he never got any money from me.

One spring, Lois Beaver (the wife of Maurice) brought their 4010 John Deere diesel tractor to the shop for an engine overhaul. Lois was always in the field working alongside Maurice. They were a very progressive farm couple, heavily involved in Farm Bureau and other farm organizations. I got the job done and sent the tractor home. Sometime later during the spring season, Lois came to the shop and told me, "You sure put a TIGER in the tank of the 4010!" I was really happy with the comments. When Lois was living at Homestead Assisted Living in Oskaloosa, she had a one hundredth birthday party. Martha and I brought a dozen red roses, and I went and asked her if she knew who I was. She said, "You are Carl who put the TIGER in the tank of my 4010!"

Ray knew I had been around a square baler a lot of times. One day, he asked if I could repair a square baler that wasn't tying knots very well and was missing several bales. I told him I would go try, so I loaded my little toolbox in the pickup and went to Larry Groenendyk's farm just north of Leighton. It was a 24T John Deere square baler pulled by a two-cylinder John Deere 530 tractor. I looked at the bad knots, looked at the troubleshooting section in the back of the operator's manual, found the picture of the knot, made the adjustments, and it worked perfectly. Larry knew I was a genius. This had to be in 1972 or 1973, when farmers were really having good years. Larry came in just before Christmas and gave me a check for $250.00 and told me how he had appreciated me helping him out during the year! WOW! And only God knew how badly Martha and I could use that money—but God always has provided what we needed.

As you can tell, the years I worked for Lee and Ray at Van Gorp Implement were real learning years for me about how to take care of farmers, how to work with others, and the importance of taking care of customers when they need work done during the busy seasons. It was very good preparation, especially for a college graduate working for mechanics wages. I think God was laughing the whole time, knowing what He had in His plans for Martha and me.

Chapter 18

Martha and Carl's Family

Our first child born to us was Judy Renee. She was born on Veterans Day, November 11, 1970, while I was stationed with the U.S. Army at Fort Bliss in El Paso, Texas. My mother took Martha to the hospital and brought Judy home to the Drost family. My sister, Annie, was only twelve years old when Judy was born, and they really bonded as "sisters." I was in the NCO Academy and did not see or hold Judy until my Christmas leave. Judy was baptized at the First Christian Reformed Church in Oskaloosa during that leave. Martha and Judy went back to Fort Bliss with me, and we lived in a little base house on Hope Street, just up the street from the base PX.

When I was sent to Vietnam, Judy and Martha lived with my parents in the basement of their home. They ate about every meal together: Dad, Mom, Dick, Tom, Annie, Judy, and Martha. After we moved home to Kirby Avenue, Judy attended Kiddy Kollege for preschool, so she could be around other kids and learn social skills. Judy attended Whittier Elementary in Oskaloosa for kindergarten, then Lincoln Elementary for first through sixth grade. Lincoln was one of the lowest-rated elementary schools of the six in Oskaloosa. She had no classmates at her math or reading level, so it was a group activity of one. Judy went to the Oskaloosa Junior and Senior High Schools. When Judy was a sophomore, we took the kids out of school for an earned vacation in Hawaii. Then Judy got the only B of her high school years in biology, and I believe to this day it was because she missed a week. If I have one regret of my years on the school board (you'll read about those later), it is that I didn't take the science teacher to task and make him, the principal, and the superintendent prove the grade correct. Because of that B, Judy was the salutatorian of the class and not tied for valedictorian.

Judy went on to Iowa State University to study animal science (pre-vet). She eventually graduated from the College of Veterinary Medicine. Judy always said, "I am going to get my education, and then I'll get a man." She married Eugene Little—a farmer from Murray, Iowa—a couple of months after she graduated from Iowa State as a veterinarian. They live on a farm northeast of Murray and have a son named Daniel. Judy worked for a few years as a hired veterinarian; then, she was taken in as a partner at the Osceola Vet Clinic. Later, she became the owner.

Robert "Bob" Drost was born on January 21, 1973, while I worked at Van Gorp Implement. I took an hour off work to bring Martha and Bob home from the hospital, and then I went back to work. Martha always took care of the kids during the night, always saying that she could do that because I worked all day and needed my rest. Bob also went to preschool at Kiddy Kollege, then kindergarten at Whittier. He spent the rest of his elementary years at Lincoln Elementary. Bob also went to Oskaloosa Junior and Senior High, where he was on the basketball and tennis teams. Bob graduated from high school and went to Iowa State University to be an engineer. He played intramural sports, went bungee jumping, and did other fun stuff.

One night, he called and told me he had changed his major to ag business. When he graduated, he worked in a Piper Jaffray office as an investment adviser. Bob married Cathy Melvin. To be successful as a financial adviser, his evenings were full of business appointments, which doesn't help a marriage relationship. Bob came to work at Drost Equipment as an ag salesman and was very successful. But as I wanted to slow down, it meant more hours, evenings, and holidays at work for Bob. He and his family decided they needed a change, so Bob went to work at Musco in the finance department. He is now the long-term facilities planner at Musco. Bob and Cathy have two children: Ashley and Taylor.

Nicholas "Nick" Drost was born on Christmas Day 1976. I dropped Martha off at the front door of the hospital, and by the time I got the car parked and Martha admitted, the baby was ready to be born. We were told by the doctor during the pregnancy that it was going to be a baby girl, so no boy names had been chosen. When the nurses asked what the baby's name would be, we responded that we didn't have one. One of the nurses suggested Nicholas for Christmas, so that was the name we chose. Nick went to the same schools as his siblings, but he got hooked on fishing and hunting and had no interest in sports. Nick caught a huge bass when he was small fishing with his Uncle Jim. He went to Penn College in Oskaloosa and got a degree in industrial technology. Nick has a daughter, Abigale (Abby), from his first marriage. He and his second wife, Jennie, have two boys: Wesley and Harrison ("Cooper"), whom Nick adopted. Nick is the location manager of Van Wall Equipment, a local John Deere dealer in Oskaloosa.

All of our children were raised with conservative views. Church was required and not an option. We told them to do their best at whatever they did, and that Mom and Dad didn't have enough money to get all the stuff their friends had. I told the children to not look at what other people visibly have, but to take a look at the parents' financials and see what they really have. The children no doubt thought Dad and Mom were just plain tight. I hope our children saw that what you are made of is a lot more important than possessions.

Chapter 19

My Spiritual Journey

Now that I am old, the Bible proves itself to be true again. Proverbs 22:6 says, "Start children off on the way they should go, and even when they are old they will not turn from it." Well, I want everybody to know that God has looked out for me all along my way in life. He even looked out for me (and my family) before I was smart enough to know God was looking out for us.

The earliest memory I have of church is going to the First Christian Reformed Church on Third Avenue East in Oskaloosa. I know it was just about a block and a half west of Grandma Valster's house. We would go to church on Sunday morning and sit in the back room, so we kids wouldn't disturb the service. All the Drost uncles also went there with their kids.

I remember we had to go to catechism on Saturday afternoon, then we would walk up to Grandma's house and go home. It is interesting to me now that all the teachers were old farmers who knew the Bible and knew God would care for them through their faith. It is amazing to me that those guys, who were fifty and sixty years old with maybe an eighth-grade education, would take off Saturday afternoon and come to town and teach the Heidelberg Catechism to us, as well as the Bible stories from the Old and New Testaments. I know they were never trained in teaching, but they had been elected elders, and it was their responsibility to teach the youngsters. (What a commitment!) I remember having Bill Memelaar, Pete Fynaardt, Tunis Fynaardt, Sam Boender, Reverend Veenstra, and Ernest DeBruin as teachers.

I think in the late fifties the church divided, and some of the people left and formed Bethel Christian Reformed Church. Our church became the First Christian Reformed Church. We moved to the new building by Forest Cemetery on North Eleventh Street. I remember our dad headed up the shingling of the new church; then a hailstorm came, and it had to be done again. This building had a big basement in it, and we would go to church every Sunday morning and evening during the summer. It was never a choice at our house about whether we were going to church on Sunday morning. I think if the thought of staying home had ever entered my mind, my dad would have known it and knocked my block off.

It was in this church that a couple of memorable things happened.

First, my brother, Jim, has always been extra smart. He's very thorough and always wants to make sure he has all the details down. It ended up that Jim and I were in the same class. Our teacher was a good old Dutch farmer. For catechism, we had homework to do; we always had a list of questions to answer. Jim always wrote out long explanations. Me being simpler, I would use only a few words. We got our homework back one week, and the farmer had given Jim a B for pages of answers, while I got an A and a note that said, "Very good." My answers were only one or two words. I know Jim will never forget it.

When I got to college and had a driver's license and car, I started going to Young People's Society on Wednesday nights. I had no interest in girls at all, but I tried to work the fundraiser events and be a part of the group. Jim and I were the only college kids in the group because nobody else felt education was important. This is the group where Keith called on me to carry Martha Vernooy around the circle. Martha liked it a lot, but I don't believe I have forgiven him to this day. I survived, but I still didn't care for girls. (I was a freshman in college.)

The young people's group would have a pancake supper or something like that, and I always got into mixing the batter and helping grill the pancakes. I think Martha Vernooy liked what she saw. And after one of those events, Janice DeBruin and a few of Martha's friends said, "I wonder what it would be like to date Carl Drost?" Martha said later that was the time she decided she needed to figure out who Carl was.

In the winter of 1968, I married Martha in the sanctuary of the First Christian Reformed Church, where we were both members. Since the church was without a preacher, we asked to be married by Dr. Lloyd Cressman, a religion professor at Penn. We were married on December 20, and we made it our church home. Even when we lived in Montezuma, we drove to Oskaloosa to go to church.

My spiritual journey really took a wild turn when I was drafted into the Army in late May 1970. I was a dumb kid who had never been any place and all of a sudden, "I'm in the Army now." I had to kiss Martha goodbye, and she was pregnant. I had to make it on my own without Martha or my dad and mom—not an easy task when you like home. I went to Fort Leonard Wood, Missouri, for basic training, and about the only time we got off was on Sunday mornings to go to church. At the chapel in the reception center, I picked up a Bible from the American Bible Society (which I still have today in my office). I went to chapel services every Sunday. It seems the military can test your faith with all the stuff that goes on there, but I was pretty good.

A real challenge came early one morning in August 1970, when I went to the orderly room at Fort Bliss in Texas. I had been told in Fort Leonard Wood that I was the luckiest draftee in the world because I was going to Fort Bliss for radar and missile control and would be in Germany in ninety days. All I remember is a big and ugly sergeant saying as I entered, "Welcome, CONG BAIT! Ninety days and you will be in Vietnam." What a shock!

My Spiritual Journey

When I finally came to my senses, I decided that if God wanted me to go, He would want me to come home. So, I really applied myself to learning how to stay alive and TRUSTING GOD. There was a brigade chapel we were allowed to attend, which I did with my Bible Society Bible. That Bible still has special prayers and sayings in the back, with notes of the time and the place I wrote them down. When I got ordered to go to the NCO Academy, I could always get an hour reprieve to go to chapel (even though I was always restricted). God and faith were still part of the military then. Martha and Judy came back with me on January 1, 1971, and we went as a family to the brigade chapel. (Though Judy was baptized in Oskaloosa at Christmastime when I was home on leave.)

In May 1971, I was deployed to Vietnam. I was in the transfer station in Oakland, California, on Mother's Day. I can remember going to a formation of ten thousand soldiers and hearing the announcement that one hundred soldiers were to fall out to go to Germany. The next formation would be three hundred to Nam. I always thought I would be one of the ones going to Germany, but my name was called for Long Biên, Vietnam. That was really a long flight—we went to Oakland, Anchorage, Yokota, and then into Long Biên, just outside Saigon. Then it was five hours to Chu Lai, home of the 23rd Infantry Division.

You'll remember I was never so scared in my life as I was the first night that I was assigned guard duty on the South China Sea. I was in a bunker with two other guys. I don't know if I had ever prayed so hard for morning to come; it was so beautiful as the sun came up over the South China Sea . . . and I was still alive. After a few days, I was flown to Da Nang and assigned to the 3rd Battalion of the 82nd Field Artillery, which was guarding Da Nang Airbase. I attended the brigade chapel just up the road sometimes. The military has an interesting way of handling religious activities, as the chaplain would show up anytime and anyplace and conduct a service and perform holy communion. They would fly in on a helicopter to the firebases on the hilltops, then be gone.

God was taking care of me in my assignments and my travels, but I was not smart enough to know it. I have to admit water was very hard to get and beer was plentiful, but I couldn't stand it, so scotch was really good. I got to come home to a loving wife and baby at Christmas 1971. Martha loved me the way I was when I came home and was not critical of me. We started going to the First Christian Reformed Church as before, but we were ignored. It might be noted that nobody from the church ever did anything for Martha the whole time I was in the military—never a visit or a call. (Hardly the way I thought church should be.) We only went in the morning. One evening during the week, a young deacon from the church came to tell us we had not paid our budget and wondered when we were going to do it. We had no money, and this guy had avoided the Army by marriage and had been making money the whole time I was gone. (Not bitter, but never forgotten.) I knew Martha was ready to leave that church, but I resisted.

In the fall of 1977, my friends, Kenny Rexroth and Bob Waal, came to the store and told me the Nazarene Church in Oskaloosa was going on a mission trip to South Africa. They invited me to go along. Martha and I decided I should go. While I was there, this group of Nazarenes showed me how to live a life for God. They had something I wanted. In a hotel room in Amsterdam on the way home, I REALLY ACCEPTED Christ as my personal Savior. When I got home, I told Martha I was ready to go to the Nazarene Church in Oskaloosa. She was so happy because she had wanted to go there.

Gary Henecke was the minister, and he was really a great preacher. Lester Fynaardt and Sam Boender (elders of the First Christian Reformed Church) came to see me at the store one day that spring and were wondering what we were doing for church because they had missed us. I told them we were going to the Nazarene Church, and they told me to go and participate. I have so much respect for them, and that has been my theory about church ever since: I don't care where you go to church as long as Christ is preached, the Bible is central, and you go and become a part of it.

We went there for several years and went on more mission trips. I taught Sunday school to teens and then adults, and I was on the board. I found out what turning my whole life over to Jesus (entire sanctification) really meant. I also found out that new members' ideas are not accepted unless they fit their mold, so don't try. Martha had also talked about tithing. I balked, but I found out that tithing works and nobody can out-give God; it always comes back many times over, but not in monetary returns. I also challenged God to prove Himself. Shortly after my return from Africa, I told God that if our company made $50,000 for the year, I would give $5,000 to missions! Guess what? That $50,000 came easy, so God proved to a dummy that you can't out-give Him.

One of the ministers who really had an impact on me was Reverend James Bearden. We became good friends, and he joked that he claimed ownership in our store. When I was the youth director (NYI president), we decided to do the live drive-through nativity. Bearden was a great supporter. I will never forget the first year; it was cold, and he was walking around the church yard freezing to death in a huge parka. I think we did that event for fifteen years. It was a huge Christmas story for the area. Bearden had a huge impact on my life because he preached the Word and cared for his people. I will never forget his wife, Nancy, coming out to see me at the store early one morning to simply tell me she believed in me when some church members were very critical of my decision to change our dealership from Ford tractors to John Deere (more on that later).

The church started having disagreements, so one Sunday morning, we turned west to Pella to go to the Nazarene Church there. Dave Lovett was the preacher. I loved Dave and Bonnie. We were talking one day, and Dave told me about being in Nam in the Engineers and having his bulldozer rocketed. He was blown off it. He was forced out of the church and went to Chariton, where he got a job working for Hy-Vee. After a couple more preachers, they were fighting, and we decided to change churches. One is supposed to be able to go to church and enjoy worshipping God in peace.

    I took out the yellow pages of the phone book and scratched out the churches I wouldn't consider. Then, I let Martha strike off some more. I left her the Catholic, Lutheran, Mormon, Jehovah's Witness, and Presbyterian Church. I always enjoyed my Sundays and giving them to God. I dealt with farmers all week long, so I wanted to pick out a church with very few farmers. (I love farmers and their lives, but I wanted a day of rest with no questions about what I did all week.) I asked Julie Fisher, an attorney at Musco, if we could go to Sunday school and church with her at the Presbyterian Church. The answer was yes, of course. Julie taught an adult class. I found out that the church was full of businessmen, retired teachers, doctors, and only one farmer. I really enjoyed the church, but Martha did not feel welcome when we first started. I again got to teach—I've found that to really grow is to be prepared to teach a lesson on God's Word and how to live it.

    Martha and I had looked at the national doctrine of the Presbyterian Church of the United States of America (PCUSA), and it was too liberal for a conservative couple like us. But Dr. Morey, the local minister, assured us that as long as he was at the church it would stay pretty conservative. Dr. Morey retired, and there was a different pastor (very liberal) and some interims. Then there was yet another new pastor, and the church really became liberal. It was getting to the point that we really didn't want to go to the church. When Martha and I were in Hawaii in February 2023, we decided we would not return to the Presbyterian Church in Oskaloosa. We would find a more conservative church to worship in and serve the Lord.

I talked to Craig VerSteegh about the local Central Reformed Church breaking away from the Reformed Church of America because the local folk could not take the liberal doctrine of the RCA. When we came back from Hawaii, we attended the Central Church (formerly called Central Reformed). We knew a lot of people there. I asked Craig if there were written beliefs of the new Central Church, and he emailed them to me. The beliefs are very conservative and are what Martha and I believe. We have not made a decision on which church to go to permanently, but we feel we have a responsibility to our family, our friends, and the people we influence to attend a church that is consistent with our beliefs.

I believe the truth of our real trust in God and our faith in Christ is to live what we believe and show our beliefs in how we live in the community. It is in the integrity of how we operate our businesses, what we do with the money we make, how we treat other people (including employees), and how we treat our spouses and families. I think the highest compliment a person can receive is, "I have been watching the way you live, and you live exactly the way you talk. You are a great example of how a businessman is supposed to live." I know money is not my god, but God honors honorable believers. I believe God rewards His faithful followers. The Bible says, "From everyone who has been given much, much will be demanded." That carries a big responsibility. I believe that when God gets a person's heart, it is not hard to live for Him. It is just the way of life, which will be more fully explained in other chapters.

Chapter 20

Ford Tractor

In early June 1974, I was working in the service department at Van Gorp Implement on the Old Highway 63 South in Oskaloosa. One day, a sharp-dressed, middle-aged man walked in the north overhead shop door and said he wanted to talk to Carl Drost. He came over and told me he was Dick Allen with Ford Motor Company's tractor division. He told me Ford was looking for a new dealer in Oskaloosa, and I had been recommended by Maurice "Mose" Van Zee, a local car dealer and a friend of my dad. I told him I had never considered that, but he suggested that we get together and talk so he could show me the prospectus of the deal. I had no idea what a "prospectus" was.

I went to the Traveler's Motel that night to listen, and it all sounded so good. Martha and I had no money, and it was going to cost $158,000.00 in cash to get this deal going. The prior dealer had their contract terminated because of lack of payment of the bill to Ford. We spent the evening going over the prospectus and the building and finances that would be required. I understood very little of it.

It really came as a surprise because Lee Van Gorp had basically told me that he would sell me and Martha the store when the time was right, but that whole deal had fallen through. It was 1974, and the ag economy was on a roll. Ag business was the best it had been in years—maybe ever. But Van Gorp was a John Deere dealer, and John Deere would not even talk to me because I was inexperienced, with no degree in ag or business. Martha and I had no money, so John Deere would not consider us as their dealer.

My mind was really spinning when I got home that night, and I decided I needed to talk to somebody about getting into business; I knew nobody at the time except Joe P. Crookham, who was a local attorney and a friend of the family. My dad had done a lot of carpentry work for him, so I called Joe and he saw me in the afternoon. I took the prospectus to him, and he looked at it. Since Joe taught accounting, he understood what it was all about, and I learned a little more. We talked for a couple of hours, and then Joe said something to the effect of, "You ought to do this." I'm sure I had told him about our desire to have the John Deere contract, but that was going nowhere. We talked some more about getting into business, and he asked, "Where are you going to get the money?" I told him I had no idea.

Our dad had told all of us boys that we should all do whatever we wanted to do and could do; the world was before us, and we were smart so, "Spread your wings and go do it." And he continued with, "Don't ask Mom and me to co-sign any papers because we are not going to do it. We ain't going to lose what we have over one of your ideas."

Joe said, "I have just negotiated a contract with the Kansas City Chiefs—professional football—for Wilbur Young. I am looking for an investment to get the maximum tax advantage we can get, and this looks good for that purpose. We would finance this operation if you want to do it."

My mind was really spinning. I couldn't believe what all had happened in less than twenty-four hours. Joe told me they would put the money into the operation. I would put the labor and time in, and we would be fifty-fifty partners. I left and went back to work. That night, I talked to Martha, and she didn't understand the prospectus any better than I did. Neither one of us knew Joe other than that Dad had worked for him. I had no business experience.

Chisel Points in the Ground

Not being very smart, we agreed that we had nothing, so it was impossible to lose anything; we might just have to start over with nothing, as we had done before.

I called Dick Allen and told him we should talk again because I thought we wanted to do the deal. A few days later, Lloyd Herwehe, Ford's area sales manager, came to Oskaloosa with Dick. They both seemed so nice. We filled out the application, which was lots of pages and spelled out what we would do. I found out later that we really had no rights—Ford had them all. The application was sent in, and it was almost guaranteed that it would be approved. Ford had done a traffic count of the ag community, and it was decided that the best location inside the city limits of Oskaloosa was on Highway 63 South, just north of the railroad tracks. Joe had made a deal with Henry Hackert of Allied Gas and Chemical, and I pulled out the plans for an equipment dealership I had drawn up while teaching at Montezuma Schools. I went to get prices on building tools and trucks, a trailer, and lots of stuff. I was trying to keep working at Van Gorp Implement, and I couldn't say anything because nothing had been approved yet.

I got a phone call the early part of July 1974 from Dick Allen. He told me the agreement had been approved and signed by Ford, so it was a go. I went to Van Gorp to work the next morning. At starting time, Lee Van Gorp and Raymond VerSteegh got all the employees together. There was a young man with them, whom they introduced as Gary Rogers. They had sold their dealership to Gary the afternoon before. Lee and Ray would later tell me John Deere had invited them to a meeting at the Holiday Inn on I-80 by Iowa City, where they were told Gary Rogers wanted to buy them. Gary's father-in-law was Lewis Martin of Illinois, and he was the world's largest John Deere dealer. Lee and Ray were told Gary wanted to buy it that day—what did they want for it? They had no financial or accounting records with them, so they went into the hall and talked and came up with a price. They went back into the room and told them the price, and Gary wrote them out a check. Then John Deere informed everybody there that Gary Rogers was the new John Deere dealer in Oskaloosa, Iowa. Gary told us that he wanted us all to stay on and continue with him. When he was done, I told the whole group that I would finish the job I was working on, then I would be gone. I would be starting a Ford Tractor dealership just across the tracks in the cornfield to the north. We would be open in the fall. It was about July 7, 1974.

In a couple of days, I had the job completed, and I loaded my toolbox in my old Ford pickup and went home. Although it was never written down, one part of the deal with Joe and football player Wilbur Young was that I would get a living wage all the time, so we could support our family. I started working all day long, every day, on the design of the building, the concrete for the floor, the overhead doors, a clay dirt base for the building, the electrical, and the heat. Joe said it had to be air-conditioned, and then there was the water service, the access road with the city and state, the building permit, and dealing with Bloom Builders. I also had to decide on the parts bins, office equipment, special tools, pickup trucks, and trailers. I had never hired a person in my life, so it was all new to me. I had no education in the field of business and no experience managing a business.

Ford had a training farm in Paris, Texas, where they offered a one-week management seminar. Martha and I loaded up our car with Judy and Bob, and off we went to Texas in mid-July 1974. The head instructor there was a young man named Mel Carr. He and his team really put out a lot of information on a lot of subjects, such as looking at and evaluating a financial statement (I had never seen one before). Mel Carr emphasized making a budget and an annual business plan, so there was a path and a general map of where the business was going and growing. (I thought I had too many other things to do to spend time on making a business plan!) When we left there after a week, my head was spinning about all the things I had been exposed to. I had a whole lot to think about and know. One thing Mel told us was, "You can sell yourself out of business." It didn't make any sense to me, but several years later, I had a hard lesson to learn.

Joe Crookham showed me in the first few months that he had lots of vision for the future. We had to look at the next twenty years when we planned and built. His ideas included air conditioning, a loft in the showroom where we could put extra displays or hold meetings (or later put a toy collection), an asphalt parking lot, and a little island display next to the driveway that turned into the dealership. At the time, I thought it was a lot of extra money, but over the years, I saw Joe was absolutely correct. I remember him telling me that farmers would be coming to town in good clothes and shoes. Why should their feet get dirty on a dirt or gravel parking lot? As I wrote this chapter, 75% of the original asphalt parking was still there because he insisted on two feet of clay dirt being compacted under the parking area. Since Joe was putting up the money, I did what he suggested; after all, Martha and I had absolutely nothing, so what did we have to lose? But we had everything to gain.

The construction started in mid-August of 1974. Jerry Van Engelhoven did the excavating and hauled in and compacted the clay. Then he laid the asphalt. Bloom Builders were to build the building, but they kept putting us off, so one day I cornered their salesman as to why. I asked if it was because he didn't get enough of our money, and he kind of said yes. I went and got him a check for more money, and they started within days. I hired Les Krusemark as my parts man (no experience), but he was also to help me on the building. Les and I formed up the concrete floor and called in the Ready Mix truck from Jess Walters on the corner of Highway 23 South. Durant Barnard came in every morning that we poured concrete to help get it laid down and struck off; then he would go farm. Jim Catherman did the sewer and water, and we had quite the time with the city inspector. We needed an inspection on Saturday before we could cover the pipes and continue. He couldn't come, so we covered the pipes. On Monday morning, here came the inspector to examine the work, and it was all covered. He told me we had broken the code and that I could be put in jail. I told him, "Call the police and get me in jail, so I can get bailed out and get back to work!" He didn't do anything, but he was always there when we needed an inspection from then on.

Wes Anderson did all the electrical work and made sure we had a big enough service and enough outlets to service what we thought we would need. Les and I framed in all the interior walls for the offices, restrooms, lofts, and shop dividers. We worked long hours six days a week. Joe told me we should sod the front yard instead of seeding it, so we called Hermann Greenhouse of Agency, and they came and looked. I asked how they wanted the dirt prepared for the sod and how deep to make the dirt loose. The expert told me to get on the asphalt roller sitting there and roll it as hard as the parking lot; they would lay the sod on top. When I questioned him about that, he replied, "It is guaranteed." So, I rolled the dirt hard. Hermann Greenhouse also had a used flagpole, which they brought up for us to put in our front yard. It was only about the third week in September, and I asked Ford for the sign for the front of the building. We were told we did not meet the qualifications for the sign. Our fancy building did not match Ford's criteria, so I went to Storm Sign in Oskaloosa, and they cut out a plastic oval in blue and put Ford Tractor in white. Then they took a tall old Pepsi Cola sign and made Ford Tractor panels for it, and we set that in the front yard. The flat iron chain link fence (which is still there) was bought from Redge Wright Salvage at $1.00 for a ten-foot roll. It was a cheap fence for the yard, and we painted it white.

We were not quite done with the building, but we were putting in equipment when Bob Durr from Williamsburg stopped in. He was looking for a new Ford tractor and had been to Shaeffer Tractor in Ottumwa; they didn't have anything, so he stopped to see us. I had never sold anything in my life, but the tractor he wanted was sitting on our lot. He looked at it, and the next day, I went and looked at his trade-ins and we made a deal. I have never checked if it was a good deal or a bad deal, but we had our first sale!

I had hired Les Krusemark to do parts. Tom Evans had worked in parts for Carmichael's (the previous Ford dealer) for years, so I also hired him. He was seventy-four years old. I hired Mick Allaman to be our service manager; he had also been a technician at Carmichael's.

One evening, a young man who lived just south of our place came to ask for a job. Glenn Knox wanted to get out of the Chevy shop and work on equipment that would have some room under the hoods and sides. Glenn had long hair past his shoulders and hair on his face. (My dad had always told us boys not to cultivate on your face what grows wild on your ***.) I wanted to hire Glenn, so I told him he had the job if he would clean up and cut his hair. He said he would, and he did. Glenn was always a great employee.

I needed a truck driver and a general yard man. Charles "Chuck" Patterson applied. He was driving an Ideal Ready Mix truck, and I hired him. We thought we could save money by having Martha do the payroll and bookkeeping, but neither she nor I knew anything about accounting. It was not working, so I decided I needed to find a bookkeeper. I told Martha to just stay home and take care of the kids and our home. (She was the first person I fired.) I called over to Bloom Builders and talked to the receptionist/bookkeeper there. Her name was Bonnie. She asked what I was doing, and I responded I was trying to keep books, but I was lost. She asked, "Do you want to hire a bookkeeper?" I said, "Yes, do you know of one?" She told me Dave in her office would be a good person, and I could hire him. She set the wages, vacation time, sick time, and all that stuff, and then she said, "If you agree to that, you hire him and I'll send Dave over." In about five minutes, Dave walked in and wanted to know if I was serious. I must have been because he was our bookkeeper from then until we sold out. He even became our partner.

We opened Drost Ford Equipment on Highway 63 South on October 1, 1974. I had a WOW moment that first morning when I stuck the key in the lock. I said to myself, "Now I have this business, what am I am going to do with it?" I have thought about that moment and the gravity of that day many times. I think it is a good thing I didn't understand it all, or I might have run away or just never started.

Ford had always been a small tractor company, but they were starting to build larger tractors. I wanted to sell the regular size as well as the big tractors. Ronnie VanVeldhuizen came in looking for a big new tractor, and I traded him a 9600 Ford Tractor with 135 PTO horsepower. What was so funny to me was that several people came to me and told me to watch out for that Ronnie because he was really hard to get along with. The people were wrong because Ronnie was one of our best customers and was soon a very good friend.

We held a field day the first fall we were open at the Durant Barnard farm west of town on Highway 163. We brought a 9600 tractor and a five-bottom plow. We got a lot of lookers. The next day, it snowed several inches. Durant went out and plowed in the snow, and the black dirt and white snow made quite a contrast. Durant wanted to get a Sidewinder for a one-pass planting operation and bought a 9600 Ford tractor from us during the winter. Ronnie and Durant were John Deere customers. It helped me a lot that Gary Rogers did not want to trade in any equipment and preferred to sell the equipment a long distance away.

We waited until the early part of 1975 to have our grand opening. We had a huge crowd of all the farmers and Ford Tractor people. Al Cook, the branch manager, was there along with Bill Templeton, the marketing manager. We had a pretty good three months in 1974, and prospects looked good for 1975. I remember Bill Templeton telling Joe Crookham as I was talking to a farmer—standing with my ankles twisted sideways and my hands in my pockets (really nervous)—"Can you believe he is just about ready to get in the farmer's pocket, and the farmer will like it?" Bill Templeton also called Joe, an attorney, and me: "The law and the outlaw."

Bill Templeton challenged me that day that if Drost Ford would do $1 million of business in 1975, he and Ford Tractor would treat Martha and me to a nice weekend trip in Kansas City. We made it! They put us up in the Hallmark Crown Center in downtown Kansas City, and they treated us very well.

Some elderly customers and friends offered sage advice. One piece of advice was "stick to your knitting," or in other words, do the implement business and do it the best you know how. Another was, "You can shear a sheep several times, even two or three times a year, but you can only skin him once." I followed those two pieces of advice, and I never purchased farmland to be in competition with the customers, and we always intended fair deals. For forty years, our goal was to do a great job serving the customers and being fair on warranties. Money and getting rich was never the goal, but it turned out to be a byproduct of the business.

In the early days of the Ford business, Ford Tractor announced an incentive trip to the Canary Islands, and they set a goal for us to sell. Bill Templeton used us in some promotions for the trip. In one newsletter, he had our kids, Judy and Bob, carrying suitcases to go to Grandpa's and Grandma's while we were gone on the trip. We earned the trip, and we flew to Tenerife in the Canary Islands for close to a week, where we got our first experience with how foolish some people can look when they are away from home. We met another young couple, Peggy and Dennis Owens from Decatur, Illinois. We spent most of our time together, and we had a good time. The language was Spanish, and I'd had enough Spanish at Penn to prove me dangerous; we got along with the people very well. The last night of the trip was the big extravaganza, and they gave us all long robes like the sheiks wear. We put on swimsuits underneath them and went to the party around the pool area and ballroom. At one point during the evening, they put a long tree trunk out over the pool with an American flag on the end. All you had to do was go out and get it. But oh, by the way, the trunk was greased heavily with axle grease. A lot of men and women tried to get it (most of them inebriated), but in the end, I got the flag. It was the start of a lot of trips to all parts of the world that we took because we earned them in the business.

During the summer of 1975, I acquired my pilot's license and joined the flying club at Pierson Field. We flew the Cessna 182 to Paris, Texas, as a family. I went back to the management class, and Martha and the kids spent the days in the pool at the motel. We didn't have enough money to do other things. Mel Carr was again the lead instructor, and he went over the same stuff as the year before, but it made more sense now that I had a year under my belt. He again covered the necessity of having a budget and a business plan, but I was still too busy (I thought) to take the time to make a plan.

Funny things can happen in the course of doing business. Neal Cambell, a farmer by the Ottumwa airport, came in wanting a four-section harrow drawbar. Neal was always a lot of fun, and he told me he would give me a baby Hereford calf for the drawbar. Of course, discussion took place, but the deal was done: one calf for one harrow drawbar, but I had to go get the calf. I took my son, Bob, along. What I didn't know was the calf was an orphan in the pasture with a hundred cows with calves. Neal had his John Deere cab tractor hooked on the manure spreader, and he took Bob into the cab with him. To the pasture we all went, with me in the spreader to open gates and "get" the calf. Neal pointed out the calf, then drove into the cows. I was to jump out, grab the calf, and walk back to get in the spreader; that was my plan anyway. Neal got close to the calf, then I jumped out and ran after and caught the calf. I picked him up, and the calf went, "MAAAAAAAAAA!" All the cows started running to the calf, and I ran fast. In one stride, with the calf in my arms, I got in the spreader! Bob's eyes were huge watching the action, and Neal was laughing his *** off watching the whole event. Neal was a great friend, and everybody laughed about the calf story.

We also sold New Idea manure spreaders and Uni-Harvesters, which were used to harvest seed corn. We serviced seed corn companies to the southeast, from Packwood with Middlekoop's to McCurdy's in Fremont and PAG in Monroe. We even served growers as far away as Baxter and Mitchellville. Pierson Seed was just west of town, but I couldn't get in the door to do business with them. They simply told me I would have to prove I could stand the test of time. After seven or eight years, I got a chance with Royce and Arvid (Shorty), and our employees proved up to snuff. They became great customers as well as friends.

1977 proved to be a real challenge in the equipment business. On the Fourth of July, the corn crop was the best anybody had ever seen, and the prospects were terrific. Then it stopped raining and the temperatures got really hot. The wind blew from the south or southwest for too long a time. It never cooled off at night, and the corn just melted. By Labor Day, the corn was all brown. Our most popular request for farm machinery was corn choppers to make silage out of the short, brown stalks that were left. When harvest time came, many cornfields were not harvested, and the yield in the harvested fields was nearly nothing. That was a huge challenge for our business. I never did tell Martha how bad it was or how near broke we were. I was invited to go to Africa on a mission trip, and I went (which was not very smart, but it was a life-changing experience). I don't know where we got the money ($1,600.00) for the plane ticket and incidentals, but I know I didn't spend much money on souvenirs. Anyway, in 1978 with no crop, business was really bad, and it is only by the grace of God that we survived.

Ford Tractor

In the summer of 1978, I got called to the bank for a meeting with the president, Mr. Russell Howard, Jr. I had many meetings with my regular banker, Rex Blom, and he was going along with us. I know it helped that Wilbur Young and Joe P. Crookham had their names on the line with Martha and me, but the year was ugly. I remember we were up against the bank loan limit of $400,000.00. We were losing money fast, but we had a crop. Mr. Howard was not nice to me, and he explained a lot of things to me about how poor a businessman I was, how I played too much, and I made bad decisions and a whole lot of stuff. Then he told me, "I should just sell you out right now, but I am going to make a businessman out of you! You are going to spend a lot of time with Rex, and either you will learn or we will sell you out." Now, if anybody asks me why I worked so hard after 1978, the simple reason is I didn't want to face Russell Howard again. Rex and I spent a lot of time together, and we made the bank satisfied. From 1978 on proved to be good years for us.

At the end of 1978, I remembered Mel Carr talking about a budget and a business plan and how important they were. I dug out my notes and made a plan. It was handwritten on lined notebook paper and was pretty simple, with the gross sales of each department, the profit in each, and then a profit number at the bottom. I even scribbled some notes of how we were to accomplish these numbers. It was a plan (not much of a plan, but I called it that), and the banker really liked it; it really helped me put my efforts where they needed to be. I made a business plan every year until 2011, when the business was expanding so fast and the numbers were so wild that records and predictions were not practical to make. Spending time to do that business plan myself was really the turning point. I really thank God for guiding me through the years and leading me to people who could help. I had faith in Him that He was with us in our business. As our business became more profitable, we always remembered to give God the portion that was His.

I was always involved in the community. The owner of Baskin Robbins was Royce Pierson, who you'll remember was a good customer of Drost Equipment and raised seed corn west of Oskaloosa. Royce planned a community fundraiser where each contestant would get pledges for each dip of ice cream they could eat in the allotted time. I raised pledges as high as $10.00 per dip, with everyone thinking I would eat five or six dips. On the day of the contest, I was hungry and ate forty-two dips of vanilla Baskin Robbins ice cream in one hour! The contributors figured out from then on that all donations would be total dollars and not per unit. I learned my lessons from the mistakes of others.

In 1979, Drost Equipment took on the Kinze brand, whose products were planters and grain carts. We also acquired New Holland, which put us in the hay equipment and combine business. This move gave Drost a full line of farm equipment; Kinze had just won a lawsuit against John Deere, so we were almost selling a John Deere planter. The Maxi-Merge unit was John Deere, and all the parts would interchange with Kinze. We sold thirty planters almost every year, and this also got us into the big planter market. Middlekoop Seed bought the largest Kinze planter we sold, which was sixteen rows wide. We also sold some grain carts. Kinze had a credit plan that was different than most; our company could pick up one load of equipment, and before another load was delivered, Kinze had to have a check with the amount paid in full. It just took a lot of cash management.

New Holland was a great line to add to meet the needs of our trade territory. New Holland had a reputation for the best hay equipment in the industry, the best parallel bar rakes, good mowers, square balers, pull-type forage harvesters, and forage wagons. The round baler left some to be desired because it was not a belt baler, but rather a chain baler with teeth on it. Our competition on hay equipment was Gary Rogers with John Deere. Drost demonstrated the equipment, and it was fun to kick John Deere around because

Ford Tractor

Gary would set the price and take it or leave it, but he never did demonstrate any equipment.

Demonstrations proved to be a very good means of acquiring business, and Ford tractors were demonstrated against all the competition. In 1974, when Drost Equipment was established, there were six other implement brands in Oskaloosa. They were John Deere (Gary Rogers Company), Allis-Chalmers (Strawn Equipment), Massey Ferguson (Bill Bone Motors), White (Whitaker Implement), International Harvester (Oskaloosa Implement), and Case (Case Company Store).

Tractor pulling among the farmers was a big deal in the late seventies. I traded for a Ford 9000 Series tractor and took it to a tractor pull. The Ford did okay, but it is a lot more fun to win. So, I decided to spend some money and be competitive—that means win! During the winter, the engine was taken apart, line-bored, and balanced. Large injectors were installed, along with larger cylinders and plungers in the injection pump. The governor was changed to provide maximum pull at 3,200 RPMs. Musco poured us a new front casting out of aluminum (instead of cast iron to reduce the front-end weight). New weight brackets were built and installed. When it was ready to compete, the tractor on the dynamometer turned 400 HP. Then the PTO mechanism was removed to get more weight gone to get us into the 9,000-pound class. A large diameter, four-and-a-half-inch chrome pipe was installed, and the tractor looked very nice.

When the tractor went to the first pull, the plan was to pull both the 9,000-pound and the 11,000-pound class. The spectators were surprised when the Ford hooked to the sled with me as the driver. It was impressive—the Ford had a lot of power, and when the power was really needed, flames came out of the chrome pipe about a foot high! It was a beautiful orange. During the year, the tractor got a lot of attention because it was only beaten once in the 9,000-pound class. It did really well in the 11,000-pound class too, but Ken Fynaardt (whose son, Russ, was operating an Allis-Chalmers 7030 tractor in

Chisel Points in the Ground

the 13,000- and 16,000-pound classes) told me one night, "You can play with the boys, but you can't compete with us men!"

I took it as a challenge and went back to the shop and helped the crew put the wide front end back on the tractor. We put the big 24.5 tires on the rear, and then the crew built more weight brackets. We were going to Monroe, and the plan was to surprise everybody and pull the 11,000-, 13,000-, and 16,000-pound classes. Ken was really surprised to see our tractor with the wide front; he was still insulting me, which was okay. To make a long story short, we won the 11-000-pound class, and we got second in the 13,000-pound class. Then the Big Man class came. A farmer from New Sharon pulled a 1066 Farmall; he had it decked out with panels over the engine, so nobody could see it. He also had murals painted on the sides. (It was very pretty!) His son would run alongside of the track and set the flag where the pull ended. He was a tough competitor. In the Big Man class, Russ and this farmer were the ones to beat.

The New Sharon farmer had beaten us in the 13,000-pound class. We had to add thirty weights to our tractor to get to the big class. Russell pulled, and then the other farmer pulled, and he was in the lead. His son set the flag along the track. It was my number, and on the way to the sled, Ken again had something to say in jest. But when the chain tightened, it was all business! The 16,000-pound class had never been pulled by the Ford, so there were a lot of variables to consider, including the speed to operate in. The Ford had a power shift high-low in it. It started in the high side, and it went well. About the time I went past the New Sharon farmer's red flag, I shifted down and the orange fire flew. I threw my arms in the air in excitement, and then I went on another thirty feet (much to the farmer's chagrin). He got second. Ken Fynaardt came over to me and asked if he could help me carry my trophies. We went together, and he did help me carry them. (We still laugh about it.) But the following day, the New Sharon farmer came to our store and told me I was nothing but a show-off and it was so insulting. He left out of the front door as fast as he came in. It was all in fun, but tractor pulling really showed the area that we were serious about the business and could stay with the best of them in the fields.

After a few years, I organized a Fall Tillage Day and invited the competition. All the dealers were invited to bring their tractors and tillage equipment to a field and let the customers see the equipment in action and even drive it. The first few years, four or five of the competitors would come. Drost Equipment demonstrated the Ford tractors along with the Glencoe Soil Savers and the Howard V-Ripper. There was no tillage equipment that could compete with them. I always took the champion Ford 9000 tractor. When the going got tough, the foot throttle was pushed a little farther and the power went to the ground. The competition finally got tired of Drost Equipment being the big winner, so then it was just the Drost Fall Tillage Field Day. We served donuts and drinks.

Accountants are very important in business, and Drost Equipment had been with an accounting firm in Oskaloosa since 1974. We really relied on the accounting firm to do the right thing with the business and taxes. The bank had set rules at the start that we could do all the tax stuff we wanted as far as write-offs and the like, but they were going to establish our credit line and loans from our income tax reporting. I went to do my taxes in 1981, and the accountant told me we were going to use a new plan called LIFO (last in, first out). He said it was going to save us lots of money, but we would show no profit. I proceeded to tell him that would put us out of business because the bank wouldn't loan us money on that statement. The accountant then said, "Look, you don't know enough to run a business! (He might have been correct.) I'll tell you how!" That was all it took. I simply told him he was no longer our accountant and to give me all the company records. He didn't want to, but I walked out with the full file. I needed an accountant, and it was determined that an out-of-town accountant would be best. There was a new accountant getting started in nearby Pella, Jerry Uitermarkt. I went to see him, and Jerry is still the Drost accountant.

Business was really doing well in the late seventies, and then we had a really bad drought in 1978. Corn yields averaged fifty bushels per acre, and the bins were empty. The farmers had been in a boom up until then, and the bankers were loaning money on net worth. The 10% inflation let farmers add 10% to their equity every year if they broke even otherwise. The banking industry made decisions in the late seventies that were devastating to the ag economy. The bankers decided that: (1) They would no longer make loans on net worth but on cash flow, and (2) they would have all their customers make a financial statement with actual values and not inflated values (basically a tax statement). These changes caused lots of turmoil in the community. Drost Equipment was not affected as much as others because we were required to use our income tax values on our financial statements from the very beginning. So, the new baking requirements had no effect on the business. But it did affect the amount of equipment our customers bought, so our sales plummeted by 50% in one year, which caused a lot of problems.

Chapter 21

Public Service: Mahaska Rural Water

In 1974, Durant Barnard asked me to go to a meeting with him, where there would be a group who wanted to provide high-quality water to the rural area. The project would be funded by the FHA (Farmers Home Administration), a government agency whose local director was named John Crumley. The group came together and agreed it was a good cause. The original group included Durant Barnard, Marion Vos, Harry Van Wyk, Sam Foster, me, and some others. Marion Vos was elected president. John Crumley guided our group, which became known as the Mahaska Rural Water Association.

Our first task was to hire an engineering firm. Then the engineer helped guide us along. We were told easements had to be acquired from the property owners as we sold meters to potential patrons. If a farmer got a meter, we needed to have an easement on their property for the water lines and a $200.00 fee for the hookup. The penalty for not providing an easement was the farmer could not hook up to the rural water system.

Most farmers were ready to give the easement and get signed up for good water. Martha and I were a good example of why the project was necessary. We had a well at home that was contaminated with nitrates and was not fit for us to drink or cook with, so we had to have water hauled in. The selling point was that for $200.00, the farmer would have high-quality water available for his home and operation, even if he never hooked to the pipe. In the cases where the easement could not be obtained, the pipe was placed in the county road right of way. It was very important to get all the users possible because the water mains would be sized by the engineer according to the expected use from the hookups, and they would be in the ground a long time. I sold Bill Carter of Carter Steel the most water meters in a potential subdivision north of the Skunk River (in the area of Lower Grove). Our engineer was working on the design and location of a treatment plant and well field. We decided to place the plant five miles below the Oskaloosa Waterworks on the paved Glendale Road. The wells were located on the Skunk River bottomland purchased from Mr. Alexander.

Soon, we'd acquired the easements, and the engineer had all the plans ready for the wells, the treatment plant, and the water distribution system with water towers and meter pits. Then there was a meeting, and the engineer expected us to just approve the multimillion-dollar project when all we saw was a stack of paper. The board was ready to do it until I said, "Don't you think we ought to study these plans and read the specifications?"

The engineer said nobody reads that stuff. I answered, "I want to look at them, read, and study it."

The Board did not go ahead but let me read it over. I discovered there was not a standby generator included in the plans. The whole rural area of Mahaska County was giving up their wells and water systems, and the Rural Water Association was to provide water to them. But if a storm struck and knocked out the power, no water could be pumped. At the next meeting, a large diesel generator was included in the plans and specifications. The project was constructed, and the rural areas of Mahaska County had high-quality water available for its residents.

I had to learn a hard lesson serving on this board. At one meeting, after the association had received and disbursed money, we learned an audit was required by the government. I suggested getting a quote from a local accounting firm. The board agreed for me to get a quote, which I did. At the next meeting, I gave the report of the quote, and the farmers all thought it was a "rip off." The next day, the accounting firm called me to hear the decision, and I told them exactly what had been said. That created quite the storm, and at the next meeting, the president dressed me down for telling the accountant that the board thought it was a rip off. I told him that was exactly what was said and that is all I told the firm. After more remarks, I told them I didn't need to be on the board any longer and walked out . . . or maybe stormed out!

After a few days, peace was made, life went on, and the system was completed. I learned that when dealing with the public and people in general, the political approach is a better model to use. The Mahaska Rural Water System was started under the original board and managed by Jim Roth, with Joyce Klein as the office manager. It has been a very successful operation and utility that still provides high-quality, safe water to most of Mahaska County, as well as some small towns outside the county. It also provides sewer systems in some small communities. Durant Barnard purchased a water meter pit for the Grandia property where Martha and I would build a new home in 1998. The rural water was connected to the property for a $200.00 investment in 1975, and it was included in the Drost purchase price.

Chapter 22

Public Service: My First Twenty Years on the School Board

In about 1976, Durant Barnard approached me about an opening on the Oskaloosa School Board. Durant was one of the first customers to buy the biggest tractor Ford built, and we were on the Rural Water Board together. The Oskaloosa School System was in a little mess because of decisions the board had made during the consolidation of all the rural country schools. Judy, our daughter, was going to enter kindergarten, so I had an interest in the school system. The hot button for education at the time was TUG (talented and uniquely gifted) students and how to educate them. It was a question in 1976 and 2021, and it is still a logical question. How do you challenge the talented student in the career area they are really interested in?

I had some opposition, but I prevailed in the election. I was sworn in and became a member of the board in September 1976. Durant was president of the board, and the other returning members were Emily Russell, Ann Morris, and Warren France. John Heslinga and Robert Randell were both new members along with me. The superintendent was Dr. Louis Sullivan, and the board secretary was Virginia Dunbar. It didn't take long to find out that one major problem was the total lack of discipline at the junior high school, which caused lots of problems with teacher morale and student educational achievement. In 1976, the Oskaloosa School

System had six elementary schools, a junior high school, and a senior high school. The elementary schools' quality was determined by the location in the city. Grant School in the northeast quadrant (in the hospital neighborhood) and Webster School on the southeast side were the best schools in terms of student achievement. They also drew what most residents accepted as the "best teachers." Whittier School on the north side toward Penn College was also a quality school. But then there was Jefferson, Lincoln, and Garfield Elementary Schools, which the community knew were "on the wrong side of the tracks."

Jefferson was on the east side of the tracks, but it was in a very poor section of town. These schools seemingly could not attract or keep the best teachers, and the schools also suffered from the socioeconomic values of the neighborhoods. I had not completely learned the lesson of being political, so I brought forth a proposal to attempt to correct some of the issues at the junior high school, soon to be named the Drost Proposal. It asked the administration to demand better discipline, to get more parents involved, and to have students study more. I was straightforward like a sergeant in the Army and told it like it was from my view. After several meetings and discussions, the proposal passed, and the administration knew what the expectations were. The administration made the necessary changes, and discipline was restored. The junior high school was a very old building, and the public in Oskaloosa would not vote for a bond issue for a new building when there were problems in the system.

The school board is sometimes looked at as a position that older people run for so they can say they held public office and did the community a service. Others, specifically farmers, usually have property taxes at the top of their agendas. People who are on the school board need to have an agenda of what is best for the education of the young people of the community with the resources available. I did not say to tax the people to death. School board members are responsible for hiring and supervising a superintendent who has the children's best interests at heart. A school board member swears an oath when they take office, and it is very simple: "Do you swear to uphold the Constitution of the United States of America and the Constitution of the State of Iowa?" This oath says nothing about education, but it does say a lot about the requirement to educate all students no matter their color, socioeconomic background, religion, intelligence level, or any other difference. It requires that at times a board member will have to vote against their own personal beliefs. A board member should always have just as good a reason to vote yes as to vote no on an issue.

The old junior high building was three stories. One section was built in the late 1800s, and the last part was added in the 1950s. The building was not insulated, and it had bad windows and tall ceilings. It needed a lot of renovation to make it efficient as a school and in its operation. The board had (quite unsuccessfully) tried to pass bond issues to build a new school. After I was elected to the board, bond issues were tried again; a vote had to be held to remodel the old building (which would have been a huge mistake).

The board had attempted to renovate the old building once, hiring an architectural firm out of Cedar Rapids, Iowa. All architects are interesting pieces of work, but this architect forgot who he was working for. When the board talked about bricking in windows to save energy, we were told by the architect that we couldn't do that because it would affect the architecture of the building. On the discussion went, like the board was working for him. It was not unusual for our meetings to last until midnight or 1:00 in the morning. After those meetings, Board President Durant, me, and maybe one more board member would go to the Coffee Cup Café and have coffee. After one of the meetings, I stated that I was ready to fire that guy! Some of the others thought it was not a bad idea.

At the next school board meeting where the architect was in attendance, he told us again, "The board cannot do that." I asked,

"Sir, who do you work for?" And then I said, "I move to terminate the contract effective immediately." Discussion was held, and the outcome was the termination of the contract. Then, the architect stood and told us the board could not do that and that there were legal ramifications. I told him, "Sir, if you go out the south door of this building and turn east one-half block, then turn right, you will see the courthouse. Go over there and file the suit so we can go on." Nothing more was heard from them.

Shortly thereafter, I brought the second Drost Proposal to a board meeting. Durant always knew what I was going to bring up. The proposal was for a new junior high school to be built on property to the south of the senior high school, which was on the north side of town on North Third Street. The proposal included buying some land from Penn College and other things. At the next meeting, when the proposal was to be voted on, John Heslinga started out with a motion to do something different. He was an attorney and a very good board member who sat directly across the table from me. John didn't want it built next to the senior high because of the concentration of students and other reasons. The motion failed, but John had a total of twenty-one motions as alternatives to the Drost Proposal. When all twenty-one failed, John looked across the table and said, "Okay, Carl—make your motion." I did and the motion passed.

Soon after that, Durant's term expired, and he had health issues. A new school board was elected. They were all progressive and wanted to see the school system and the quality of education move forward. Bruce Smith and John Pothoven were new board members, and I was elected board president. Under the new board and the new superintendent, Harold Westra, the architectural firm of Dana, Larsen, and Roubal was hired to put a plan together on the site south of the senior high school. Oskaloosa would lose the community auditorium when the new school was built, since it was in the old school. There were dreams of a new community auditorium being constructed in various parts of town. The board decided to leave room between the new building and the senior high for a future auditorium when the community decided it was a need.

Penn College agreed to sell the school all their property on the east side of North Third Street, which was around three hundred acres. That purchase was made part of the expansion plan, as well as athletic fields and practice areas. The board told the architects that the building had to have a pitched roof, not a flat roof. The new school was put to a vote of the community; like all bond issues that affect property tax, there is a 60% passage requirement. The proposal passed. It was the eighth bond issue for a different junior high building.

The plan was not a cheapened version, but a high-quality building. It was the most expensive bond issue to date, and it would serve the community well for the next fifty to seventy-five years. At the time, every school board member wanted the Oskaloosa School System to have a middle school, so we would have a K–5 elementary school, a sixth through eighth grade middle school, and a four-year high school. The plan was made so the building could be converted into a middle school at the appropriate time.

Merit Construction from Cedar Rapids won the general construction bid. I was at the building site every day from the first day McAnich Construction moved the D-9 Caterpillar in with the dirt scoop until the students came for the first day. A couple of days before Thanksgiving 1983, the contractors served a Thanksgiving feast to all the workmen. I was the only school person invited. It was served in the home economics classroom. Some of the construction company owners, superintendents, and workers I met became lifetime friends. This was the first big construction project I was involved with from start to finish. When the building was ready for occupancy, I and board member Bob Randell helped move the furniture and equipment from the old building to the new building with the Drost Equipment flatbed semi delivery truck. "Vinny" and other custodians helped with the move of all the student desks, teacher desks, bookcases, and other items. It was a three-floor building with only stairs (no elevator), and it was lots of work. My delivery semitruck was loaded and unloaded several times at the new building, where everything was put in the classrooms. A big dedication was held in August 1986. I had the privilege of presenting the "key" to the school and the students.

Under the direction of a great superintendent, Dr. Harold Westra, the Oskaloosa School System became a high-quality education system. It was rated at the top with Pella Community Schools, and the board was very supportive of top-quality education. Dr. Westra and I had a great working relationship, which is vitally important if a school system is going to move forward. I served as board president for several years. Then, after one election somebody else was nominated by a new member at the organization meeting, and that person became president. It seemed prearranged. It was a very difficult pill to swallow, as the other board members had said nothing about a change of leadership. I learned a lesson that friends do matter, and when several of the board members have spouses who work for the district, things like this will happen. I was elected president the following year after a difficult year. LESSON LEARNED—don't trust your supposed friends because they sometimes will work behind your back; or rather, trust but verify.

I had a good working relationship with the Oskaloosa Education Association, but at election times, the union would put a candidate on the ballet to get a different board member. There is a law in Iowa that states that during an election, no new advertising can be placed after the Friday before an election; the only ads that can be used are the ads already being used. For the school board election in 1993, I was unopposed until the Friday before the election when the union's candidate, a farmer's wife, was announced as a write-in. One must realize that the union controls close to eight hundred votes along with their own votes. With all the family members added on to that, it makes an election controlling block. The Tuesday of the election was also the day John Deere introduced the 8000 Series tractors nationwide, and Drost Equipment had a huge customer event planned for the night with dinner for eight hundred friends. I got several volunteers to canvas the rural area and encourage people to get out to vote. I had run one ad of my family that could be printed for distribution. Farmers were calling from the voting places asking us to keep the food warm so they could stay and vote. The show went on with the election. I won by a few votes, getting over nine hundred votes (two hundred votes would usually win the election).

Harold Westra resigned and took a job as the administrator of the Area Education Agency in Ottumwa the following year. The school system hired a new superintendent, Dr. Tucker Lillis from Wyoming. When Dr. Lillis came to Oskaloosa, he informed me that his wife had refused to move to Oskaloosa. He had dropped her off in her hometown in Nebraska, and he moved to Oskaloosa.

It became obvious with the sale of the old junior high building and the loss of the auditorium that the community needed a performing arts center for the various band, orchestra, and vocal concerts, as well as for the drama departments from Oskaloosa Schools, Penn College, and the community. The George Daily Trust had just come into existence. I was board president, and the board was very supportive of trying to get a new community auditorium. That space was reserved between the new junior high and the senior high school. John Pothoven, a board member, and I worked on the project along with Joe Crookham and Nick Williams, who were trustees of the George Daily Trust. A separate chapter will talk more about the George Daily Auditorium, but in September 1996, the deed to the new seven-hundred-seat auditorium was presented to Oskaloosa Community Schools at the last school board meeting of my first term. I had been on the board for twenty years.

Public Service: My First Twenty Years on the School Board

When constructed, this building was the junior high. Today, it's the middle school.

Chapter 23

Live Drive-Through Nativity

In the early 1980s, I was elected Young People's President at the Nazarene Church in Oskaloosa. The group decided it would be better to get the young people involved in a project for the community rather than in projects for themselves. Someone presented the idea of doing a live nativity, with the young people of the church being the actors in the set. The idea was expanded to be a nativity set up on the church yard that the community could drive by to see without getting out of their vehicles.

It was November, and all involved thought it was a great idea and that the group should do it before Christmas. A couple in the group exclaimed, "It can't be done for this year!" I took that as a challenge, and the dates were set for the week before Christmas. Four scenes were planned: Mary and Joseph traveling to Bethlehem, baby Jesus in the manger, the shepherds, and the wise men with the star. The driveway would be lit with paper bags that had sand in them supporting a lit candle. An older church lady volunteered to lead the group of ladies in making the costumes to match the biblical characters. The actors would be dressed up and could warm up in the basement under the parsonage between shifts. (The parsonage was in the center of the parking lot where the nativity would take place.)

The sets were quite simple. For example, the angels announcing Jesus' birth to the shepherds were on the deck of the parsonage, and the shepherd scene was below it. The young people had a great time. With limited advertising, over nine hundred people drove through the display. The nativity was put on for two evenings. Everybody called it a great success and said it should be done again.

I was the elected director, and planning started earlier for the next year. A one-hundred-foot backdrop was painted on eight-foot sheets of plywood for the traveling scene. A donkey was found for Mary to ride. The inn scene was added, and the sand-filled bags once again held candles to light the walkway. The youth did really well and were excited about all the visitors. (Close to two thousand folks visited the live nativity.) Proceeds from the offering was given to the local Diamond Shelter, a home for special needs children. The Drosts funded the nativity.

The nativity became a community event expected by the locals. The sets grew in size and quality. For example, the wise men set was expanded to a traveling scene with a one-hundred-foot painted backdrop and the star shining over the house. We contracted with an exotic animal farm located at Cape Girardeau, Missouri, to bring a donkey for Mary to ride, Joshua sheep or goats for the shepherd scene, and camels dressed in garments fit for a king for the wise men. They brought the animals for several years. The paper bags with sand and a candle were replaced with plastic bags with an electric light bulb string in each.

As the nativity expanded, it was extended to three hours per evening, with a shift change every thirty minutes. The crew of actors grew to over one hundred young people, and the ladies of the church prepared food for the whole group to include supper, hot chocolate, coffee, pastries, and popcorn. It takes a large church to provide that number of volunteers for a three-night event. It was a great party, but it was all serious when the actors were in the sets. One year, a Musco public relations employee named Bonnie Bailey offered to write a short article and submit it to the AP as a news release. That article brought Todd Magel from KCCI TV out of Des Moines for a live report. The attendance really went up, and the show had to be extended by thirty minutes to an hour to accommodate all the people in line. The police had to come to help control the traffic.

There was a fire for Mary and Joseph to stay warm, as well as a fire for the shepherds. Heaters were put in each of the small buildings to keep the actors warm. It got to ten degrees below zero one year, and the nativity went on as scheduled. The outside shifts were reduced to twenty minutes to keep people warm, but the crowd was still there. It was beautiful to see the little children gleefully looking through the window of a car or the window of a bus, as they were seeing the true Christmas story.

In future years, the nativity was expanded to four nights so more spectators could see the event. A final scene was added after a few years depicting the return of Jesus. Jesus was dressed in a bright silver gown, suspended in the air with a strong light on him. It was a very powerful scene that made the Christmas story go full circle from Jesus' birth to the end of times when Jesus will come again to take His believers to Heaven to be with Him. The best year was when about ten thousand people came and visited the nativity. Sometimes the wait would be over thirty minutes. One of the preferred jobs was to be the person to tell people thanks for coming and to turn their lights back on. Those people got to hear all the positive comments and see the faces of the children.

The nativity continued for several years until it got to be work and duty instead of fun and a mission. The Nazarene Church in Big Spring, Texas, did a nativity similar to the Oskaloosa show. Bemidji, Minnesota, also did a live drive-through nativity.

Chapter 24

A Huge Transition

Drost Equipment was losing a lot of money in 1982 and 1983, and it appeared it was going to be several years before the ag economy got readjusted to the banking requirements. There were a lot of closing-out sales on farms, several Chapter 11 bankruptcies, and farmers going to town to get a job to supplement their farm income. At one point, I went to Rex Blom, who was the banker at Mahaska State Bank, and had a heart-to-heart discussion. I told Rex what the situation was and offered the keys to the store to him. Rex asked, "What would I do with them?" The outcome of the discussion was that Mahaska State Bank was going to stay with Drost Equipment until the end of the economy bust, but we agreed that neither of us knew what the business could look like when the economy changed. Mahaska State Bank stayed true to their word. Drost did not make much money, and the $400,000.00 loan limit at Mahaska State Bank was the amount of our loan for a few years (for sure in 1983).

During the spring of 1983, the John Deere area sales representative, Greg Frazier, stopped by Drost Equipment, asking questions about the business and what I thought the future held. Greg would stop by every three weeks or so, and he was a nice guy to visit with. Dr. Sydney Smith, my doctor, came back from a Canadian fishing trip and told me that in the fish-cleaning house, a group of John Deere big wigs had asked who the new John Deere dealer in Oskaloosa should be . . . because they were going to cancel out Gary Rogers. I also found out that Greg Frazier was going to the farms in the area

A Huge Transition

and asking farmers who they thought should be the next John Deere dealer in town. I found out later that they unanimously said it should be Drost Equipment.

In the early part of July 1983, Greg Frazier stopped at the dealership and asked me if Drost Equipment would be interested in becoming the new John Deere dealer. Greg said it was highly unusual to take a competitive dealer and convert them. This situation would be an exception, but John Deere was prepared to do it. Joe Crookham and I are two of the few people in the world to have John Deere come and ask them to be their dealer.

Here are the facts:

1. Drost Equipment was losing a lot of money.

2. Drost Equipment was at the loan limit at Mahaska State Bank.

3. The area was in the midst of a drought.

4. The prime interest rate was 22.5%.

5. I'd talked to Ford about how tough things were at Drost Equipment. Their simple reply was, "There isn't anything you can do about it!"

6. Gary Rogers wanted $1 million for his operation, without the used equipment.

I knew the future in the farm equipment business in Iowa was with John Deere, but this was an impossibility. I wish I could tell you that I prayed about this for hours a day, or that I opened my Bible to a verse that said, "Buy Gary Rogers!" I don't believe I even

Chisel Points in the Ground

had the nerve to ask Martha about it, because she did not know how bad the financial situation was in our business. Martha only knew that every Thursday morning, she could stop by the store and pick up a paycheck to provide for our family. I know I asked our partner, Joe Crookham, about it; of course, he knew we should pursue it. But humanly, I could not figure out a plan to take to my banker and convince him how this would ever work.

Still, I went to Mahaska State Bank one afternoon in early August to talk to Rex Blom about the John Deere/Gary Rogers deal. We talked about the weather, the kids, the school system, and a lot of other things first. I finally got up enough nerve to bring up the John Deere deal. Rex asked how much Gary wanted, and I told him $1 million! Then he asked if I wanted it. I told Rex that I knew the future of the farm equipment business in Iowa was with John Deere, because all or most of their equipment was manufactured in or near Iowa and it had a huge market presence in the area. Then he asked a really strange question (or so I thought). I was thirty-six years old, and he asked, "How is your health?" I know I responded, "Pretty good—I take an aspirin now and then."

And then he asked, "Do you want it?"

And I responded, "Yes." I asked why he would ask about my health, and I will never forget his response: "We know that if you get it, you will really have to work because of all the increased business. The bank board has already met and approved the loan, so go get the deal done!"

I knew I had heard him correctly, but I was amazed and in shock. I had not even applied for a loan, and he just told me to go spend $1 million! I know the Bible states that angels go before us (Genesis 24:7). I am certain a whole group of angels was at work in this situation.

Over the next few months, I had several meetings with Gary and Karen Rogers and Greg Frazier from John Deere. One night at the Gary Rogers' Company facility, I (being a good Dutchman) asked if they would accept $900,000.00 for the whole deal. Gary looked across his desk, slammed closed the notebook he had in front of him, and said, "NO!" I didn't know what to say, but Karen came to the rescue when she said, "Now, Gary, you know Carl is our only buyer, so we do need to talk." So Gary opened his notebook again, but he still got the million dollars for the real estate, parts inventory, special tools, office equipment and fixtures, rolling stock, and costs of the new inventory.

Rex Blom attempted to get me a Small Business Administration loan, but it proved to be too much paperwork and too many limits on the capital; so Rex took the loan to several participating banks (I didn't understand, but I didn't need to understand). The loan interest rate was 22.5%, or $225,000.00 per year in interest, which had to be paid first. The whole deal was put together so all that was left was our trip to Moline, Illinois, where I'd meet with the John Deere Moline branch manager (who had the reputation for being "hard"). Joe Crookham and I went to the meeting, and John Deere really spent a lot of time telling us about the benefits of being a John Deere dealer and how good the company was. I asked if John Deere had any incentive trips for sales rewards, and the branch manager took great pride in telling us John Deere dealers made enough money to go on vacation wherever they wanted to go, how they wanted to go, and with whom they wanted to go! I just said okay.

John Deere wanted us to move our store to where Gary Rogers had his location, and they were adamant about it. I finally had to ask, "Why should we move to his location when we basically started in business the same day as Gary? He had the support of John Deere, and I had Ford. We set our location on the quarter mile of highway where the most farmers travel by traffic count. We designed our building ourselves. You helped Gary, but I have kicked him all around the area in market share. We want to keep our business where it is in Oskaloosa." (I knew we could have been thrown out for saying it, but it was all true.)

The John Deere group told us they were going to meet for a little bit. I figured we were going to be thrown out, but instead they came back and said, "Let's be partners in this business. You guys go back to Oskaloosa and operate it from where you want and how you have operated in the past, and we both win." I thanked them, and we drove back to Oskaloosa.

The switch to John Deere was set to take place just after Thanksgiving 1983. We informed the employees of the change. Late one afternoon, I got a can of white paint and painted all the blue trim on the buildings white. I removed the blue oval Ford sign from the front of the building. The next day was the change. I took a can of John Deere green paint and painted all the trim on the buildings green! Needless to say, there was a lot of talk around the community. On the transition day, our employees drove the Ford equipment out to the Rogers' building on Highway 63 South; then they drove the John Deere equipment back all in one day.

Ford Tractor was less than happy when they got our termination letter and really tried to make things difficult. Some of the Ford customers were very unhappy. About ten customers were so mad about it they opened their own Ford dealership just down the road. I told them if they wanted to do that, they should open it up adjacent to Drost Equipment because that was where the ag traffic was going to be, so they could make use of it. Most of our customers and the ag community were extremely pleased that Drost got the John Deere dealership. Ron Van Veldhuizen was one of the most loyal Ford customers, and he was the first to trade a Ford off for a John Deere 4450 MFWD (mechanical front wheel drive) tractor. Ron told me he was going to get all his Fords traded off while they still had value.

There was one very disappointing aspect of the switch. Two of the customers I called my very good friends got mad and wouldn't speak to us, even though we went to the same church. They didn't even care that Drost Ford Equipment was going broke; Drost had to spend its last dime helping them and Ford succeed. I told them that if the color of machinery I sold determined our friendship, it was not friendship. So, I replaced those people with about five hundred new friends.

Chapter 25

Thirty Years as a John Deere Dealer

When Drost Equipment made the transition to being a John Deere dealer, it was decided that our territory manager would be Greg Frazier, the same person who had been coming to see us for the past six months (so we already knew each other). Greg and I went to the Traveler's Motel in Oskaloosa for a day, and we ordered equipment all day. John Deere required us to order forty tractors, and that was a huge number for me. We had only been selling seven or eight tractors a year, so to have thirty or forty tractors in inventory really didn't make sense. We also ordered combines, planters, hay equipment, and tillage equipment. We had just borrowed $1 million at 22.5% interest, and now the parts department and the service department needed to be enlarged to house the parts inventory. The shop also needed to be expanded to take care of the service needs.

An addition was built on the south side of our parts department, and the wall was taken out between the old building and the new addition. The parts bins were moved up from Gary Rogers' building. Roger Taft, the parts man at Rogers', was hired to help in the parts department. We also hired the equipment salesman from Rogers', Bernard "Junior" Meinders, to help me sell equipment.

In the spring of 1984, a service department addition was added to the west end of the old Ford building. It included a huge overhead door, which was fourteen feet high and twenty-four feet wide and would be large enough for "forever." Jay Bruxvoort—who worked at Hoeksema's, the John Deere store in Pella—was hired as a technician. Randy Roose was hired, as he had been the setup person at Rogers'. Finally, John Schippers was hired as a technician; he had been a technician at Hines Westburg in Knoxville, the International Harvester dealer.

One has to realize that all of this took money: the additions, the extra parts, the extra staff, the overhead, and the money to finance the trade-in used equipment. Our debt increased another $1 million at the rental rate of 22.5%. (Total, it was $2.4 million dollars at 22.5%! That's an extra $450,000.00 interest per year to the banker first.) It really is a miracle of God that we survived. I was told by my banker that every time the bank examiners came for their inspection, the Drost Equipment file was the first one they wanted to look at. The examiners told the bank we wouldn't survive! After we became successful, the examiners still wanted to see the Drost file, and they were surprised to see the results of a banker who had trust in an individual.

Back in 1978, Drost had started selling Kinze planters and grain carts manufactured in Williamsburg, Iowa. We were very successful with it. We were also the dealer for New Holland, which sold hay equipment, manure spreaders, forage harvesters, forage wagons, combines, corn heads, and bean heads. When I announced to New Holland that we were going to be the John Deere dealer, our sales representative told us they would just leave because of the conflict, and I agreed. Kinze Manufacturing took a different approach. Their sales manager TOLD me I was going to stock the same number of Kinze planters as I had John Deere planters. At that time, John Deere planters came in for stock with terms of a year, while the Kinze inventory was due before thirty days or before another truckload was shipped. That demand didn't make much sense, so I asked him, "Whose name is on the front of this building?" He said, "Drost." I told him that when his name appeared on the front of the building, he could tell me what I was going to do. Until then, no bananas. He then told me to write a letter to them terminating the Drost agreement with Kinze. Again, I asked him, "Why? I don't want to terminate the agreement—you do! So, you write the letter of termination." He didn't want Drost to get the rights under the Iowa law to return parts and other rights. The sales manager kept asking for the letter, and I kept telling him no. So, Kinze finally sent us a letter of termination. I have often wondered if Jon Kinzenbaw knew about the discussion, but in the long run, it didn't matter.

We got off to a very good start in the fall of 1983. The strong part of the dealership was always the employees. I was the owner (fearless leader), but my right-hand man was always David DeJong. He was the bookkeeper by title, but he was also the "do whatever needed done guy," from unloading trucks to fixing stuff, arranging equipment displays, or mowing the grass. David was also the pessimist (along with Martha). I swear their position in life was not only to warn me of the risks involved, but to keep me humble. Roger Taft was in charge of the parts department and had several helpers over the years. Roger had knowledge about what parts were needed, and he did a good job of keeping the farmers happy. Glenn Knox, who was one of my first employees in 1974, was our service manager. Nobody will take care of customers better than Glenn. He knew how to schedule work, keep the employees busy, and keep the customers happy all at the same time. I know there were days when Glenn just absolutely didn't want to see me because of the demands I put on him. Brant Bruxvoort drove our truck. He was a retired farmer who knew the farmer language and could explain the simple operation of equipment.

Drost Equipment was blessed with terrific employees over the years, and the business tried to operate as a big family. As a John Deere store, it became apparent that service and parts were going to be the driving force for growing the business. Jay Bruxvoort and John Schippers were on Glenn Knox's service team. Jay was a very experienced John Deere technician, and John was a very good technician no matter the brand. John worked really hard and only spoke when he was asked a question. Otherwise, he did what he was paid to do—work. Dean Reese joined them as a tractor tech, and he didn't care what was put in front of him to do. He would get the job done and never complain. Dean Hoksbergen had started for Drost as a truck driver under the Ford sign, but he had moved up to being an implement technician and developed his skills in that area. Dean really liked square balers, and he could make one work well and make the knotters tie. As mentioned, Randy Roose came from Rogers'. He started in the spring of 1984 as a setup person and was later promoted to combine and implement technician. Randy was always fun to watch because he worked so hard. If you asked Randy a question, you would get a very straight answer.

Jacob Hemann came into my office in August 2003 and said he wanted a job. He was a graduate of the John Deere tech program in Calmar, Iowa. The John Deere dealer at Cresco had told him to come to Oskaloosa and get a job. Jessica, Jacob's wife, had taken a music teaching job in Albia. Jacob told me he really liked the AMS (Ag Management Solutions) and GPS farming technology. The GPS stuff was really just starting, and I didn't think I needed anybody at the time. But Jacob was hired because he was available, and he was the key to the success of the Drost Equipment satellite farming department. Jacob loved this stuff, and he could get people to understand how to use it. I did a good job of selling the equipment because of the convenience, the money it would make, and how it would take the stress out of planting straight rows. Jacob also excelled in all the new electronics that came on the equipment, and he helped our "old-time" employees learn how to navigate the computers. Just for your information, the S Series combines introduced for the fall of 2012 carried more computer equipment and storage than the space shuttle, and we had to teach eighty-year-old farmers how to use it! Jacob did a swell job.

We had lots of employees over the years. I had a little sign behind my desk with my simple employment plan on it: "Work or be fired." All the great employees knew that I knew what was going on. They didn't need to tell me, but I would ask the question to see if my assumptions were true.

We hired Dustin (there will be more about him in another chapter) to do equipment clean up and just "do dirty work." He was promoted to truck driver and delivery person. Dustin could switch semitrailers in less than ten minutes and be on the road. He was very good at his job and never dallied. If he was on the road, you could time him at an average of fifty miles per hour, and he would be home ahead of time. Dustin told me once that he would never stop with a load, instead driving straight from Moline home. Once, Dustin took his wife, Jennifer, along with him to get a new trailer in Mitchell, South Dakota. They stayed in Sioux City for the night. The next morning, Dustin headed the truck to Oskaloosa. At about Des Moines, Jennifer needed a restroom; he told her the next stop was Oskaloosa, and so it was.

The employees were always very loyal, and we found out that a lot of competitors tried to hire our best employees. The employees knew that April 15 was the time of year for raises (after the slow winter months). They also knew there would be an employee meeting to discuss the past year, the way the new year was looking, the insurance, and the raises. We started out in 1974 paying 100% of the insurance plan for employees and their families to include the doctor, hospital, major medical, drugs, short- and long-term disability, and some life insurance. We did so until the sell-out on December 31, 2013. The insurance coverage was a big deal to most people. The employees also knew that if I told them that there would be no raises until we saw how the year turned out, I would make it right at the end of the year; they knew they would be taken care of. In hindsight, it worked out well because the bonuses took care of the difference in salary; the wages hadn't increased, so the wage scale didn't jump a bunch. When employees were offered another job by a competitor, the best ones would come and tell me we needed to talk. They would tell me about the offer, and I would make adjustments if necessary. The employees knew that if I told them they would get a raise or a bonus on a certain date, it would be on the check. I believed that good employees could never be paid enough, and poor employees were always overpaid. Only the best, most qualified, most trained, and trustworthy employees would stay. The employees knew Martha and I treated them like family and that they would be taken care of.

Drost Equipment always had a Christmas party. It started out as a dinner at the Stonehenge north of Oskaloosa. Then we decided to go to Des Moines and rent all the married couples (not the single guys or gals) a nice room in a nice motel. We'd have a nice dinner catered in, do a white elephant gift exchange, then give out the Christmas money and bonuses. After several years, we decided that the money put stress on the evening, so the money was all sent out in the paychecks the Thursday before the party. That way everybody knew what they were getting ahead of time. This really made the party fun and a whole lot less stressful for me. On Sunday morning, everybody could have breakfast at the motel and spend the day in Des Moines shopping with the Christmas money and having a good time. I would head down early to visit with the couples as they came down (and drank too much coffee).

At Christmastime, Drost Equipment also took a token of appreciation to the loyal customers, both small and large. We learned the ladies of the house really enjoyed fruit baskets, and so for the last several years, 350 fruit baskets were delivered to customers as far west as Monroe, north to Tama, east to Packwood, and south to Blakesburg. It took a ton truckload of fruit, and Martha and some other ladies assembled all the baskets. It took the employees three days to deliver the baskets with four routes per day.

Even though the farm economy in 1984 was in the dumps and there were lots of horror stories, I found out we had moved up to the big leagues. As a Ford dealership, we had been the number-three dealership in our town, behind the John Deere store and the International Harvester store owned by the Hugen family. The Hugens and I were good friends. We tractor-pulled together for many years, and they were just very good people. There were still seven farm equipment brands represented in Oskaloosa when my other friends opened the Ford location. I read one time that it is a lot easier to be number two than it is to stay number one. I never realized what that meant until Drost Equipment became the number-one ag dealership in town. Everybody compares to you; the expectations just become higher, and they get higher every year. When you are number one, you get a target put on your chest, and everybody shoots directly at you. The comparisons they make are often cruel.

Our salesman, Junior Meinders, and I had opportunities to sell farm equipment, even in depressed times. We traded in lots of competitive equipment, so the used equipment lot was full. It took a lot of money to cover our equity in the used equipment. During this period, Drost also sold the same short lines as we had before the switch: Glencoe tillage equipment; New Idea manure spreaders, hay equipment, and uni-harvesters; Killbros wagons; and numerous pieces of equipment from catalog attachment businesses. Almost every day, there would be a sales representative coming in from one of these short lines, and they all took an hour (which I really didn't have). I had already quit eating lunch to gain at least an hour per day. Since John Deere was nearly a full line of farm equipment, the short lines were nearly all eliminated over a period of time.

The farm economy hit its low sometime in 1985. Then, it slowly and gradually increased until 1988, when it was about a normal atmosphere. John Deere was offering some pretty good incentives to keep the market rolling. On December 31, 1987, Junior and I sold six new tractors, which was the best tractor sales day in the history of our company. I went home tired that day. At supper, Martha asked, "What did you do today?"

"WE SOLD SIX NEW TRACTORS TODAY!"

Her response was, "That is nice. Pass the rolls."

Martha did her part in keeping me humble!

During this time, John Deere also offered sales incentive trips. The way the programs and sales incentive numbers were put together, Drost Equipment could earn trips about every other year. When we earned multiple trips, they were shared with the employees.

Service clinics became a part of the schedule for the year at Drost. We put on planter clinics in the spring before planting, then combine clinics in the fall before harvest. Tractor clinics were tried without much success. The first several clinics were taught by John Deere territory service representatives. Then John Deere didn't want to commit to them, so the local employees had to do them. Drost always got a good turnout for those clinics. Basically, Randy Roose and Dean Hoksbergen were responsible for the clinics, and neither of them felt comfortable teaching, even though they were very qualified to lead the groups. As a group, we decided I would lead the groups in a discussion of the operation of the equipment and guide them in the meeting. Then I'd ask for follow-up questions in case anything was missed. Using my education in teaching, I'd write a regular lesson plan to follow, and it worked well. All the clinics were operations clinics, so they were intended for the farmers to come and be refreshed on the operation of their equipment. After all, it had been eleven months since they had used it! Drinks and Jaarsma pastries were always on the menu.

When we began, you had to host a John Deere Day to be a dealer. Around 2005, it was no longer a requirement, but it was a tradition for customers to come to town and go to John Deere Day. It was usually held in early February, and several wives would come along to enjoy a delicious catered meal at the shop. It forced us to really clean the building up one day a year. After the meal, we'd show a John Deere Day film. At intermission, there would be a drawing for some prizes. It was always a lot of fun, and it was enjoyed by the customers, the employees, and the employee spouses who would volunteer to help serve the food and clean up. Drost would have over three hundred for lunch and about two hundred who stayed for the film, which was screened in the back shop of the main building. My father was always around the store, and he would get mad about the "freeloaders" who would come early for a free meal. I told him we would feed them early and get them out of the way before the good customers came. I told my dad that if they needed a meal that bad, we could afford to feed them. It was quite humorous to watch the "freeloaders" stuff two or even three sandwiches in their coat pockets before they left.

Over the years, Drost Equipment held several special events to celebrate special times, like reaching twenty-five years in business, my big birthdays, and the introduction of new equipment. The introduction of the 8000 Series tractors was memorable because the shape and models were to be kept secret until a certain day and evening. The tractor that came to Oskaloosa was in a big canvas cover, so it could not be seen early. The celebration and all the tables for eating were set up outside on the south side of the main building, and we served a huge meal. Then after dark, the tractor was unveiled. We had contacted Musco Lighting, and they had one of their mobile light trucks set up in the Hawkeye Lumber lot so the light could come over the top of the building, which really added excitement. It was also a stressful night because it was the night of the school board election. This was when I was up for reelection and the teachers had run a write-in campaign. Remember, some of the customers were in line to vote, and we had to keep the food warm until they got to town. (I won, but not by a bunch.)

A qualified accountant is invaluable to a business, and I always felt that tax laws should be stretched in a way that's explainable and legal. When Drost Equipment took over the John Deere franchise, Martha and I were not financially secure enough to guarantee all the debt. So, others with net worths to guarantee the debt were required by Mahaska State Bank and John Deere to obtain the required financing. When a lot of risk is involved, compensation should be included. Our accountant, Jerry Uitermarkt, found a Thor Tool case that explained guarantor fees or money paid to those for their guarantee of debt. Jerry thought it applied to Drost Equipment and filed it on our income tax. Yes, you guessed it! Drost was up for an IRS audit, and the item they looked at closely was the guarantor fee. The IRS accepted all the travel expenses, the contributions, and the owner's compensation, but they wanted big penalty dollars for the guarantor fee deduction. Jerry recommended that we appeal the decision, and he filed the appeal. I thought the appeal would be four or five days at the federal building in Des Moines, but Jerry informed me that we would have thirty to forty-five minutes to explain our case and that it was best if the client did the explaining.

Now, I had sold a lot of expensive equipment, but this would be an all-cash settlement. If we won, the deduction could be used for the rest of the years of the company. At the appeal hearing—with only the IRS agent, Jerry, and me in a small room—I explained why the deduction was necessary for business continuation. I explained how I was a Vietnam veteran who was financially broke when the opportunity came around to open a business, and how I as the owner worked harder than any other employee and wanted to see the business succeed. Without the money and guarantees from outside people, the company would be forced to close, leaving fourteen employees without jobs and a company that doesn't exist and pays no tax. It took twenty-five minutes, and the auditor asked Jerry, "Can you provide me with financial statements to back up what Mr. Drost has told me?" Jerry's response was, "Yes." The IRS auditor said he would rule for the deduction. Jerry could have two weeks to send in the financials because the auditor was leaving to go fishing in Canada as soon as we left. Drost Equipment used that deduction every year as long as we were in business and saved a huge amount of tax. The IRS came to audit Drost Equipment four more times after that, and it was always the guarantor fees they looked at. When I told them that deduction had been won in appeal, the auditor's comment was always, "You ruined all the fun."

When the farm economy finally straightened out a little, we decided that to get new employees and retain present employees, Drost needed to provide a retirement plan. Dave DeJong and I researched retirement plans and came up with a profit-sharing plan through Mahaska State Bank. Lynn Howard from the bank was invited to a company employee meeting to explain the plan. I will always remember well-dressed and sophisticated Lynn standing and doing the presentation when a "big" mouse scurried across the floor right in front of her! (It was hilarious!) Our profit-sharing plan was designed so that when the company had a good year, Drost would put money in the trust fund at the bank, and the bank would divide it up amongst the employees as their percentage of the total payroll. It was not top-funded. I will always remember when the employees were asked if they had questions or comments. Randy Roose spoke up and said, "I don't know about the rest of these **********, but we depend on our Christmas cash to have Christmas at our house, and I want to see us get the Christmas cash first and then this plan!" We did start the profit-sharing plan, but true to Randy's words, each employee got a $1,000.00 bonus before Christmas in cash until the IRS told us it had to be counted as payroll. Then, our employees got a check as an extra part of their payroll at Christmastime.

Drost Equipment did other things to motivate employees to work hard and stay with us. I remember the first month we did

$1 million of business. Everybody had busted it to get all the work done. So, Dave went to the bank and got an Uncle Ben for each employee (no matter their position), and we had a time clock meeting at starting time. It was a surprise for everyone when I presented each of them with the $100.00 bill. The time clock meetings were usually used to keep employees updated on business practices, but many times the employees received cash.

One of the activities our employees and spouses enjoyed was the Mystery Trip. Drost Equipment would charter a bus from Daryl VandeGeest, and the employees would all come and get on. The only people who knew where we had reservations for dinner were me and Daryl the driver. We would spend the evening on the bus and at a nice restaurant. Daryl would usually drive a detour course to the restaurant. My favorite memory of these trips was when we were on our way to Crossroads Depot in Grinnell, and Daryl pulled up in front of the Apple Basket in Montezuma and stopped and opened the door. Our daughter-in-law, Cathy, got up out of her seat and I said, "Surprise, this isn't where we are eating!" It was a priceless moment. (Sorry, Cathy, but it is a great memory.)

In the eighties, most of the children of the employees were young, and Drost purchased a used travel van for the employees to use for vacations. All the employees had to pay for was the gas during the trip.

In 1987, Wilbur Young needed some money, so he decided to sell off half his interest in Drost Equipment. Martha and I bought half of Wilbur's shares, and the deal worked out well even though the timing could have been better. I had to take another mortgage paper home and point to the X where Martha needed to sign her name. She always trusted me and never asked any difficult questions. Joe Crookham still owned his shares, so it was still a three-person shareholder corporation. A few years later, Wilbur needed more money, so we bought his shares out, but we allowed David DeJong (our longtime bookkeeper) and his wife to buy half of those shares. The partnership was made up of me with 87%, Joe Crookham with 5%, and Dave with 8%. The ownership never mattered because we never had a vote on decisions; Joe just went along with what we did, and Dave and I would talk about any major purchase or decision, and then we would act on our joint decision. We were very fortunate to have business partners we could enjoy both in business and personal relationships.

Joe always told me that at any time I wanted to own the whole store, I could purchase his shares. Joe was always a great person to seek advice from. Most Saturday afternoons, one could find Joe at the John Deere store, where we would talk about our community projects and discuss our future projects. If someone asked what we were discussing, our standard answer was, "We are solving the world's problems . . . and also the world problems nobody knows about yet." Just for information, Joe came up with this "crazy" idea to build a recreation trail circling Oskaloosa. You'll learn more about it in another chapter, but the plan was completed on a Saturday afternoon, with maps taped together on the floor of the showroom of Drost Equipment and three of us crawling over it with markers and highlighters. There was even a post in the newspaper by a person who claimed that all the major decisions made in Oskaloosa were made in a dark room at the local John Deere store. The poor person was misinformed because it was really at the parts counter, with Joe on a stool on one side and me on the other. We always had popcorn and a can of pop (though we started out with a twelve-ounce bottle). And during the busy spring and fall seasons, Joe would answer the phone, gather up parts, and set parts outside the front door for later pickup. I tell all of this because the mystery with people downtown was how we got together, how we got projects done, and how we are always in agreement. The answer is in another chapter or two.

Over a period of years, the competing farm equipment businesses started closing in Oskaloosa and the surrounding area. I was blamed for most of them because Drost took their business, took their employees, and just kept expanding. The Ford tractor dealership was short-lived. Hoeksema's, the John Deere dealer in Pella, closed when John Deere wanted only county seat locations. The Allis-Chalmers store closed after two or three owners. Bill Bone Motors, the Massey Ferguson dealer, closed after Bill's death. Whitaker Implement, the Oliver/White dealer, closed after White had financial problems. Charlie from that store and I were always good friends, in spite of the fact Charlie disagreed with the Drost business model. Courtney's, the John Deere store in Ottumwa, also closed. Then, the Hugens sold Oskaloosa Implement to Mr. Boot from Pella. Remember, the Hugen family and the Drost family were always friends . . . even though each of us wanted the other's customers! In 1974, Drost delivered the first Ford tractor on Bob Hugen's truck with the International signs on the doors. We are still friends with the Hugen family remnants. Eventually, the only competing dealership left in Oskaloosa was McKim Tractor, the local AGCO dealer.

As bad as business was in the eighties, we made a pretty good living in the nineties and early aughts. When the price of corn went over $3.00 a bushel in September 2005, the volume just kept increasing at 10% a year or better. During the years of rapid growth, it was important to have employees who could see the big picture, knew their jobs, and were willing to stay and get the job done. In the year 2004, when I had my knees replaced (I could hardly walk anymore), we sold a large number of used combines. One night, every employee stayed, and all we did was change tires and duals from one combine to another to get the wheels and tires on the proper combine to get them delivered. We also cleaned combines, and I stayed and ran the power washer. Everybody remembers the raccoon poo that covered me after cleaning out one combine.

I always worked more hours than any other employee, and during the long hours of the busy season, I took my turn. It was not unusual for Martha and the kids to show up with supper, and we would have the family meal on the parts counter. Martha was a great partner, and we both had the same end in mind: to take good care of our customers, our employees, and our family, and to be able to live a comfortable retirement, all the time giving God the praise for what He allowed us to do.

The fast expansion of the farm equipment market made the equipment very hard to get from John Deere. For several years, combines had to be sold to a customer fifteen or sixteen months ahead of use; planters and tractors were sold at least a year before the next season. John Deere started evaluating dealers based on market share numbers, but they couldn't provide the equipment in a timely fashion. For tax reasons, Drost customers bought other brands of equipment. During the "glory years," John Deere also added more requirements to the dealer contract, which made it very difficult on single-store operations. John Deere wanted to get to multistore operations, and I firmly believe (in my own mind I know) that the new requirements were pushed on single-store operations, while multistore operations were not under the same requirements.

These are the facts as to what made me get out of the ownership of the single store and sell to a multistore operation. For the last several years, Drost Equipment had a very high CSI (customer satisfaction index) with John Deere. We had this number because John Deere would send all customers who had purchased a new piece of equipment a survey form to fill out. The Drost score was so good that John Deere came and asked what all we did to perform so well. I think they thought I was filling them all out; but in fact, I only filled out the ones I could get my hands on! Drost Equipment had one of the five highest CSI scores in the United States, and that score paid off big time when the time came to sell out.

Chapter 26

The Sell-Out

In every business owner's mind is the question of how long the business can sustain itself. My motto had always been that a person wants to get out of any situation on a high, not a low. In about 2001, my knees were so bad that walking was very difficult, and Martha and I talked about the future of the business. At that time, we decided that when it happened, we wanted to change the ownership to a company who would provide for the current employees and provide the parts and service support our customers required. After looking at all the viable John Deere dealers around, we decided to try to make an agreement with the Van Wall Equipment Group because of their reputation.

I had a visit with Don Van Houweling a few months later about any possibility of Van Wall buying Drost Equipment. John Deere required the territories to be contiguous, and we were not. Don told me he would really be interested at the right time, but he stated, "It really scares me to buy a store like yours because we can't do all the things you have done over the years to take care of the customers and your employees."

I had both knees replaced in 2004, and the surgeries were very successful. The business grew and was very profitable. The Bible says in Luke 16:10: "Whoever can be trusted with very little can also be trusted with much, and whoever is dishonest with very little will also be dishonest with much." And then again in Luke 12:48b, the Bible states: "From everyone who has been given much, much will be demanded; and from the one who has been entrusted with much, much more will be asked." Martha and I have always believed that God has promised to look after His children. We have a responsibility to use what God has given us to glorify Him, help others, and further His kingdom on earth. Because of all the business our loyal customers did with us, we tried to do as God laid on our hearts. We made sure that our family was taken care of, that our loyal employees were provided with enough to raise their families, and that we provided for mission work of the kingdom. Our goal in life was never to get rich; our goal was to have a business that was run honestly and to take really good care of our customers. If that happened, we would be able to take care of our employees and do God's work.

Drost Equipment was blessed over the years with excellent professional advisors, including our accountant, Jerry Uitermarkt from Pella. He became our accountant when he became a CPA in 1981. Jerry is very good at what he does. In about 2006, he said in one of our tax appointments, "You have done really well creating this monster . . . but how are we going to get you out without giving it all to the government?" Over the next year and a half, Jerry and I worked on a plan to put in effect when the right time came. One of the things Jerry suggested was that we take dividends out every year. We paid some tax as we went, which worked really well. We were giving over 20% to God's work through charities, and that amount increased as we took money out of the company. Jerry put together a plan for selling the business and the approximate value, the contributions we would make, and a plan forward into the future. It was probably done in 2007. We reviewed it every tax time.

Business really boomed in 2010, 2011, and 2012, and it was off to a great start in 2013. In early February 2013, I got a phone call from Don Van Houweling of Van Wall Equipment. The conversation went like this: "Hi, Carl! This is Don. I'm gonna make this short. I want to buy you!" I was surprised, but in a few moments, I said,

"Martha and I are leaving for Hawaii in a few days. I'll call you when I get back so we can talk." Martha and I did go to Hawaii, and we had some very serious conversations around the pool and at the beach about the future of our company. We'd had nine record years in a row, and it looked like number ten was coming. I told Martha that it couldn't stay that way. (All the projections were a straight line up at about 15% a year through 2020.) I would turn sixty-five years of age, and there were a lot of things we wanted to accomplish in life after business. We decided that I should talk to Don when we got back. We had told John Deere back in the mid-nineties that we would one day sell our store and would not expand into a multistore operation, even though it could have still been an option. Mom Drost had always said that I "knew when to hold 'em and when to fold 'em."

In late February 2013, Don and I met at the conference room of the Newton airport and discussed the potential of Van Wall acquiring ownership of Drost Equipment, as well as the real estate owned by us under the name Young Equipment Buildings. In that first meeting, we decided how to come up with the value of the business and determined that both parties were interested in getting it done. The appraisals were ordered, and I met with Jerry when the values came back. I wrote it all down on a piece of notebook paper, including what the salary would be if Van Wall wanted me to manage the location for a period of time. We made a few extra copies.

Another meeting was scheduled with Don in April at the Newton airport. (Isn't that a good place to do a multi-million-dollar deal?) When I got to the meeting, there was Don; his son, Matt; the Van Wall attorney; his accountant; and maybe somebody else. When I walked in, Don introduced me to his team, and then his attorney asked where the rest of my team was. I said, "I'm here." So, I passed out the copies of the notebook paper where I'd handwritten all the value breakdowns. I went over the numbers and how we had arrived at those numbers, with the documentation and the total at the bottom. Don's attorney wanted a non-compete clause, and we discussed what that would cost. I responded, "You don't need to pay me for a non-compete clause. If I wanted to compete, I wouldn't be here trying to sell the business to you."

The agreed turnover date was January 1, 2014. The meeting went very well, and Don's final comment to Matt was, "Well, son, we now know how much money we have to get ready for January 2." Then the meeting ended. After I left, I called Jerry, who knew the meeting was taking place, and he asked, "How did the meeting go?" I responded, "It went well, and the business has been sold."

Of course, he asked in response, "What did you get?"

I told him, "Everything on the sheet of paper!"

Jerry responded, "In all my years, I have told business owners to sell their businesses that way (selling the stock), but you are the first to have gotten it done!"

It was a simple matter that Don and I trusted each other. In later discussions, the attorney wanted to know how much money we would leave in escrow until Van Wall was sure they were getting what I had told them. I just told him, "Why don't you just keep $1 million? Does that satisfy you?" I had never had a million dollars before, so what would it matter if it took three or four weeks to get the last one? Then the attorney wanted to know who the lien holder was on the property, and I simply told him, "There is no lien holder. It's all paid for."

Of course, John Deere had to approve of our agreement. The Iowa sales manager for John Deere was a very aggressive lady. I didn't like her, and the feeling was mutual. What I did not know was that Van Wall was also in negotiations with Southard Equipment, which had locations in Grinnell, Marshalltown, and Tama; that deal would make Drost contiguous with Van Wall. That John Deere sales manager was very difficult, and I finally told her

I would no longer talk to her, but I would talk to the branch manager, who had already committed to me that the deal would be approved. The sales manager was a lady with something to grind, and her role in Iowa was a step up the corporate ladder.

I had told my employees that when something concrete happened about selling the business, I would tell them. Every five or six months, there would be a new rumor floating about who Drost had sold to and when. True to my word, after the meeting in late February with Don, I called an employee meeting and told the employees about the potential sale. I asked them not to breathe a word about it because it could ruin the business for a period of time. Another meeting was held in April to tell the employees it looked as if the sale was going through and that we had agreed on the methodology of the value. When the final deal was signed in early May 2013, corn was at $7.50 per bushel. We held another meeting with the employees, telling them the deal was complete and that on January 1, 2014, they would have a new employer. We expressed the need for confidentiality, and the employees all did a great job of keeping it under wraps until November, when we all agreed the announcement would be made. I did tell my two brothers who farm when the deal was done, and they told me that the markets couldn't stay where they were forever. What goes up always comes down. I did not ever get asked by any customer about a sale to Van Wall, but I was asked about a sale to Sinclair Tractor and Agri-Vision.

About mid-November, before the public announcement, Van Wall announced to their employees that they were purchasing Drost. I went and told Jim Scott and John Ryken, who were two of the first customers Drost had in 1974 and had been the most loyal customers for all those forty years. Then, the public announcement was made in Oskaloosa. December was very busy with the year-end sales, and the customers were asking, "If I give Van Wall this prepay, are they good for it?" As a result, Dave DeJong opened a trust account at Midwest One Bank under my name and deposited all the money in that account. Then Dave would withdraw the money and pay the bill at Van Wall for the piece of equipment or the repair that was prepaid. It worked very well, and everybody was satisfied, but that account held several million dollars.

The last Drost Equipment party was held at the Wildwood Lodge in Des Moines in mid-December 2013. Dave and I had already distributed the bonuses and the 401(k) amount, so the employees were expecting good food and a good time with the white elephant gift exchange. But Dave and I had decided to give the employees $200,000.00 as a loyalty going-away gift. It was divided up so the employees who had been there over twenty-five years would each get $10,000.00. Those who had been there five to twenty-four years would get $5,000.00. (There were no employees between fifteen and twenty-four years). Those who had been with us under five years would get $1,000.00. It came out to exactly $200,000.00, and nobody was close to the year cutoff. The employees were very shocked and surprised because they got their checks that night. There were several people around the room with tears in their eyes, but every one of the loyal employees deserved it very much.

On January 2, 2014, Dave and I made the final trip to the Newton airport for the closing and to pick up the checks. It was a great day. The teller at Midwest One Bank about had a coronary when I asked her to deposit the three checks. At the end of January, when all the inventories and accounting was complete, Don and I each had the value calculated; it was a $37.00 difference on the multi-million-dollar deal. Don paid me the $37.00 (his value was that much more than mine!).

It was an unbelievable year for Martha and me. I had started in January 1972 working at Van Gorp Implement, when we were a pair of bankrupt kids (if we had known how to figure it). Then to have a dream come true . . . TRULY, THE AMERICAN DREAM. As the Bible says, "Trust in the Lord with all your heart and lean not on your own understanding; in all your ways submit to him, and he will make your paths straight." All of that proved true—God blessed us beyond anything we could imagine. Martha and I never could have dreamed that our John Deere store would be worth so much money with the real estate included. With the intent of leaving a legacy of Drost Equipment in the community, $400,000.00 was donated to fund a new competition soccer field in the Lacey Recreation Complex. At the field dedication, customers of Drost Equipment and the Drost family cut the ribbon. The soccer field is named Drost Field, and it is one of the best collegiate fields in the Midwest.

Chapter 27

Being NICE to Others

I had excellent examples and teachers in the areas of helping others, providing them with food, and giving back. When I was growing up, if a neighbor needed help—whether they were young or old—my father and us boys were there. You have already read about the supplies we picked up after a heavy snow, but it went further than that. When the neighbors were getting older, we'd help them out. When Emmett next door was mowing hay, we'd go help him get his hay cut. We were pall bearers at a huge number of funerals and went to help widows. We took trips to the hospital to visit relatives, friends, and neighbors, and we always asked if there was something they needed or what we could do to help. The four boys knew that if we accepted money or payment, our arms would probably have been broken. Our mother, Ada, was a great cook, and food was always sent to the neighbors who needed it—the sick, the preacher, and even the family doctor were given garden produce or frozen chickens. In our father, Richard's, later years, he spent every Saturday afternoon in a nursing home visiting his friends and acquaintances.

Richard and Ada didn't preach about generosity to the family from the Bible, but they lived it by example. The Drosts never had much money, but the other kind of giving usually means more.

The Bible has a lot to say about helping others and generosity:

- **1 John 3:17–18:** "If anyone has material possessions and sees a brother or sister in need but has no pity on them, how can the love of God be in that person? Dear children, let us not love with words or speech but with actions and in truth."

- **James 2:14–18:** "What good is it, my brothers and sisters, if someone claims to have faith but has no deeds? Can such faith save them? Suppose a brother or a sister is without clothes and daily food. If one of you says to them, 'Go, in peace; keep warm and well fed,' but does nothing about their physical needs, what good is it? In the same way, faith by itself, if it is not accompanied by action, is dead. But someone will say, 'You have faith; I have deeds.' Show me your faith without deeds, and I will show you my faith by my deeds."

- **1 Timothy 6:17–19:** "Command those who are rich in this present world not to be arrogant nor to put their hope in wealth, which is so uncertain, but to put their hope in God, who richly provides us with everything for our enjoyment. Command them to do good, to be rich in good deeds, and to be generous and willing to share. In this way they will lay up treasure for themselves as a firm foundation for the coming age, so that they may take hold of the life that is truly life."

- **Matthew 25:34–40:** "Then the King will say to those on his right, 'Come, you who are blessed by my Father; take your inheritance, the kingdom prepared for you since the creation of the world. For I was hungry and you gave me something to eat, I was thirsty and you gave me something to drink, I was a stranger and you invited me in, I needed clothes and you clothed me, I was sick and you looked after me, I was in prison and you came to visit me.' Then the righteous will answer him, 'Lord, when did we see you hungry and feed you, or thirsty and give you something to drink? When did we see you a stranger and invite you in, or needing clothes and clothe you? When did we see you sick or in prison and go to visit you?' The King will reply, 'Truly I tell you, whatever you did for one of the least of these brothers and sisters of mine, you did for me.'"

- **Proverbs 11:25:** "A generous person will prosper; whoever refreshes others will be refreshed."

- **2 Corinthians 9:6–7:** "Remember this: Whoever sows sparingly will also reap sparingly, and whoever sows generously will also reap generously. Each of you should give what you have decided in your heart to give, not reluctantly or under compulsion, for God loves a cheerful giver."

I have found that it was easier to manage money when Martha and I had very little. God blessed our lives, and it became much harder to manage the money when there was more than enough for our daily needs. It has always been a question of who to help and how many to help because of the many needy folk in the area, city, or state. My philosophy is to help those God has pointed out to me, whether they are a person in church, a car along the road, a person along the street, a friend, or a relative. Help when God says, "Help this one or that family." I have always tried to carry cash in my pocket. If God says to give something to this person, I do it right then. If the person goes and buys beer, so be it; the money was given to God for His purpose. If someone asks me if I could be taken advantage of, the answer is yes, but a person is better off erring on the side of giving than passing up a real opportunity to witness for God by providing for real needs.

Many years ago, a noted religious author named Tony Campolo spoke at Penn College. Martha and I went to hear him. Toward the end of his presentation, he told the group, "The worst people at a restaurant come in on Sunday at noon. They have just come from church, and they pray to God before eating. They are very rude to the wait staff, are very demanding, and are the worst tippers of any group." What an example for the people, usually young, who are trying to make a living, and we claim to love Jesus! The other thing Tony said was, "If you are in a restaurant and you really get great service at your table, the wait staff is friendly, and they really went beyond to give you good service, if you are able and you have an Uncle Ben in your pocket, leave it as an anonymous tip." I have tried to take these messages to heart, so when we go out on Sunday after church and pray for the meal, the whole table will be respectful and the tip will always be very good. I have been able to carry an Uncle Ben and give one away occasionally, a few times to wait staff.

For example, we ate lunch at Lambert's in Springfield, Missouri, with my Uncle Short and his wife, Mary, who live in Republic. That afternoon, a very delightful young lady was our waitress, and we struck up a conversation with her. She was a medical student at Drury University in Springfield. My uncle was an old, retired farmer, and his comment to her was, "You got to be rich to go to Drury!" Her response was very simple. She told him that she'd studied hard in high school, got several scholarships, and was working to make money to stay in Drury. The young lady just kept coming back to our table to give us free food and chat. It was an all-cash restaurant, so we had to pay at the cashier. Before I left the table, an Uncle Ben was hidden (but I made sure it was visible enough so it would not go in the trash). I went and paid in cash, then went to the restroom. When I came out, the waitress was standing there in tears and hunting for me. I got a great hug. She thanked me and said how badly she needed that and how much it meant to her.

Chisel Points in the Ground

In 2022, Martha and I were on a driving trip, and we stopped one evening in southeastern Alabama. We went to a fried chicken restaurant for supper. It looked good from the road and there were lots of cars, so it had to be a good place to eat. Martha and I went in, and it was a buffet with chicken, fish, and the extras for $9.95. It was under $20.00 to pay cash. The plates were filled by waitresses behind the glass, and there was lots of food and lots of people. I observed that hardly any tips were going in the tip jar by the cashier, but all the ladies were working really hard. They said "please" and "thank you" and were doing a very good job. I decided to take one of the Uncle Bens out of my wallet and give it to the cashier when we left, no record of the giver. When the cash was given to the cashier and we told her to divide it among the workers, someone screamed and ran to the working manager. Martha and I were out the door. "The least of them" was ringing loud and clear.

The amazing thought comes to me that when we take time to help others, God multiplies the time, so the giver gets more time in the day or the accomplishments are greater when others receive our help. Stop and help an elderly couple change a tire along a country road in the rain, and God will allow us to accomplish more that day than we ever thought could be done. I have found that God returns everything that is given away in some form of a blessing, whether it be personal or material. The gift is always returned many times over, in one form or another.

When Drost Equipment was sold, the accountant and I had a plan for the money that included approximately 30% of the proceeds being given to charities. Most was to be given in major contributions to Child Evangelism Fellowship, Biblica (which used to be the International Bible Society), Bibles for the World, Back to the Bible, the Bible League, and the Mahaska Community Recreation Foundation (MCRF). These continue to be the major charities that the Drosts support.

Child Evangelism Fellowship is an international organization designed to help children under the age of twelve accept Jesus as their Savior through the Gospel message, disciple them in the Word of God, and get them established in a local church. The vision is to reach EVERY CHILD in EVERY NATION on EVERY DAY as children grow in their relationship with the Lord through the Word. They reached over 15.6 million children a day in 2022 in over 206 countries around the world.

Biblica is an international organization whose mission is to provide the Bible in accurate, contemporary translations and formats, so that more people around the world will have the opportunity to be transformed by Jesus Christ. The New International Version (NIV) is a major translation by Biblica. The Bible still needs to be translated into 3,712 languages.

Bibles for the World is an international organization with the intent of sharing the good news of God's love through Jesus Christ by ministering to unreached peoples. They have a strong influence in India.

Back to the Bible is an international organization whose mission is to help ministries and individuals move closer to Jesus today than they were yesterday, leading to life transformation as people become biblically engaged disciples of Jesus. Back to the Bible wants to see thriving local churches around the world, offering salvation, life changes, and hope through biblically based training and resources that meet the spiritual, moral, and social needs of communities. A new innovation for Back to the Bible is an app for smartphones called GO TANDEM, where people can get a daily devotion and update for their individual needs. The aim is to grow spiritual fitness by having users read the Bible at least four times per week.

Bible League is an international organization whose mission is to serve the under-resourced Church with Bibles and training to transform lives worldwide through God's Word. Similar to Back to the Bible, the Bible League wants to see thriving local churches.

Chisel Points in the Ground

MCRF, or the Mahaska Community Recreation Foundation, is a local group who works to facilitate and promote recreation opportunities in Mahaska County. They provide recreation for youth in particular. Martha and I have not only contributed money to the organization, but also hundreds of hours of time and equipment usage. (Remember Drost Field from the previous chapter?)

Sometimes friends inspire us to give. Michael Vos is the son of Don and Bonnie Vos, who were our neighbors as Michael was growing up. Michael had a very good position with Ag Leader, a major company in electronic farming. Michael told me one day that he had given up his position at Ag Leader because he had been called by God to use his knowledge and talents and serve as an Antioch missionary for BILD International in Ames, Iowa. BILD's mission is to train networks of leaders—from grassroots to the national level—in the way of Christ and His Apostles, in partnership with church-planting movements in each of the nine major civilizations. Michael still farms, but he also travels all over the world training pastors and church boards on how to multiply the kingdom of God. This neighbor man deserves and gets the Drosts' support because he is one of us—a farmer, friend, Christian, and customer. The Apostle Paul was a working missionary who made tents and was a promoter of Jesus. And so, BILD was added as one of our major charities to support.

I learned from Martha long time ago about tithing (I can learn!). Malachi 3:10 says, "'Bring the whole tithe into the storehouse, that there may be food in my house. Test me in this,' says the Lord Almighty, 'and see if I will not throw open the floodgates of heaven and pour out so much blessing that there will not be room enough to store it.'" I learned that the 10% tithe is the minimum, and the blessings roll in when one does what God lays on our hearts. It is crystal clear what we are to do for others. Martha never goes along for the dreaded tax appointment, but when the return is complete, she always asks, "Did we give at least 10%?"

Chapter 28

Coffee Time With Friends

I never eat breakfast or lunch, but Martha thinks the farmers' wives do a good job of keeping her husband healthy. Where do you start with so many good places to get coffee and cookies?

I was blessed to have a real mom, plus two or three other mother figures who claimed me too—maybe more. The first was Betty Barnard, who was married to Durant Barnard. They were the folks Martha and I bought our first place to live from when I got home from Vietnam. After Durant died, Betty's house was a great place to get a cookie and a cup of coffee on the road west, since she lived on Highway 163 on the way to Pella (across the road from Pierson Seed). Before Durant died—when he was at Methodist Hospital in Des Moines on his way to surgery—he asked me to look after his wife and his farm ground. I told him I would. Betty was always interested in our children. When we attended the Nazarene Church in Pella, we would stop occasionally on Sunday evening on our way home. Betty lived in the house she had grown up in; she also married Durant in that house. When Highway 163 was to become a four-lane highway, she was told it would take the house. Betty asked me to negotiate with the Iowa DOT and settle for the loss of her buildings and the ground. I negotiated, and the State of Iowa built Betty a very nice home on her ground. I often had coffee with Betty and Juddee, her second husband. My uncle, John Drost, joined us when he moved in with Betty in her later years. Betty lived in her new home until she was ninety-two years old.

The second "mother" who claimed me was Ruth McGee, who lived a few miles south of Cargill by Eddyville with her husband, Donald. They farmed with their son, Jim. I had worked with their other son, Mike, at Van Gorp Implement in the early seventies. Then I did business with Donald and Jim on farm equipment. Ruth always had the coffee pot on and a cookie or cake to eat. After Donald passed away, Ruth always welcomed me. She always said she and Donald had gotten married when she was sixteen years old and lots of people just knew she was pregnant . . . but it took over two years for that baby to be born! Martha and I were invited to special birthday parties for Ruth. When her health failed, Ruth went to a nursing home in Albia. The day of Ruth's funeral, Martha was in the hospital in Des Moines. It was not a good morning for Martha's health, so I missed the funeral.

My third claimed "mother" was Pauline Hutchinson from Montezuma. I started doing business with the Hutchinsons in 1996 after the John Deere dealer closed in Montezuma. (Remember, I had taught junior high and high school industrial arts in Montezuma before I went to the Army; therefore, lots of farmers around town knew me.) Maynard and Pauline lived on Highway 85 east of Montezuma. Coffee time was at 9:00 in the morning in the office of their machine shed, around a cable spool. They farmed with their son, Dennis (Denny). It was always a good place to stop for cookies, coffee, and a good visit. The friendship grew, and we would go out to eat with the Hutchinsons and their neighbors, the Rempps. When I was in the hospital in Des Moines for knee replacement, one evening the door opened and it was the Hutchinsons and the Rempps. They drove to Des Moines to visit the invalid. Martha and I were invited by the family to special birthday and anniversary parties for Pauline and Maynard. The coffee times continued with Denny and his wife, Margaret, after his parents passed away.

Another coffee spot was the Augustine farm, and most of the coffee times were at Esther and Keith's kitchen table. Most of the coffee times were during the off season, so extra time could be spent visiting about lots of issues and future farm equipment needs. Esther always had cookies or bars along with the coffee and iced tea. At times, coffee was at Howard and Wanda's house or in Dan and Teresa Augustine's kitchen. (Howard is Keith's brother, and Dan is Howard's son.) A lasting memory I have of Keith Augustine came after Young's Ponzi scheme in Lamoni. I asked Keith if they had any cattle down at Lamoni. Keith's response was short: "Now, Carl, if anybody is stupid enough to believe you can feed cattle for ten years and never have a run of cattle that loses money, you deserve to lose it!" Howard was a Korean War veteran, and it was at the Augustines' home that I first met Matt Strasser, who had just returned from Kosovo with the Iowa National Guard. That has turned into a long-term relationship with Matt and his family. It was always best to call ahead before visiting the Augustines to make sure most of the family would be present. When the new farm shop was built, coffee was there and prepared by Teresa most of the time.

The VerSteegh family coffee is at 9:00 in the break room by the office. I always checked the schedule to be certain most of the farm crew would be there, and then I would normally bring Jaarsma donuts and other pastries. This was always an interesting stop because there'd be lots of questions about a wide range of subjects (not necessarily farming). It was an opportunity to bring out your true beliefs about how to live a life. I have a couple of favorite memories of the family. The first memory is when Howard bit into a Jaarsma sugar-cream-filled Bismarck... and the cream went all over his mustache and chin! The picture will be in my mind forever. The other memory is when I presented Bob the deal on putting auto-steer in a track tractor; Bob's response was memorable and short: "Now, Carl, what are those boys going to do in that tractor if they are not driving?" There was no auto-steer sale.

Coffee Time With Friends

I started doing business and coffee breaks with Goosen and Jane Van Utrecht in 1976. They had Art's Way grinder mixers and a small tractor. Goosen and Jane were both Dutch immigrants. They'd been teenagers in Holland. The Germans invaded in 1940 and took Goosen to Germany as a forced laborer, while Jane was left with the Germans occupying her town and the rest of the country. Goosen told me how the Germans treated him in the munitions factory he was forced to work in. Jane would talk about "being a little mouthy" to a German soldier. The soldier put a gun to her head, and she told him to shoot her. Goosen would also tell the story of how glad he and his fellow forced workers were when my father, Richard, and Patton's United States Army came over the hill so fast the Germans couldn't shoot the slave workers. Goosen would talk about seeing the American flag on top of the U.S. Army tanks. They immigrated to the United States in 1948 and worked extremely hard to be successful American farmers. They came legally and became American citizens speaking English. It was always good for me to spend time with them, even after Goosen stopped working on the farm.

When Goosen and Jane had first come to America, Walter and Wilma Vernooy (also Dutch immigrants) invited them to a Thanksgiving dinner at their home. The Vernooys' daughter, Martha, was crawling at the time. Of course, Martha is now Mrs. Carl Drost. Goosen was in the North Mahaska Rehabilitation Center one Christmas Day. Martha and I went to Hardee's to get coffee and spend Christmas morning with him. We had a great morning. It was always a good, welcoming feeling at the Van Utrecht home.

In about 1978, Steve Boender called late in the day and told me that his 715 International combine had blown up and he wanted to talk about a new combine. In the evening, Steve and his wife, Jan, came to our home and traded for a New Idea Uni-Harvester 708 hydrostatic drive power unit with a Model 717 combine and heads. That is the only piece of equipment ever traded in the Drost home. Steve and I were friends before, and we still are. Coffee time at the Boenders' office on the farm can take place as early as 6:30, but usually no later than 8:00. The whole family is there most mornings, including the hired employees and even sometimes the neighbors. It is not unusual to be treated to Jan's baked rolls, cake, cookies, or fresh egg sandwiches. The Boenders are seed dealers, and the office is a great place to catch up on seed traits, trends, and plant populations for both corn and soybeans.

Roger Abel became a very good John Deere customer, and I was always welcomed at his home with his wife, Beverly. Roger traded combines every two years, and the combine never had enough power. Roger and I had a hard-to-explain relationship, but we always worked hard and enjoyed what we were doing. Roger also sold feed, tires, and Westendorff farm equipment. Beverly and Roger had three daughters, and Roger raised them like they were boys; they would go in the truck to get feed and attend livestock auctions. Roger was mowing weeds in the summer of 1996 when his tractor rolled over and he was killed. Beverly, Martha, and I are still good friends and spend an occasional evening together.

Across the field were the Abel brothers, Randy and Rick. They were always friends with me. The Abel brothers started farming when I was a Ford tractor dealer, and they got to be friends with Ron Schott, the John Deere dealer in Sigourney. Randy, Rick, and I stayed friends, but they bought their machinery from their friend. I always told the Abel brothers that where they bought farm equipment should not define our friendship. When Ron Schott got out of the John Deere business, I became their dealer, and the loyalty began with me. John Deere toys and older John Deere tractors were always on the discussion block over a cup of coffee with the Abel brothers.

Dorothy and Paul Groenenboom live northeast of Oskaloosa on Paul's boyhood farm—a full lifetime spent there. Paul and Dorothy have been world travelers, doing a river cruise in Russia and a trip to southeast Asia and the Baltics and many other parts of the world. I take a few Jaarsma donuts once in a while, and the coffee and the discussion are always great. We talk about many subjects. Paul is now eighty-seven years old, but in 2022, he took a delivery of a new John Deere S760 combine with dual wheels, four-wheel drive, and a folding grain tank cover with extension. He operated it himself.

Tracy, Iowa, was another coffee stop that I found out about when Lloyd Havener came to the store in 1986 to buy a John Deere combine and trade off his Massey. Lloyd liked to keep "new paint" on his combine, and he planned to trade every year. I sold Lloyd, his wife, Beverly, and their son, David, thirty-one combines with heads, starting with that first one in 1986. In the early years of doing business, it would take fifty minutes to drink coffee and eat cookies and ten minutes to trade combines and heads. In 2021, Lloyd was ninety-one. He and his son took a delivery of a new John Deere S760 combine with four-wheel drive, a new soybean head, and new corn head. I also sold them numerous other pieces of farm equipment. Coffee at Bev's house was at 8:45 in the morning. At Christmas, Beverly always made me a batch of peanut clusters for home and a batch for all the employees to eat at the store. The peanut clusters were great, and Beverly did it for many years until it just got to be too much work when she was in her upper eighties.

John and Delores Ryken's home is always a good stop for coffee and a nice visit. The Rykens were some of Drost Equipment's first customers and have been loyal ever since. When farming got to be tough business in the late seventies and early to mid-eighties, the young farmers (like the Rykens) and I all had to watch every penny if we were going to keep doing what we were doing. John and I shared a lot of notes, and he worked at Drost Equipment assembling farm equipment several winters to supplement his farm income. It has been a very valued friendship, and spending time over a cup of coffee is always a pleasure.

Chisel Points in the Ground

Ron and Judy Kielkopf's house is a stop for exotic coffee! You can usually find their son, John, there too. He lives just west of Hedrick. Ron is a member of a coffee club, so the flavors and strength of brew are varied. I would bring coffee back from Hawaii to drink there. Ron and John are very progressive in their farming operation and try to stay on the cutting edge. As such, the discussions over coffee and cookies are about what was new and what was coming in equipment, equipment trends, planting attachments, seed technology, and chemicals. Ron and John can ask questions that require research, but they are always great questions. When Drost Equipment's CSI (customer satisfaction index) score with John Deere got very high compared to other dealers across the United States, John Deere asked me why and how. I told them about the coffee visits. Our John Deere sales rep was told by his superiors to ask if he could go along on some of the visits. I limited him to one visit, and the visit was to the Kielkopfs to show how varied the discussion could be—not just a sale of farm equipment.

Jerome Fynaardt graduated from North Mahaska High School, then attended Indian Hills Community College to study ag mechanics. Jerome completed his on-the-job training at Drost Equipment, and then he was employed at Drost for a few years. Jerome had the opportunity to work in the portable lighting section at Musco. Martha and I attended Jerome and his wife, Linda's, wedding at Central Reformed Church in Oskaloosa. The coffee pot was always on the burner at Drost Equipment, and Jerome's responsibilities at Musco meant he had to go into the office. So, Jerome would stop at the John Deere store for a cup of coffee on his way to work. We tease each other about the "work" part for both of us.

Coffee at my brother Tom Drost's can be very interesting because we go to the "corporate office" in the machine shed. Family can be very interesting to do business with, but I found out one must separate business from just talking about family, friends, trips, and other events. The coffee or tea is always good, but the goodies are special: muffins warmed up with butter, waffle and ham sandwiches, homemade cookies . . . and who knows what else Tom might pull out of a pan, a cooler, or the refrigerator! With the advent of all the new technology and a cow herd, making arrangements in advance is a better idea.

Bill and Marge Rempp's place was always a good stop for me to have coffee at 9:00. The Rempp children, Denise and Kevin, were in my classes when I taught in Montezuma. When the John Deere dealership closed in Montezuma, the Rempps became Drost Equipment customers. They were also in the New Idea Uni-Harvester business for seed corn. The coffee, cookies, and discussion time was always good. When there were warm cream puffs on the table, it was to "butter me up" because the Rempps were ready to buy farm equipment.

In the summer of 1997, Bill and Marge invited me and Martha to their home for an evening meal and a crop tour. Martha and I went, and Bill grilled a half salmon and Marge prepared a large meal to go with it. This "threshers dinner" was great! Then we all got in the Buick, and Bill showed Martha and me every field of corn and soybeans they had planted. Bill drove the field roads and the waterways. (He and his son, Kevin, had mowed all the fence rows, ditches, and waterways so the car could get close to the crops.) It really gave me a good indication of the crop because we made numerous stops to do ear and kernel counts in the corn and pod counts in the beans. After the crop tour, it was back to the house for lemon meringue pie, which was baked using lemons from the tree at their winter home in South Texas. The meal and crop tour became an annual tradition that continued through fall of 2018. The next year, Bill got cancer, and some of his last words were about how he missed not having the crop tour. Bill called me one afternoon and told me that the oncologist had just been in and the cancer was really bad. He told me it wouldn't be long before he would be in the arms of Jesus.

I have all these and many more great memories of being welcomed to sit down around the kitchen tables at customers' homes, where we enjoyed life and being friends doing business.

Chapter 29

Real Estate and a New House

I have been involved in several real estate opportunities. My first try at real estate was the Marje subdivision on the southern city limits of Oskaloosa. In 1985, Joe Crookham approached me about the need for affordable housing for working people in Oskaloosa. The Shaw farm was for sale on the south side of South Fifteenth Street, and it was purchased by the Drosts and the Crookhams. To keep Joe and me from getting into trouble with our spouses, Martha and Jeanie, we decided to name the subdivision Marje (the first letters of both their names).

Robert Nielson of Garden and Associates designed a subdivision for the land, including the streets, sanitary sewer, storm sewer, and electric supply. The city requirements for streets, sewers, and water supplies made the development of a subdivision very expensive. For example, the city required all the streets to be paved and be a specific width. The city water supply and fire protection also made the development costs extremely high. The city required us to connect the eight-inch water main to a loop to provide fire protection to a larger part of Oskaloosa than just Marje. The first homes were built on lots along South Fifteenth Street while the streets and utilities were constructed in the rest of the development. The old farmhouse was remodeled, and six other homes were built. The homes were not profitable because the contractor didn't get all the costs included in the estimate. A townhouse with four homes

Real Estate and a New House

was also constructed, and there was no profit there either. The contractor was changed at that point, and other speculation homes were built.

We sold building lots to an apartment complex (which turned into a low-rent district) and a senior living facility. Casey's also wanted to buy a lot to put a gas station on the south side of Oskaloosa. Joe and I determined that Oskaloosa needed an assisted living facility to provide full care for the community. A realtor tried to sell the building site to the care company, and the realtor gave up. I called the developer directly and negotiated a sale for the property. And yes, the realtor demanded his commission! The assisted living facility was called Maple Ridge Assisted Living (though it is now Homestead), and it proved to be a very valuable addition to the Oskaloosa community. It constantly remains full and has a waiting list. The Casey's convenience store also remains very successful. It took several years to fill all the building lots in the first area of Marje. Musco bought me out of Marje after a period of years and has since added more acres to the east. Marje has a recreation trail along both sides of the creek on the land in place of sidewalks, which was new for Oskaloosa and approved by the city.

Another real estate venture started when I was at Mahaska State Bank doing business and the topic of the abandoned Continental Overall Factory came up. John Pothoven told me that the Oskaloosa Development Group wanted to give the seven-eighths block with the old factory on it to somebody who would remove the factory and make it tax-bearing. I took possession of the property and contracted with Al Wicker to demolish the building. The factory had employed mostly ladies to make the clothing, so the ladies' restrooms had twenty-four stalls on each floor. One of the buildings had a red steel frame with aluminum siding that I took care of tearing down. My daughter, Judy, and Ronda, my niece (Jim's daughter), were given a summer job removing the aluminum roof and siding. They were given a choice for pay: take all the aluminum or $8.00 per hour. Judy and Ronda took the sure payment of $8.00 per hour. They learned a very hard lesson because when the aluminum was sold, they saw they could have gotten four times more. Risk usually carries a reward!

My father and I seeded the property on Labor Day, and the lot soon turned green. During the winter, the city needed a new location for the United States Post Office for downtown development. The city purchased the property to put the post office at the intersection of South Market Street and Sixth Avenue East. The funds were put in my and Martha's new house fund.

Then Drost Equipment purchased the John Deere lawn and garden store from John King, and we needed to find a new location. The name was changed to Yardware by Drost. The Kingma Motors building on Highway 92 West was for sale, so I purchased the building the day before the property would have gone into foreclosure. The lawn mower store was moved there. Directly east of the Kingma property was an old Fina gas station and another property with an old greenhouse on it. I acquired both these properties. During the demolition, an abandoned underground gas storage tank was discovered. Howard VerSteegh and I dealt with the DNR on the "orphan" tank and contaminated dirt. After several years of the lawn store being unprofitable, I decided to close it and combine the lawn equipment as a department of Drost Equipment. The Yardware by Drost property was sold to the Earl May Garden Corporation, and the building was renovated to sell plants and garden supplies. The profit from the real estate was also put in our new house fund.

In the late nineties, it was determined that Oskaloosa needed a new motel because there was no motel of any quality in town. A group of local investors got together with a motel developer and constructed a Comfort Inn Motel on Highway 92 West, next to the new Walmart and along the new Highway 163 bypass. The investors were Joe Crookham (Musco Lighting), Charles Howard (Mahaska

State Bank), Young Equipment Buildings (me), Robert Lynn, Joan Kunz, Jean Argo, and the developer, Charles Klinkhammer. The group elected me president. The motel proved very successful and had occupancy close to 80% average, but the employee situation was always a problem. After twenty years of ownership, the group decided that when a potential buyer was located, the motel should be sold. A buyer came to town, liked the operating numbers of the Comfort Inn, and made an offer for the property. It was sold in 2015. Our profit from the motel was placed in the Carl and Martha Drost Charitable Foundation, which was utilized for many years to donate to charities.

Martha and I had moved into our first home on Kirby Avenue in December 1971, and we always had a dream of building a new home. We decided the new home would be built when it could be paid for with cash. I drew several sketches and plans of what the home should be and the size. Our daughter, Judy, took architectural drafting in high school, and she added to the house. Our sons, Bob and Nick, also took the class and edited the plan (not exactly the design Martha and I desired!). In 1996, I contacted an architect in Des Moines, Mike Stodala, to come and meet Martha to make sure they could communicate. It was a hit at first words. I hired Mike to take the plans and sketches we provided and make a house that was efficient and had load-bearing beams and walls. Mike suggested turning the house to six degrees to the southeast for maximum use of the sun for heat in the winter and less exposure to the sun in the summer to lessen the air conditioning cost; we took that advice. Mike also planned on doing the preliminary work and letting an AutoCAD employee do the plan; but when he got into the home project, Mike did all the drafting himself with a pencil. When the complete plan was done, and the money was in the bank, Martha said, "I'm sorry, but I don't understand how it will look." I made a model of the house out of fiber board to scale, complete with a removable roof, a removable first floor, a removable chimney, an elevator, a spiral staircase, a retaining wall, and the circle drive. When the model was complete, Martha said, "I like it—let's build it." And so construction started.

I had a guaranteed maximum price from Mike Stodala for the architectural services, and the services provided were lots more than the guarantee. Much to my surprise, Martha had a "secret stash" of money she had put aside from babysitting and selling vegetables and fruit. She had over $20,000.00 in the fund, which was enough for all the cabinets in the kitchen, built as the cook desired. The house was built by selected contractors on a time and material basis, with the exception of the elevator and the bricklaying. It took a year from the day Voss Concrete excavated the hole until Martha could move into a completed house (only the basement still had to be finished). Move-in day was July 4, 1999. It was built as a house, but Martha and I have made it a home for all who visit. It was paid for every Friday when the laborers presented their bills. Three years later, the basement was finished and paid for at the time. The pool table was from Rec Room Plus in Urbandale, and it cost a new John Deere lawn tractor. In about 2010, geothermal heating and cooling was installed. Then in 2019, solar energy was added to the location. The combined electrical, heating, and cooling bills are very minimal (close to the meter rental)!

Chapter 30

One of Three: Joe Crookham

I only knew Joe P. Crookham as a name before 1974. My dad was a carpenter when he wasn't farming, and he was pretty good. It always amazed me that he could square a building project using the one-two-three method. I found out in school that he knew all about the Pythagorean theorem, but he sure never heard about it when he went to school. I have no idea why, but Joe P. Crookham called my dad and brothers to do a remodeling job in the old Hensyl building somewhere near the old Iowa Power generating plant. I was married and in the Army, but the story goes that my dad and Joe laid out the plans for the remodel with a lumber pencil on some sheet rock. That was how they worked. My dad did several jobs for Joe over the years.

The day Dick Allen of Ford Motor Company walked into the old John Deere store, my head was spinning with all the numbers they had laid out and the business prospectus (a word I couldn't even spell). I needed to talk to somebody, and I decided I would call Joe P. Crookham because he was the only attorney I had ever heard mentioned. I called Lori, who was Joe's secretary, and made an appointment to see him. I went up to the old Skelly building and met with Joe, and we went over the Ford Tractor prospectus and the required $158,000.00 cash to put the plan in progress. Joe told me it looked like a good deal, and he thought I should do it! It never occurred to me how much $158,000.00 was, but it did to him.

One of Three: Joe Crookham

He asked where I was going to get the money, and I told him I didn't know. Then he told me about negotiating the Wilbur Young contract with the Kansas City Chiefs and how they wanted to invest in something to get the maximum tax advantage they could. He was interested in financing my operation.

Joe was my mentor in business. He gave me permission to go out and build a new facility, but he knew how to get traffic counts and the size we needed, and he located the plot of land we needed to buy from Henry Hackert. He allowed me to lay out the building like I had drawn in the architectural drafting class I had taught in Montezuma, and I also laid out the grounds. It was Joe who designed the raised island at the entrance to display equipment on, and he also told me we needed to hard surface about two acres of our parking area so customers and their vehicles could stay clean. Joe added the upstairs mezzanine to our showroom so we could have events upstairs. (We had an organist up there for our grand opening!) Joe shared his vision and told me we should not just look at today or tomorrow but down the road ten or twenty years into the future. We needed to build for that situation.

When Joe and Wilbur put up the money for the dealership, I had never sold a single item, nor had I ever had employees, handled inventories and cash, or experienced any other aspect of business. I often wondered what our business would have been like if I had a degree in business. I have told people that if I knew then what I know today, I probably would have said there were too many problems and it would never work. But Joe was my business mentor, and in the startup, he took care of the banking, loans, and mortgages. I wasn't even a partner for the first five months we were in business. Joe would look at our financial statements, then ask the hard questions about why something was this way or why this ratio was out of whack. He made me think about what we were doing and how to make the business better. Dave DeJong was our bookkeeper, and once he was so mad at Joe's questions that I thought

Chisel Points in the Ground

he was ready to beat up on Joe or maybe worse. But Joe's mentoring is what made our business what it was. I can tell you that through the thirty-one years we were partners, there was never a written contract between us—we trusted each other at our word.

We were business partners, but over the years we developed a very close relationship. Even my blood brothers will tell you, "Carl and Joe are closer than brothers. It would be very dangerous to be between them." My brother, Tom, puts our relationship this way: "The Bible says they are closer than brothers, and believe it that these two are." I have always cherished that relationship built on TRUST. In 1978, Joe and Myron Gordin bought the bankrupt Muscatine Lighting Company. Joe was telling me of his vision to go into sports lighting. He told me that college football games needed to be played at night under the lights. I know he went to NBC Sports in February 1981 and told them of his plan to light college football games so they could televise at night, and he got a signed contract from them. They didn't own a crane truck and didn't have the program ready to aim the lights, and the first game was in early September 1981 (Michigan versus Notre Dame). It was hectic around Musco Lighting that spring and summer, so I tried to help get stuff for them (which was just a small part).

I stopped by one evening at the old plant, where they were assembling trucks. They were ready to set up the lights for a test at Penn College on the east side of the highway. Nobody there had a commercial driver's license to drive the crane truck to Penn, but I did. They told me to get in and drive. It was huge, and I had no idea about the transmission, air brakes, and such, but we got it started and I herded that big, white, stub-nosed Freightliner with the trailer generator out to Penn. We set up the lights, and they sure made the night into daylight. I think Joe breathed a sigh of relief. When the game was approaching, Joe asked if I would go along to help if they needed it. I said I would, but I wanted to be home on Sunday morning to teach my Sunday school class. The

Musco airplane picked me up at the Oskaloosa airport late on Saturday afternoon, and we were soon in South Bend, Indiana, at the home of Notre Dame. It was a very uneventful evening for me because the light system worked perfectly; the only "hitch" was that some of the portable generators in the parking lots stopped. Most of the people outside the stadium were so stoned they never realized it. I believe there were more people outside the stadium than in it. The plane brought me home after the lights were off.

As I mentioned in a previous chapter, John Deere wanted us to change from Ford to John Deere. Joe was very positive about the switch and just plainly said, "We got to do it." He was very instrumental in getting the financing guaranteed because Martha and I certainly could not have done it. All this was still done with no written agreement.

Joe married Jeanie Bieri, and they hadn't been married long when we earned four cruises along the Mexican Riviera on the Holland America Line. I asked Joe if he and Jeanie would like to go with us, and they agreed. We had a great time, and the good news was that Martha and Jeanie got along better than sisters. Joe and I kind of did our thing when at sea. One day, we sat on the top deck of the ship, and our responsibility for the day was to figure out how much farther away the horizon was on the top deck than on the first deck. We worked on it all day, without a calculator or a computer. (It is easy, except accounting for the Earth's curves!) So, we found out the horizon is many times farther on the top, which (to us at least) explains why the pilgrims coming to America in the early 1600s said, "The pirates came upon us out of nowhere." It was because the pirates always had the lookout in the crow's nest, and they could plan and come in the wind for the attack.

Joe came out to the store almost every Saturday afternoon when he was in town to help me operate. I always stayed open on Saturday afternoons to take care of our customers if they needed something. During harvest, he would answer the phone, take parts to sit outside, and do whatever needed to be done. Then we would discuss the international lighting business, the challenges of finding key employees, the farm equipment business, or politics. Joe's favorite saying to people who came in was, "We are solving the world's problems of today, plus the problems the world doesn't know they have."

Joe was always a great encourager to me, and he was always loaded with compliments. The one that probably meant the most came after I started making an annual business plan in 1978. Every year, I did it with very little help. By the mid-eighties, it was about fifty pages and covered all aspects of our business, including a one-year plan, a five-year plan, and a ten-year plan, and then a look into the future beyond. I would always give Joe and John Deere a copy, knowing it would stay confidential. Joe would tell me it was the best business plan he had ever seen, and he wished his company could put something together like it. I had created it all by myself with the information necessary to operate our business. I was at a John Deere meeting once, and they popped our information on the screen; John Deere never got another copy after that, and I told them why.

I don't know why Joe and I have always clicked it off, but a lot of people in the community wonder how we are so tight. As you will read in the following chapters, there have been many projects we've worked on and completed together. Our personalities are very different, and our ideas are totally opposite sometimes, but we have always been able to sit down, put out our ideas, and blend them together for a solution. I asked Joe once why he would ever invest his time and money in a young man like me, and he said: "I knew the family, and I knew Richard had taught all his boys to be honest and to work hard."

In the previous chapter, I wrote about Joe and I working together on the Marje subdivision. I believe I found out more about Joe's vision and long-term planning during this project, and I believe Joe learned a lot about the knowledge I have in construction (and that I really like to move dirt with a dozer). We learned a lot about dirt as we graded the area, put in the mud seams, filled a small creek, and put fly ash under some concrete to stabilize the base. But the biggest lesson we learned was to have the correct costs on any project we participate in. Joe and I both came to realize we were very good with numbers, and our math was not only fast but very accurate. Joe taught me how to add a column of numbers by beginning with the left columns and moving to the right.

I think the first community project Joe and I worked on together was planning for a community auditorium, which became the George Daily Auditorium. You can read more about it in Chapter 32, but here is the quick story. I was on the Oskaloosa School Board, and we needed a place for our student performances. John Pothoven, president of Mahaska State Bank, was also on the school board. As John and I discussed the auditorium, Joe and Nick Williams convinced George Daily to give his oil wealth to the community in a trust for community projects. John and I approached Joe about the community needing an auditorium for all kinds of performances, and he agreed that maybe the auditorium could be built as the big project from George Daily. Enter Bob Neilson, who was an engineer and partner in Garden and Associates. Now there was a group of four: Joe, John, Bob, and Carl. We all agreed that the need existed and that the area between the new junior high and the senior high was the logical site, but the money was the big issue. John and I made the first request to the Daily Trust Board, asking them to help fund the community auditorium and offering for it to be named for George Daily. The project went ahead, and the auditorium opened in September 1997.

I have taught adults and youth in Sunday school, and I have told my students that it is great to have lots of friends. But when it gets right down to it, if you have three really good friends you can trust, confide in, and tell anything to without getting criticized, and if those friends will help you through a tough situation, you will be BLESSED. Joe is one of my three! (Or maybe two.) After I gave up managing the store, I no longer stayed on Saturday afternoons, and I still miss those times when we could plan projects, discuss our businesses, and (in the later years) discuss how we were both going to make our businesses sustainable and leave a legacy into the future. John Deere sealed our future by requiring multistore operations or else selling out, but Musco is a much larger and more complex operation. The major contribution we both made to our operations was that we both had a vision of what we thought the future (or at least the next twenty years) would hold. That is a key to business. The Bible states in Proverbs 29:18a (KJV), "Where there is no vision, the people perish." And I believe that is the main reason Joe and I were and are such great friends. Joe and I can disagree and talk issues through, but it has never gotten to the point of a personal attack. The Bible also says in Proverbs 18:24, "One who has unreliable friends soon comes to ruin, but there is a friend who sticks closer than a brother." If anybody has ever been in a meeting where Joe and I are present, they'll see our disagreements have already been worked out or else we just think alike and explain our position.

Joe and Jeanie are great traveling companions. As stated earlier, our first trip was the Mexican Riviera cruise, but Joe and Jeanie also came to Hawaii, to the island of Kauai, with us for a few days. We have learned that Joe's schedule on vacation usually keeps him occupied until close to noon, and then we can do things together (unless it is a scheduled tour, and then Jeanie sees that they are punctual). Joe talked to the pool bartender one night and was told of a great picnic spot. So the next day, we set off in the car with a picnic the girls had prepared. We went down a back road, walked through the sugar cane, and came to a river with a huge rock in the middle next to a small waterfall. Joe had been told it was part of the movie *Raiders of the Lost Ark*. We spent the afternoon on the rock, playing rummy and eating.

One of Three: Joe Crookham

We also earned extra cruises on the Baltic Sea. Joe and Jeanie agreed to go with us. We got coach seats on the airplane to Copenhagen, Denmark. But before the cruise, Jeanie stopped by to ask about the tickets, and she told me they only fly first class on international flights; they wanted to upgrade all of us to first class on Scandinavian Air. What service we got! The cruise was a tour of Stockholm, Sweden, then on to Helsinki, Finland, and into St. Petersburg, Russia, overnight. I didn't know it, but it was a Radisson Cruise, and the ship only had 175 cabins. We even had a king bed and a balcony. We toured Catherine the Great's summer palace; the Peterhof, where presidents go to visit; and the Hermitage, which is the famous art museum. After a dinner of Russian food on the ship, we went for the white night canal tour (like in Venice, Italy). The tour left at 11:00 p.m., and since it was the last of June, we could take photos at midnight without a flash. The most memorable part of the whole trip was Joe and I visiting with our tour guide, who was an electrical engineer by day and tour guide by night; she was a thirty-five-year-old female living in government apartments. We tried to explain to her how capitalism worked and how she should open a travel agency. She couldn't understand how you could do that without paying somebody off.

There are always some things to remember from each trip. There was a John Deere dealer from Illinois on our trip, and he was overbearing and pushy; he always had to be first and was just quite obnoxious. When we got on the airplane in Copenhagen after our short flight from Stockholm, we boarded the plane and took our seats in the front first-class section, and we had our drinks. Down the aisle comes Mr. Know-It-All. "How did you get seats here?" he asked. I replied, "This is where they told me to sit." I shouldn't have enjoyed it so much, but he would have been really upset if he had seen the ice cream sundae I got for dessert after a very nice meal in my big seat!

Chisel Points in the Ground

The biggest trip Joe and Jeanie went on with us was the Panama Canal cruise, which left from San Diego and ended in Fort Lauderdale. It took seventeen days to do the cruise. Joe and Martha don't like to plan trips, so Jeanie and I planned our shore excursions. In Cabo San Lucas, it was a Jeep tour through an area like a national park (Jeanie was our driver). Then an authentic Mexican meal was prepared for us in a school in a desert ranch area. Finally, we drove a dry riverbed back to the coast. We did a shopping stop in Huatulco, Mexico, which was a town that only opened up when the ship came in. We went on a coffee plantation tour in Guatemala, which was all hand work. The trip took us through the ancient capital of Antigua, and we went on an aerial gondola ride through the rainforest of Costa Rica.

It took all day to traverse the Panama Canal. The canal from the Pacific Ocean to the Gulf of Mexico goes northwest (yes, northwest and not northeast or east). The most amazing side trip was arranged by Jeanie in Cartagena, Colombia, where we were met at the port by the contractor who installs Musco lights in Colombia. His name was Romey, and his wife, Adrianne, was very pretty. She was also the daughter of the Colombian ambassador to Great Britain. They drove us through old Cartagena, which was built in the late 1500s. The city had tall walls along the sea, with tops wide enough for chariots and canon holes. Underneath were barracks for troops, which have now been converted to tourist traps. Then, they drove us through new Cartagena, which was built after 1960 and is as modern as can be. Adrianne asked what we wanted to do for lunch, and of course, our answer was that we didn't have a clue, but she could pick the place. We went back into old Cartagena, which had only one-lane roads and four-story buildings with a blooming flower box in every window.

We stopped at a restaurant. The door was short, just four feet tall. That way in old times, an attacker would have to come through bent over and was easily overcome. I knew we were in the right spot for lunch when we got in and the owner said, "Oh, Adrianne!" And the rest is history. The meal and service were great!

Joe and I surprised Martha and Jeanie with a marriage vow renewal ceremony that we'd booked before we left, which was to be performed on the ship. It was held in one of the lounges, and the ship's orchestra was there, along with the photographer and the captain, who performed the vow renewal ceremony. We got a photo book of the ceremony. The vows were really nice and meant a lot to all of us. (This was all prior to the Panama Canal day.)

We found out that before our arrival, Adrianne had asked what she should show Americans, and one place she was told to take us was a jewelry store. After lunch, she took us to the jewelry store, and I bought Martha a piece of jewelry and brought it along to the ceremony. I saw Jeanie looking around the store, and she picked out a really nice ring and brought it to Joe and asked him if he liked it. He said, "SURE!" And she said to Joe, "Give me your credit card!" It was the slickest way I had ever seen a man treat his wife to what she wanted.

When it got to be time to go back to the ship, Romey pulled up to the gate of the port and spoke to the guard. The gate opened, and we drove down the aisles between the containers, then onto the pier and down to the ship. We made a U-turn, and Romey stopped right by the gangplank. Now, Joe and I always wore John Deere caps, and the crew knew we could be counted on to do and find different things, so I doubt if they were surprised by our front-door service.

When we arrived in Fort Lauderdale, it was a real mess at the airport. I saw eight cruise ships lined up, and everybody went to catch a flight. There was a huge snowstorm in the Midwest, so we flew to Minneapolis. About over St. Louis, Joe told me we were going to miss our flight home, and the last flight out was also full, so I thought it would be overnight in Minneapolis. Joe told me that Musco One (a jet) was going to be waiting on us and we would be going home, but our bags would be at the Des Moines airport. We walked out of the terminal to a waiting van, then to the fixed base operator, where we had cookies and coffee. Then down the runway we went. Martha got in the copilot's seat, and the pilot let her fly us to Oskaloosa. I have never flown a jet, so I am behind! It was a very memorable trip.

In future chapters, you will read about more of the projects Joe and I have worked on. I like to say, "I helped put feet to his dreams." Joe and I have a very unique relationship that nobody understands, but I treasure the good times we have had together, both individually and with our wives. I hope that Oskaloosa is a better place because of our relationship.

Chapter 31

MCRF and the Multipurpose Recreation Trail

In 1998, Joe Crookham told me we needed to develop a recreational park in Oskaloosa where the kids could come and play all types of sports, but we needed to start with soccer. I said, "What is soccer? That is a European sport." Joe said that if we built it, they would come (the same as the motto for *Field of Dreams*). I told Joe that he must be crazy with an idea like that. But he already had the eighty acres picked out on the northwest corner of Oskaloosa, next to the old Vander Wilt apple orchard. The property was owned by Wayne DeBruin, who was my customer. I made the initial contact about them selling the land for the recreational park. The DeBruins were receptive, so Joe and I met around a kitchen table in Wayne's home, and we explained the "dream" (or the idea). We completed the purchase of the eighty acres in 1999. About twelve acres was sown down to blue grass for the first soccer field in Oskaloosa. Adult volunteer soccer coaches were found . . . and the kids came.

It was then we decided that a 501(c)(3) nonprofit organization was needed, so the Mahaska Community Recreation Foundation (MCRF) was established in 1999. The original founders of MCRF were John Pothoven, who was president of Mahaska State Bank; Bob Nielsen, who was a civil engineer and part owner of Garden and Associates; Joe P. Crookham, who you know was part owner of Musco Lighting; and me, Carl Drost, part owner of Drost Equipment. The mission of MCRF was to provide recreational opportunities for the young people and residents of the Oskaloosa and Mahaska County area.

Shortly after the organization of MCRF, Joe came up with the crazy idea of planning and constructing a multipurpose recreation trail completely around Oskaloosa. Joe believed Oskaloosa didn't have enough recreation options to attract and keep the young, skilled, and highly technical employees that Musco, Clow Valve, Oskaloosa Foods, and other companies needed. MCRF had just hired Marie Ware as the first executive director for organizing and planning the future of the organization. On a Saturday afternoon, before Marie officially started employment at MCRF, Joe brought plat maps of the entire area around the City of Oskaloosa to the showroom at Drost Equipment. Joe, Marie, and I took markers and outlined the proposed multipurpose recreation trail, which would go completely around Oskaloosa without going through developed areas. It was sixteen and a half miles in length. The proposed path went along creeks, through timbers, through Edmundson Park, through an abandoned railroad right of way, along the creek in the Marje subdivision, and along three sides of the newly acquired eighty acres of the MCRF park.

We knew it was possible, so we started getting the landowners to provide easements for the trail. The first section of the trail to be developed was along the creek in the Marje subdivision. I had a D8 Caterpillar bulldozer that I had purchased when I built our new home. The D8 was used to clear the trees and level the dirt for the route of the trail. I owned a 12A Caterpillar road grader (an old gear jammer with no hydraulics); it was used to level out the trail before paving. I did the final pass with the road grader early on the morning of the paving. It was determined that the trail would be ten-foot-wide, fiberglass-reinforced concrete poured five inches thick.

The next question: How to pave the trail? We found a six-foot-wide slipform paver near Davenport. We purchased it, and the Musco fabrication department widened it out to ten feet. The contractor we purchased it from said a small tractor would pull it because it slid on the ground. The first day to pave the original 3,000 feet was November 11, 1999. I soon found out that the paver held three cubic yards of concrete and a small tractor would not move it. The first trail to be paved was along a creek between some trees. A concrete truck could not get close, so we used two concrete pump trucks. They could be moved as needed to fill the paver. A large tractor was used the first day to pull the paver, but idling in first gear was too fast a speed. Volunteers were asked to come and help on the holiday (Veterans Day). About three hundred people showed up. (It was only necessary to have fifteen workers to accomplish the job!) The volunteers wanted water or soda to drink, snacks, and lunch. Marilee DeCook, a fifth-grade teacher at Webster School, brought her class down to watch. They were all allowed to write their names in the concrete close to the beginning of the trail. Jeff Greenhalgh, the Musco facilities manager, and I were in charge. It took three people to run the paver, three or four to bow float the concrete, and two people to pull the burlap mat across to put texture in the concrete. We learned a lot that first day, including that a cubic yard of concrete would lay down six feet of trail on average.

Larry Stevens, the city engineer at the time, was very supportive of the recreation trail project. He helped determine the size of the pipes we needed for drainage, and he also helped Joe and I get the city's approval on using recreation trails in new developments like the Marje subdivision in place of the required sidewalks. Larry helped a lot in getting easements across the city parks, the use of streets, and other city property. Larry also allowed the city employees to help with city equipment when we could use it.

Like I said, we learned some lessons the first day. The paver didn't move the aggregate to the edges very well, and it needed to be pulled slower. A conveyor was needed to load the paver, and the shoulder of the trail needed to be wide enough to drive a concrete truck alongside so the truck could dump concrete in the conveyor. The pump trucks were very expensive and took too long to move the required 250 feet. The Musco weld shop put a hydraulic-powered auger in the bottom of the paver to move the aggregate to the edges, and they installed vibrators on the rear panel of the paver to assist in getting the concrete to the ends of the paver. A slow-speed tractor was needed to pull the paver. Research showed that John Deere and Case IH both had tractors with a creeper gear, but John Deere's were very expensive. I found a Case IH tractor with a super-slow creeper gear in it from Leaman Tractor—a wholesale farm equipment dealer in Pennsylvania owned by Ed Leaman. It was red, of course, and my John Deere dealership was all green and yellow. But the speeds were correct, and the price was right. I told Ed that I would take the tractor, but it had to be green and yellow when it got to Oskaloosa, Iowa. It was green and yellow when it was delivered, and the decal said, "Experimental." Kelderman Manufacturing in Oskaloosa built a hydraulic-powered conveyor that sat perpendicular to the paver, with two dolly wheels at the bottom to carry the load. It could be set on either side of the paver.

 During the winter, we acquired easements for more trail along the proposed route drawn on the maps. My helpers and I worked on clearing the trees, leveling and compacting the soil, and getting ready for paving day. When paving day came, it was determined that Jeff Greenhalgh and I would invite people to come and help. Of course, Jeff and I were there, and so were the eight employees from the Musco facilities department. Daryl VandeGeest and Reverend Alvern Boetsma (who was nicknamed "Vern" and "Preach") were also invited. Daryl and Preach were in charge of pulling the burlap material to put the final texture in the concrete. They were both very faithful in coming to every paving day until

Chisel Points in the Ground

Daryl passed away. Preach scratched his initials in every section of the trail he helped pour.

For every foot of trail we put down, we needed to grade and seed ten square feet of shoulder (five square feet on each side), so it would look nice and could be kept mowed. Lowell Lenarz volunteered to do the shoulder work, and his group was called "Lowell's Disciples." Lowell was a retired junior high school principal, and his group used provided equipment to prepare and seed the shoulders for several miles of trail.

The amount of paving we got done was related to the amount of concrete that could be delivered. The longest trail section completed in a day was approximately 4,800 linear feet, which required 800 cubic yards of concrete. That section of the trail starts at the northeast sewage treatment plant in Oskaloosa and goes along Spring Creek to almost North Third Street. On the day this section was laid, the paver was ready, and the concrete had been reserved; the shoulders were all wide enough for the concrete trucks to drive alongside the proposed path, enter from the east end, and go out the west. The trucks could empty their loads in the conveyor on the paver. All the concrete for the recreation trail came from Ideal Ready Mix in Oskaloosa, and it drew quite a lot of attention. On that day, the concrete was coming slow and sporadic, and we were behind schedule. Martha and her friend, Ilene Wymore, brought a very nice lunch, and we could stop and eat because there was no concrete. We ate under the trees of the timber between the trail and Spring Creek. Shortly after lunch, a pickup arrived with "Ideal Ready Mix" on the door, and out came Johnny Johnson, owner of the entire corporation. He inquired about how things were going. He certainly was impressed with the trail, and Jeff and I told him everything was going well, except we were not getting enough concrete to keep the paver going. A lot of times it is not how much you know but who you know! The concrete trucks started rolling in. At one time, there were seven trucks in line waiting to unload. The trucks would unload while moving, so the paver didn't have to stop. Like I said, that section of the trail was completed in one day. Ideal Ready Mix has always given MCRF a discounted price for all the materials we get from them.

Joe Crookham took care of acquiring most of the fifty-eight easements for the land where the recreation trail goes in Oskaloosa. Some of the largest easement lengths were from the City of Oskaloosa, the Oskaloosa School System, William Penn College, MCRF itself, Mahaska County Conservation, and an abandoned railroad right of way. We acquired fifty-eight easements without paying any money, but putting the property back in order was important to the owners. Some fences had to be put in place, barriers built, golf tees moved, and other small stuff. One easement from a city councilman (who voted "no" on everything, but never had a better idea) required MCRF to pay a huge amount of money for creek and scrub land. (I think the councilman should have paid MCRF for taking it off his hands.) One easement in University Park was very expensive because the only land they would allow the trail on was inside a badly eroded creek. A five-foot diameter culvert had to be installed, and then clay dirt hauled in and compacted to get the trail through. It got paved, but the shoulder was a challenge. On almost all the places where fencing was required alongside the trail there was a five-foot shoulder. On this property, only twelve inches were allowed, which made it the most expensive easement of all. But it was needed to complete the trail connections. Joe or his employees also worked with the Iowa DOT and the Union Pacific Railroad to acquire construction permits to place the trail under the highways and the railroad.

The first time we crossed the trail under Highway 92 was on the east edge of Oskaloosa. Spring Creek flows under the highway, and there are three cast-in-place concrete culverts that are fourteen feet by fourteen feet. Joe convinced the DOT to allow MCRF to put a two-foot false bottom in the west culvert, so when Spring Creek gets higher water, it covers the trail. It is very safe because the trail crossing is under the busy highway.

The second time we crossed the trail under Highway 92 was on the west edge of Oskaloosa. There was an eight-foot-by-eight-foot tunnel under the highway where MCRF could get access on both sides. This tunnel had very little use until there was heavy rain in the northwest corner of Oskaloosa. Joe asked the DOT if MCRF could bore a two-foot diameter pipe under the highway for normal water flow, and then the eight-by-eight tunnel would only be used in heavy flow. The DOT approved the plan. I talked to Vermeer Corporation in Pella about navigating the pipe under the highway. MCRF would have to get the pipe and a pulling head, but Vermeer would donate the machine, manpower, and time to install it. I also contacted Gene Miller of Miller the Driller in Pleasant Hill by Des Moines, and he arranged the pipe and had the pulling head made. Vermeer told me they could drill and pull the pipe in a day, but Gene Miller said it couldn't be done in that short of time. The day Vermeer did the work, Gene Miller came to observe, and he lost a bet of a Big Meal with me because it was all done in less than a day!

The largest challenge for the recreation trail was to get a tunnel or underpass under the Union Pacific Railroad on the north edge of Oskaloosa. The trail was already in place on the west side of the tracks, but city streets had to be used to get back to the trail on Penn College property. We knew the railroad underpass would be much safer because no city streets would be involved, and it would be shorter. It would also be good for Penn athletes to be able to use the trail to get to the Lacey Recreation Complex and their new stadium.

Adam DeJong, a Musco employee who had a relationship with the engineering department of Union Pacific, started this project. The railroad was agreeable to do a tunnel under the railroad if it met their specifications. I contacted Miller the Driller in Pleasant Hill to see if they could put a twelve-foot diameter tube under the railroad, and Miller assured me that they could. The tube was to have a 144-inch inside diameter and a 147-inch outside diameter, but the railroad line was to be kept open for rail traffic. The price of pounding the pipe under the railroad was about $450,000.00. About 22,000 cubic yards of dirt had to be hauled into the west side to connect the tube to the existing recreation trail. DeLong Construction from Washington, Iowa, was doing the dirt work at the new Community Stadium, which was a little over a half mile west of the railroad (another MCRF project you'll read more about in a later chapter). The dirt was hauled from the stadium with a Caterpillar rubber track tractor and a dirt scoop. About the time all the permits were in place, Miller the Driller filed for bankruptcy. An agreement was made with the court that Miller could do the work, but the checks for the project would all be third-party checks. Miller brought the equipment to the site, and the boisterous foreman said they would pound the pipe through in one good day. They found out that the fill was put in during the late 1800s, and it was very hard. The job was accomplished in about ten days, and the hydraulic pounder could be heard to the very southeast corner of Oskaloosa. The pounding stopped when a train went on the tracks above the tunnel. Peterson Construction from Reinbeck subcontracted with Miller, and they poured the concrete retaining walls. The Musco crew and I put approximately two feet of fill in the pipe and poured the five-inch concrete trail. It is about ten feet wide through the pipe. Altogether, the underpass cost around $800,000.00.

When the trail needed to go across property owned by the Mahaska County Conservation Commission, their directors were all in favor of bringing people through their outdoor area and close to the new educational center they were going to build. One area that would be the nicest route was on the bank of a large creek and very steep. An engineer told me that it was too difficult and that the trail could not be put there because of the terrain. Taking that as a challenge, we excavated lots of dirt from there with a John Deere 9630T track tractor and a seventeen-yard Ashland

Chisel Points in the Ground

The recreation trail underpass under the Union Pacific Railroad.

pull-type dirt scoop. The dirt was transported to the south to fill in along the west side of the University Park sewage lagoons and connect to University Park. The trail was paved and is now a wonderful place to observe wildlife at any time of the year.

We had fun! Originally, the recreation trail was to go through the timber at Vennard College in University Park on the east side of Oskaloosa. The timber had not been taken care of, so there were large trees and brush and undergrowth where the trail might go. To get the route started, we had to walk through and get the starting point and ending point established, then try to find a route through the trees, leaving as many large trees as possible and keeping the grade to no more than 5% to meet the handicap regulations. One nice afternoon, Joe Crookham and John Pothoven were going to walk ahead of me with my D8 Caterpillar and push a proposed route through from start to finish. John and Joe were not far enough ahead when the tall, small-diameter trees started smashing down beside them. They really started moving then because I could not see them from the dozer! We made a route through the timber, but the leadership at Vennard changed and a new route had to be found. The story is still a great conversation topic.

Alan Fender, the Rotary Club president, called to talk to me about building a gazebo along Highway 92 on the west side of Oskaloosa. He thought we could connect the gazebo to the recreation trail and install a parking lot to be a trailhead. This idea was the first time a local group came forward with a concept to improve the trail system. I assisted them with the trail route and design, but the Rotary Club members did most of the work. The MCRF paving crew laid down the concrete, and MCRF paid for half of the concrete. The gazebo and trail are a great addition to the trail system. A few years later, Alan Fender and his wife donated the money to pave the parking lot and the driveway off the highway.

When the Fairfield Inn was constructed on the western edge of Oskaloosa near the bypass, the owners wanted to bring the recreation trail to the new motel for their patrons to use. We had a discussion with the nearby Nazarene Church, who provided the easement. The city was requiring the church to provide a sidewalk in front of their property, and the trail was approved by the city to be that sidewalk. The church was asked to pay for only half of the concrete, while MCRF paid for the other half and provided all the construction costs. It was a great deal for all parties involved.

The latest addition to the recreation trail is just west of the Lacey Recreation Complex. A large pond has been constructed on the property, and the trail was paved across the dike and around both the west and east sides of the pond. A 1904 A-frame bridge was moved to the north end of the pond, where it crosses the water entry point. When the pond is full to capacity, there should be approximately two feet of water under the bridge. There is a walkway under the bridge on both sides, so people can walk under the bridge and observe the construction. The bridge was purchased from Jim and Jan VandeVoort of Pella when the county abandoned a road on their property. It was built by the Oskaloosa Bridge Company and moved to the site by DeLong Construction. The wood floor and railings were recently cut from white oak trees. Five of the beams are eight inches by twelve inches and twenty-nine feet long, cut from the center of the log to take care of any warping. The railings were added because of pedestrian and trail tram traffic. All the oak was cut by Raymond Yutzy of RJ Lumber from Drakesville, Iowa.

Presently, there are thirteen and a half miles of trail poured in concrete, and the trail goes around three quarters of Oskaloosa. There are many access points to the recreation trail, and the people of Oskaloosa use it a lot.

MCRF and the Multipurpose Recreation Trail

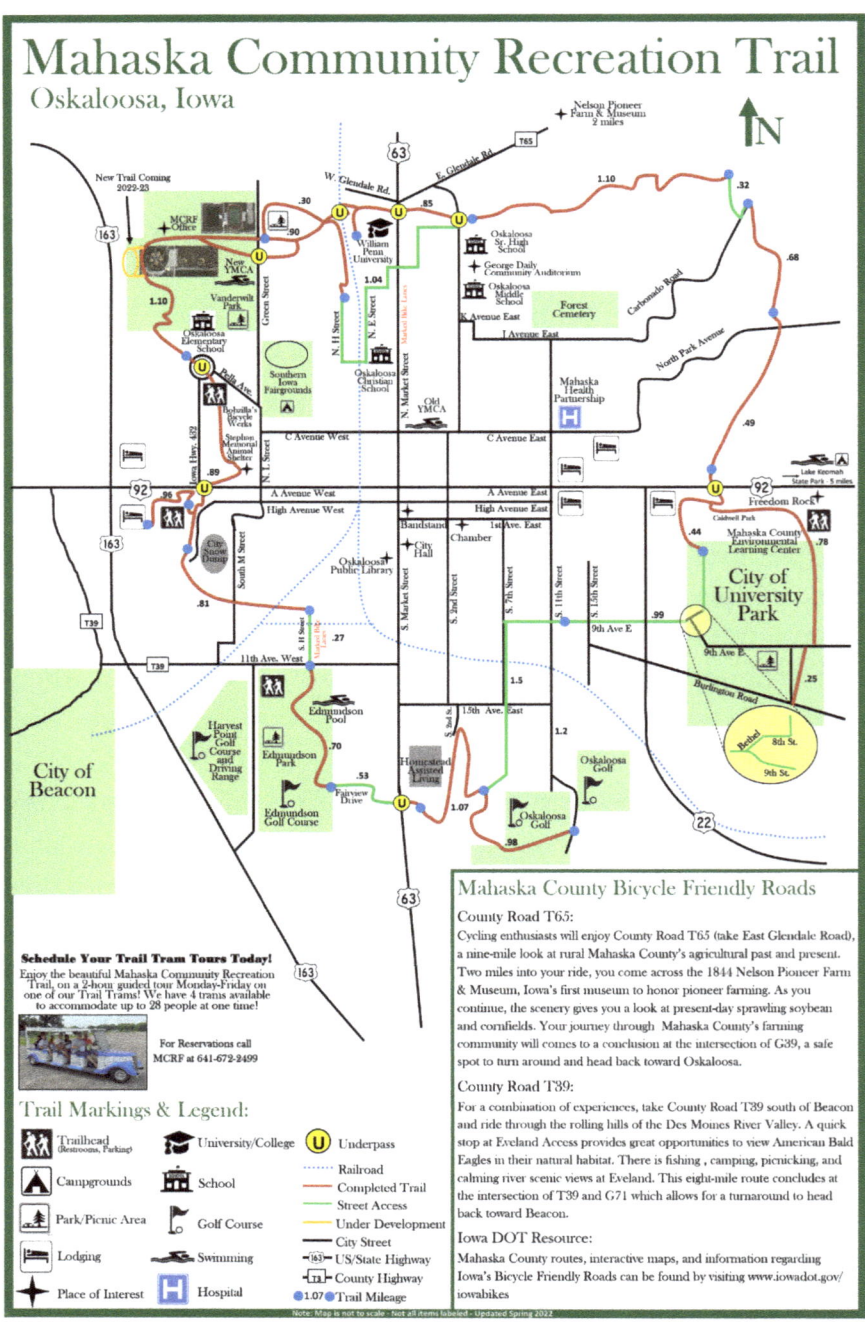

A map of the recreation trail circling Oskaloosa.

Image courtesy of MCRF, March 2024.

Chapter 32

George Daily Auditorium

I was elected to the Oskaloosa School Board in 1976. At the time, the old Oskaloosa Junior High School was in use. The original construction happened in approximately 1898 with some additions. The junior high housed the community auditorium for musical and drama productions. All band and orchestra concerts and all drama productions in the district were held there.

In 1983, the voters passed a bond issue for a new junior high school to be built on the south side of the senior high. When plans were made for the new junior high school, there were no provisions for an auditorium. Gymnasiums would have to be used, but a space was left for an auditorium to be built between the senior high school and the new junior high school.

The use of gymnasiums for school and community activities was not the standard Oskaloosa was accustomed to after having had an auditorium with a stage and a balcony. Many committees were formed to study the problem, and several solutions were offered, including renovating a building on the west side of the square downtown into an auditorium. But downtown was completely distant from any schools or children.

The Oskaloosa School Board was all in favor of solving the problem by using the land between the schools, so the auditorium would be close to half of the students in the district. There would also be parking for evening productions and performances. The big problem was funding the project.

In the early nineties, a man in Oskaloosa named George Daily found out he owned land in Louisiana and that the property had oil on it. The property was listed as past due taxes, and Nick Williams—a friend of George Daily—along with local attorney Joe Crookham persuaded George to let them help him get his property rights under control. Then he could donate the property to the community of Oskaloosa for the betterment of the town. George agreed. A trust with a board of directors was established with several million dollars in it.

I was president of the school board. John Pothoven, another school board member, and I approached the trust about providing funding for a new community auditorium to be named after George Daily. The trust's board discussed it and asked the school board to do a presentation. The school had previously hired an architect and had a preliminary plan for a seven-hundred-seat auditorium. John Pothoven and I presented the Daily Auditorium proposal to the board; it was the first presentation by any group.

The trust committed to contributing $2.5 million out of the $4 million proposal. John Pothoven volunteered to be the fundraising chairperson, and I was named the construction committee chairman. John raised over $1 million from companies and individuals in the community. Those who gave $500.00 had their names put on seats in the auditorium.

The remaining funds came from the school system. The Oskaloosa School System had its central administration office in an old post office at the main intersection in town. The school board decided it was time to get the central administration closer to students, and the perfect location would be in the front portion of the Daily Auditorium. Working with the architect and the trust board, the school proposed a new central office with a meeting room for school and community activities. The Oskaloosa School System would put in $300,000.00 toward the office and meeting room complex. The plan was completed.

The school board selected Merit Construction of Cedar Rapids to be the contractor. It was a design/build contract that allowed for changes as construction progressed. In addition to seating seven hundred people, the auditorium has a wide stage proscenium opening, an orchestra pit, two green rooms, a fly loft with rigging to lift four elephants' weight in sets, a rear stage, the community meeting room, storage space, and the school administrative offices. The construction of the auditorium was paid for in cash; the profit from the trust investments paid for the increased cost of using higher quality or additional amenities.

The deed to the George Daily Auditorium was presented to me, president of the Oskaloosa School Board, at the September meeting of 1997 (which was also my last meeting after serving twenty years on the board). The auditorium was dedicated that month with special programs by local theater groups, a concert by world-famous opera singer Simon Estes, and a motivational speech by Charles J. Plumb, who was a Vietnam prisoner of war for seven years. This wonderful presentation was given at 3:00 in the afternoon for employees of the sponsors, then again at 7:00 in the evening for the community. The auditorium was full for both presentations. The Friends of the Auditorium was formed, which brings in national talent to perform and present at the auditorium. The school uses the auditorium for assemblies, award nights, plays, and concerts. The Daily Auditorium is used over five hundred times per year.

The motto of the George Daily Trust is "A Seed for Growth," and this project was focused on the growth of Oskaloosa and furthering George Daily's legacy. The auditorium was a major contribution to the community and is truly a tribute to George Daily.

George Daily Auditorium

The statue on the bench is of George Daily, the main contributor to the auditorium. He's playing checkers, one of his favorite pastimes.

Chapter 33

Trail Trams

Here's another one of Joe Crookham's crazy ideas. One day in 2010, Joe said, "Carl, we need to get an electric vehicle to take elderly folks from the nursing homes for a ride on the recreation trail. It will be good for them to get outside and get fresh air and take in the sights." That was an idea!

A John Deere six-wheeled, gas-engine-powered Gator was repurposed into a tram that carried ten passengers. It was the first trail vehicle. With a little research, we found out Club Car makes an eight-passenger, extended-battery-powered electric vehicle that would be very quiet on the trail and wouldn't scare the wildlife away. This vehicle can be seen at almost any passenger terminal at an airport, transporting passengers between gates. We purchased one of these vehicles with funds donated by a couple who thought this would be a good service for the homebound folks. The big question was how and where we could find a person to direct the tram tours, set up guidelines, and ensure the safety of the riders.

I was sitting in an adult Sunday school class at the Presbyterian Church when Charles Argo, a retired physician, spoke up. I thought, *There is the tram director!* After class, Charles and I talked, and after giving it some thought, Charles agreed to do it. He asked what his directions were and how we wanted it done. We told Charles it was his project to plan and organize and to let us know if we could help in any way. Charles set it up, and he took eleven trips that fall with forty-seven people from the nursing homes. Charles made it a requirement that each tram would have a staff member from the facility ride along in case of an emergency. It proved to be a very desirable service.

The following year, Charles continued to plan and organize the tours out of the nursing homes and assisted living facility. Martha was added as a volunteer driver. A narrative was added to the tour to explain to the riders the sights and the locations around Oskaloosa that the tram was traveling past, because some of the areas are not seen by any means other than the trams. The spiel covered some construction notes about the trail. Family members of the elderly passengers were allowed to ride with them. It became a known community activity, and the tram tours were expanded to include people over the age of fifty-five.

Another tram was purchased by a donor. The donor decided that the vehicle would be a custom-made, eight-passenger electric vehicle. Streetrod Golf Carts in Montezuma was given the contract to fabricate a custom golf cart in the design of an old car, with a fiberglass body and a nice vinyl cover to keep the sun and elements off the riders. The vehicle is blue and white, and it has an "oogah" horn, which is sounded when the tram goes around a sharp curve in the trail or near a tunnel. Of course, more volunteer drivers were needed, and people came forward. Again, the tours were open to fifty-five-year-olds and up, and the group requests were very popular. Yet another custom electric vehicle was added, this time red and white in color. Then more volunteer drivers were needed.

The trail tram tours were eventually opened up to any age and any group, but the nursing homes and assisted living facility continued to request tram tours. It was determined that another tram was needed based on the number of tours given (the riders were about 1,300 per year). Martha and Jeanie Bieri got together and said we needed a patriotic tram that would be red, white, and blue and have stars on the hood. The patriotic tram was donated by General Tom and Kathy Franks, Joe and Jeanie Crookham, and

Carl and Martha Drost. Streetrod built the tram and painted it patriotic colors, and the Musco sign shop made and installed the stars. When there are veterans in the group, they get to ride on the patriotic tram.

The trail tram tours are very popular. The groups include riders from all the nursing homes in the area: White Oak, the Christian Opportunity Center, and Homestead Assisted Living. The second graders from the Oskaloosa Elementary School take an annual field trip with the trail tour. Preschools and daycares do tours, and out-of-town groups also book tours. With the picnic area available a short distance away, groups can plan a picnic lunch as well. The scheduling has been done for many years through the Mahaska Community Recreation Foundation office and can now be completed online too.

Chapter 34

Lacey Recreation Complex

The Lacey Recreation Complex was named after John Lacey, who was a representative from Mahaska County in the United States Congress in the early 1900s. John Lacey helped author the Antiquities Act, which founded the National Park System. When you look at the buildings and the signs around the complex, you'll notice the national parks' architecture, materials, and colors in the design.

As I shared in an earlier chapter, the Mahaska Community Recreation Foundation acquired the first eighty acres for the complex in 1999. The land was on the south side of 238th Street, then it went west of the city street called Green. It was bordered on the south by the old Vander Wilt apple orchard and to the west by the Welch property. Shortly after the acquisition by the Daily Real Estate Trust, MCRF decided to build a Little League softball complex with five 200-foot fields on this land. Before this time, the Little League played ball on fields in various sections of town. With this facility, all games could happen in one place. Joe Crookham again told us, "If we build it, they will come!" We envisioned a pentagon design, with the concession stand in the center surrounded by the fields. We contracted Iowa Athletic Field Construction out of Webster City, Iowa, to do the building. MCRF had previous experience with the owner, Kurt, and his sons when they helped move the sod where the elementary school was to be built to the new soccer field (you'll read more about those projects later in this

Lacey Recreation Complex

chapter). Many volunteers helped with the project, working on tiling, performing general labor, hauling the grass sod from Riverside, Iowa, and laying the sod. Of course, Musco donated most of the money to create the fields and also all of the lights. A large irrigation system was installed to irrigate the new fields as well as any future development.

In 1999, Joe and I stood on the south eighty acres with a writing pad and a pen and drew a sketch of the projects that were planned for the entire property. On the sketch was the five-field wagon wheel Little League Complex; the Babe Ruth Fields east of the Little League, so all the fields could use the irrigation; the new elementary school; a new YMCA that hadn't yet been proposed along Green Street; the soccer fields north of 238th Street; a new turf stadium for football with a track and a press box facing the field; and a soccer stadium on the opposite side of the press box. The sketch also showed the streets and parking lots.

At the same time the Little League fields were being built, the soccer community wanted more area to play, so Martin Roepke and I started to level twelve acres to sow grass in for soccer. Martin is a retired veterinarian in Oskaloosa and enjoyed volunteering at the complex, operating farm and construction equipment. The area was seeded to bluegrass, and soon the young people were playing on it.

We soon discovered *Field of Dreams* had it right—we built it, and they did come. Soccer had really taken off in Oskaloosa, and we needed more space. To the north was another seventy-eight acres owned by Donald and Pat DeBruin. Don was the brother of Wayne DeBruin, who sold the original eighty acres to MCRF. We contacted Don in 2000, and he was willing to sell his property for the recreation area, which doubled the size of the complex. Don retained the right to farm the undeveloped land and pay rent for it. He planted soybeans on the area where the proposed stadiums were to be built for seven years, and then the decision was made to build the football field.

At about the same time, the Oskaloosa School System wanted to build a new elementary school that would replace the five smaller elementary schools. Daily Real Estate donated the land on the south side of the original eighty acres purchased for the new school. Martin Roepke and I started leveling off the soybean field that had been purchased from Don to make a much larger soccer field. I purchased a thirty-six-foot landplane to do a better job making the fields flat. Martin pulled the landplane for days with his favorite John Deere 4450 tractor and leveled the soccer fields. Martin and I, along with a few other volunteers, drilled the bluegrass and rye mixture for the soccer fields, and it was a very nice stand. It turned out to be a very dry summer; the grass was going to die, so an eight-inch water main was dug in throughout the entire 120-acre complex. Two reel-to-reel irrigators were purchased to water the grass. Each of the irrigators had a gas-powered engine on a pump with a four-hundred-foot hose reel. When connected to the water main, each irrigator puts out 106 gallons of water per minute. The grass was saved.

Daryl and Gwen VandeGeest had their home in the corner of the seventy-eight acres from Don, as well as the office and truck parking lot for Oskaloosa Grain. MCRF asked if the lights and crowds were affecting them, because if so we would buy their property. The property included the old brick home, where the VandeGeests lived, plus a five-year-old office and parking lot. The VandeGeests found a new property east of Oskaloosa, and MCRF acquired their property in 2005. The Oskaloosa Grain office became the MCRF office and conference room, which was large enough for community groups (though it was mainly used for members of MCRF to hold meetings).

The Babe Ruth League was playing baseball games at Edmundson Park in Oskaloosa, where there was only one field. MCRF decided to build new Babe Ruth baseball fields east of the Little League five-plex. Iowa Turf of Des Moines got the contract to build the baseball fields, which included irrigation, Shakopee clay for the infield and warning tracks, chain link fencing, and dugouts. Bleachers were added, and a smaller concession stand was put by the fields. Of course, a Musco lighting system was installed. The grading of the second Babe Ruth field was completed at the same time the first field was completed, as well as the irrigation, but it took a couple of years to complete the fencing and lighting.

We made a plan for the new football and soccer stadiums. A large volume of dirt had to be removed to level the terrain and the parking areas. At the same time, the railroad underpass was being designed for the multipurpose recreation trail, and we needed 20,000 cubic yards of clay to make the fill on the west side of the railroad track. DeLong Construction of Washington, Iowa, moved the dirt. A rubber track Caterpillar tractor and a pull-type scraper hauled the dirt the half mile from the stadium to the railroad underpass trail. Sometimes, there were two units of equipment.

The football stadium is turf with a rubber track around the outside of it. It also has seating for 2,500 spectators in the home section and 800 spectators on the visitor side. The press box was designed as part of the stadium project and has four floors (the second floor at ground level). The lower level is locker rooms, with showers and storage. There are tunnels out to both the football stadium and the soccer stadium. The second level of the press box has the public restrooms, the concession stand, and public areas to access the bleachers for the home spectators. The third level is a luxury suite, which is air conditioned and has tables for spectators to watch and enjoy the football or soccer game (or both if there's a game on both fields).

The soccer stadium was graded flat by hauling the clay dirt out, then hauling in twelve inches of black dirt and grading to specifications. Iowa Turf from Des Moines came and helped place the sand in the underground drainage ditches where Mahaska Rural Water had dug the trench for the drainage system. Real soccer players came and told me that the field needed to be 50% sand, so eight inches of clean sand was spread over the field and tilled into the black soil. The seed was very expensive, but it was a high-quality athletic turf combination of seed. The volunteers refused to operate the drill to put in the seed in because too many spectators would see it, so I had to operate the John Deere tractor with the Brillion grass seed drill while the volunteers opened the bags of seed and dumped them in the drill. It was doubled-drilled to get excellent coverage. The field is irrigated from a water main and the reel-to-reel irrigators, so there are no irrigation nozzles in the grass to injure any players. When Martha and I sold Drost Equipment in 2014, our donation of $400,000.00 allowed the field to be completed with fencing, signs, and bleachers. The soccer stadium is named Drost Field, with a sign saying the customers of Drost Equipment made the donation possible.

In 2011, the eighty acres directly north of the Lacey Recreation Complex were purchased from Don and Pat DeBruin to make certain the property was not developed into a housing subdivision. This land is the full width of the Lacey Complex and has Chew Cemetery on the far north side, with no public easement access to it. There are still three Chew tombstones in the cemetery from the 1860s.

In 2020, I was on the Oskaloosa Schools Facilities Committee. We discussed the ticket booths at the old Community Stadium, which needed a lot of repairs since the stadium had been built in 1929. The roofs needed to be replaced, the wood supporting structure was rotten, and the bricks all needed tuck pointing. The repairs were going to cost a lot of money for a stadium that got very little use (and most of the use was from the middle school for practice). I approached MCRF about moving the ticket booths from the old stadium to the new stadium in the Lacey Complex. No permanent ticket booths had been constructed at the new stadium yet.

At the same time, the City of Oskaloosa, the Oskaloosa Community Schools, and local contributions made it possible for a new $31 million construction project: a new early childhood facility with a community YMCA in the southeast corner of all the MCRF land (the same spot on the sketch Joe and I had made!). In the construction documents, it was written that MCRF would receive the dirt and have it placed within one mile of the project without any cost. MCRF decided that a large new parking lot could be built south of the new stadium, on the south side of the road. The plan showed it would hold 250 vehicles. It would require a lot of dirt, but it was now available, and the only real cost would be the gravel to cover it (about $50,000.00). MCRF decided that a new entrance from the south to the stadium would make the large parking lot more accessible. The old ticket booths would make a very nostalgic entrance and would preserve the history when the new roof and tuck pointing were completed.

The MCRF Board and the Oskaloosa School Board arranged for the ticket booths to be available, but MCRF would pay to have the new concrete and fence put up at the old stadium to make it safe and secure. A contract was secured with DeLong Construction, as well as a subcontract with Goodwin House Movers from Washington. They were to move both the west and south ticket booths the four miles to the new site. It took five hours to move the brick ticket booths out of the north side of Oskaloosa and west on 230th Street. The booths were put in place, a new handicap-accessible ramp was added to the second level of the press box (where the concession stand was), and the new entrance enhanced the stadium. The south ticket booth from the old stadium was placed at the north entrance of the new stadium. Some members of the community were not excited about the project, but now that everything is in place, the community likes them and the criticism is over.

In 2019, MCRF decided that more softball fields were needed, as well as larger fields for tournaments. We made a plan to add one 250-foot field and two fields with 220-foot sidelines. They would be added to the south side of the Little League five-plex, around the children's playground. A huge amount of fill dirt would be needed. Again, the excavated dirt from the new YMCA building project was utilized to raise the new softball fields to the planned elevation. Musco had just purchased Iowa Turf from the Iowa Cubs organization, so they were in charge of the project after the fill dirt was hauled in and the black dirt placed on the outfield. The recreation trail had to be moved out of the scope of the new softball fields, so it got paved and landscaped. The old recreation trail, which would be under the new fields, was taken out by Wayne VerSteegh of VerSteegh Brothers. Wayne's family farms a lot of land along the Des Moines River, and they take concrete to dump on the riverbank to control the erosion.

Joe and I had bought the Welch property in 2012, which was adjacent to the MCRF property to the west. A three-acre pond was constructed on this property and was filling up in 2021. About 80,000 cubic yards of clay fill dirt had been sold or donated off the property over the years, and the new recreation trail came very close to the pond. Joe thought it would be good to construct the trail around the pond and across the pond dike, which would mean a lot of liability for the owners. Daily Real Estate purchased the land from me and Joe in late 2021. The timber to the south and just north of the old Pella highway is a great place to observe birds, deer, and other wildlife. A nature trail was already cut and seeded through the timber, so a walking nature trail is now open for the public to enjoy. The nature trail connects to the concrete recreation trail.

In its entirety, the Lacey Recreation Complex covers over 320 acres, and the land cost alone is over $5 million at acquisition cost. The Lacey Complex covers land from Kirby Avenue on the west to North Third Street by the Oskaloosa Senior High School (with a small section owned by Penn University). It stretches from the animal shelter on the south side to the city limits on the north. The property on the east side of the railroad can also be developed and is connected by the trail underpass.

Lacey Recreation Complex

An aerial photo of the Lacey Recreation Complex taken by Abby Drost, my granddaughter.

Chapter 35

William Penn Activity Center

In the spring of 2005, Joe Crookham called me before 6:00 in the morning, which was very unusual (meaning way too early). His reason for calling was to tell me that he had decided that William Penn University needed an indoor practice facility for all the athletes and students. (Penn graduated from being a college to a university in 2000.) Joe told me we needed to build them a "hoop building" with a vinyl roof like the ones we see on farms to put hay and machinery in. We thought it would cost about $400,000.00. He thought it should be built on the far west side of campus, near the railroad, where it would be approximately a half mile from the center of campus. I told him it was great idea (albeit another crazy one), but nobody would use the building because it was too far away from where the students normally spend time. In fact, a couple of hours later, I called Joe and told him I had recently been to Dordt College in Sioux Center, Iowa, and their recreation center was in the center of the campus.

Before noon, and after several phone calls between us, Joe and I had a plan together for the Penn Activity Center (PAC), which would be in the center of campus like I'd suggested, attached to the north end of the gymnasium and connected to the old campus heating plant and smokestack (for nostalgia). It would include an indoor football field.

Building the PAC would entail demolishing the industrial technology building and constructing a new building for industrial tech. The original idea of a $400,000.00 hoop building had grown to at least a $10 million project. Those associated with Joe and me are never concerned with project creep, but always project LEAP! The Penn board approved the project when all the costs were established, and they dealt with the funding along with the university.

There were many listener group sessions and discussions with university and city voices. The project was approved, and Merit Construction was selected to be the design-build contractor. Jeff Greenhalgh of Musco Lighting worked closely with Merit on the plans and design. The design included geothermal heating and cooling for the main part of the building and required fifteen miles of underground coolant loops to be placed at depths of fifteen, thirty, and forty-five feet. A groundbreaking ceremony was held on April 28, 2006. The 150,000 square foot building has a forty-five-yard football field, two full-size basketball courts, a three-hundred-yard running/walking track, a workout area on the second floor overlooking the field area, a lounge, locker rooms for both men and women on the first floor, and classrooms on the second and third floor above the locker rooms.

The main entrance was built around the entrance of the old heating plant and the smokestack. The main floor of the PAC can be used for large gatherings like banquets, concerts, and graduations. The PAC turned out to be a $25 million project, but it is used a lot. The PAC opened in August 2008 in time for the new school year.

Thanks to its location at the center of the campus, the PAC is used by students to stay in condition. The athletic department uses it for conditioning and games (including all volleyball games). The community uses the running/walking track for cardio exercise.

Because both the industrial technology buildings were demolished to build the PAC, the 50,000 square foot Musco Technology Center was constructed to house industrial technology classes. The building includes the laboratories for metals, woods, and drafting, as well as classrooms and labs for computer science. There are also classrooms for broadcasting and two production studios, one small and one large enough to bring vehicles in for props. There is a large lobby where smaller meetings are held. The Musco Technology Center had a construction cost of approximately $7 million.

Chisel Points in the Ground

Front of the William Penn Activity Center.

William Penn Activity Center

Rear of the William Penn Activity Center.

Chapter 36

Public Service: Second School Board Term

In August 2013, the superintendent of the Oskaloosa School System stopped at Drost Equipment to get parts for his lawn tractor. He told me that nobody was running for the open school board seats in the upcoming election in September. Several board members had resigned, which created several openings. Over the years, more than a few citizens had asked me to get back on the school board (and even Martha had told me that I needed to get back on the board). After some consideration, I took out nomination papers and ran for the Oskaloosa Community Schools Board of Directors. After I took out papers for the at-large seat, three other citizens took out papers for the spot. After several open meetings with the candidates, I won the election and was sworn in. The next nomination was for me to be school board president; the motion passed, which was not what the superintendent wanted. It was a shock! It had been years since I had led a meeting, but I took over the rest of the agenda. After the meeting, I remember Charlie Comfort—a very young board member—told me I had done a good job.

After I'd spent a few weeks on the school board and had some discussions with a couple of members who had been on the board for a few years, it seemed to me that the quality of the school system had fallen drastically in terms of academic standardized tests. I felt the superintendent was running the school system and the board as a coach instead of an academic. The test scores had fallen from the upper eighties to the upper fifties between 2008 and 2012. It was found that in 2008, Oskaloosa's scores on the Iowa Test of Basic Skills scores were on the same level as Pella (a very good district). By 2013, the same test scores had fallen significantly. These numbers were totally unacceptable. The number of students open enrolling out of Oskaloosa was also extremely high. Close to 10% of our students were seeking their education in other school districts; this was allowed by Iowa law.

I asked the superintendent how we could have an independent evaluation of our school system, so we could see if and where the deficiencies were in our education plan. No help was given by the superintendent. I found out that the Iowa School Board Association had a group of educators who would come to the district and visit classes, ask a lot of questions, and then give a report to the board. The superintendent was never enthused about the evaluation, and the board was very polarized on any issue that mattered.

The School Board Association's evaluation of the Oskaloosa School District finally got to the board for a vote. The vice president voted "no" on the $8,000.00 evaluation to see if the group could help us improve the quality of education. But it passed, and the evaluation was done and a report given. However, the superintendent refused to take any action on the report.

All the board members would agree if I said serving on the school board for the next several years was literal hell. The superintendent's three-year contract was not extended year after year, so the contract would terminate on June 30, 2018. However, the board would still have to act to terminate the contract. The superintendent knew what was going to happen with the newly elected board (led by Shelly Herr as president). So, the superintendent told the board by letter that he had accepted a position in another district.

It was good that Shelly was elected board president because she is a strong leader who is very careful with her words and will not upset many people. I've found that a board member has a lot more latitude to influence outcomes than the board president because the president's responsibility is to keep the school district open. So, presidents are somewhat restricted. As a board member, you have a lot more freedom in discussing and making motions. I assumed the role of "kids first and watch the dollars!" I have to admit that amongst some board members—and some of the community—I was not very popular.

The board employed a search company to find candidates for the now open superintendency of the Oskaloosa School System. We received fifty-six applications. When we hired the consulting firm, I had asked if board members could look at all the applicants' resumes, and the answer was affirmative. Later on, the consulting firm was not going to allow me to look at them until they were reminded of what they had said during the interview process. I studied all fifty-six of the applications from both coasts of the United States and all places in between. I took a whole weekend to read and analyze the resumes, making piles from not acceptable to acceptable, who we should interview, and my top candidate. Martha will verify that I selected Mrs. Paula Wright from Chariton, Iowa, as my top pick.

The firm narrowed the fifty-six to twelve applications (including Mrs. Wright). Then a video of each candidate was presented, and we narrowed the twelve to six (again including Mrs. Wright). In-person interviews were held, and the six and were narrowed down to two candidates: Mrs. Wright from Chariton and a man from Minnesota. A full-day meeting was set up for each candidate (but on the same day). I prayed for wisdom about this major decision. My prayer that day was very simple: "Please, Lord, make it crystal clear which of the two candidates is the right person for the position in Oskaloosa." The superintendent's values, morals, mode of operation, and philosophy carry all the way through the system.

During the final interview, I told both candidates that the Oskaloosa School District had a lot of problems, from the present administration to the teaching staff and curriculum ... and that was only a start. It was very clear when the evening came that Mrs. Wright was the choice of the group. The one thing that everyone spoke about was Mrs. Wright's philosophy of KIDS FIRST in every decision that is made. Mrs. Wright came to Oskaloosa effective July 1, 2018. She worked very hard to improve the education of Oskaloosa's students. I told Mrs. Wright I would give her the best I had for the three years left in my school board term.

The board basically told Mrs. Wright that we would support her in decisions that would improve the school district. My personal thoughts were that the district administrators were very weak and that Mrs. Wright would be busy trying to train them or counsel them out. To condense three and a half years of change is very hard. But Mrs. Wright (she always wanted me to call her Paula, but out of respect for the position, it was always Mrs. Wright) changed and greatly improved communication between the superintendent and the board, the administration, staff, parents, and the community. We found out early on that we didn't need to waste any time checking on the accuracy of her communication because it would be accurate and truthful, whether it was good news or bad. Mrs. Wright's integrity is beyond question—she was a breath of fresh air in the schools.

Mrs. Wright also initiated board committees. Each board member was on a committee focused on a topic they had knowledge of, expertise in, or a desire to improve and learn more about. It really proved beneficial because in the monthly committee meetings, adequate time could be spent studying an issue so we could make a quality recommendation at the full board meeting. It took a short time for the board members to trust the committees' work, and it really shortened board meetings. Mrs. Wright also earned the respect of community leaders and members. I am not sure how many meetings in the community she attended—whether large or small groups—but the community was in full support of her efforts to improve the education of the students in the Oskaloosa School System.

As I said, Mrs. Wright inherited an administrative team that a lot of us thought was very weak. She evaluated all the administrators that were in place when she came to Oskaloosa and made her decisions about them. Mrs. Wright had told us she very rarely terminated any person; instead, she counseled them out. I don't know many details because of the confidentiality laws, but as of this writing, every administrator in the Oskaloosa School District has changed without any terminations. As of 2021 and 2022, I felt the administrators in the district were very good at what they did. Our standardized test scores were on the rise and beginning to look more acceptable.

And then COVID-19 struck the country in February 2020. In my view, some really bad decisions were made by the president of the United States and the governor of Iowa (though they were probably good with the unknowns at the time). The schools were required to stop in-person learning. Classes were online (or virtual), but attendance was not required, grades couldn't count, and the time and grades couldn't be used for class rank or graduation. So, it was a real challenge to do a good job educating young people. KIDS FIRST was really tough, but Mrs. Wright got it so every student had the opportunity for a Wi-Fi connection and a computer at their home. The good students took advantage of the available virtual learning. In the homes where education did not take a priority, the students really suffered.

When August 2020 came, Mrs. Wright and the board had agreed that the students needed to be in their seat with COVID-19 protocols, such as required face masks, no open drinking fountains, students eating lunch in their rooms, and a whole lot of disinfecting. Mrs. Wright also monitored the infection rates, and the high school and middle school were shut down a couple of times because of the positivity rate. The face mask mandate proved to be educationally unsound in the lower elementary grades. No one could see the lips of the teachers or the students, and that is extremely important when students are trying to learn to pronounce words. During the summer of 2021, Mrs. Wright and the board decided that the best education of the students takes place in a classroom, face-to-face and without masks. That is how 2021 started. Mrs. Wright left most of the other protocols in place; we were buying disinfectant by the fifty-five-gallon barrel. The community bought into the plan, and Iowa's Governor Reynolds also issued an order that mask mandates were outlawed in the state.

In late September, a judge in Georgia issued an order that Iowa's mask mandate was unconstitutional because it discriminated against the handicapped. It was funny to me that in the spring of 2020, people were saying face mask mandates were not good for handicapped students. Some members of the community came forward and spoke at board meetings about how we had to put the mask mandate back in place. It was a contentious time. A vote was taken at the board meeting in October 2021. It was six votes to leave the policy with no masks and one vote to require masks. That settled the discussion down a lot, and our students got along quite well with a very low positivity rate. The COVID pandemic and all the rules and regulations put a lot of stress on good people, mainly the superintendent and the administration. As a result, Mrs. Wright resigned as superintendent effective June 30, 2022.

After serving twenty-eight years on the Oskaloosa School Board, my last meeting was on December 14, 2021. At the start of the meeting, Joe Crookham took the floor during the public comment time and presented me with a check to the Oskaloosa School District for $28,000.00 to be used in my favorite (but neglected) department of industrial technology. It was really a surprise, and I was left very dry-mouthed. I suppose Joe thought I had spent a lot of time doing the work for kids and the community. (By the way, school board members in Iowa do not get paid.) It was quite the way to leave after twenty-eight years! I also received my second lifetime pass to all Oskaloosa school activities.

Chisel Points in the Ground

My final School Board meeting after serving 28 years. Superintendent Paula Wright presented me with a plaque.
Photo taken by Kathleen Butler.

Chapter 37

Dozer Day and Picnic Area

In 2007, fourteen acres of land owned by Bill Fallis on the east side of Green Street became available. It included a big old farmhouse and a couple of outbuildings, and the land was hilly. The recreation trail had already been put in an easement along the south side of this property. Because it was contingent, the land was acquired by the Mahaska Community Recreation Foundation for the Lacey Recreation Complex. The original plan was to make a parking lot on it or practice fields for various sports. Nothing was done with the site until MCRF decided to level it off because a wildflower trail was being planned to go from the railroad underpass toward the new stadium on Green Street, along the north side of the property. It was estimated that about 24,000 cubic yards of dirt would need to be moved to balance the dirt and have a level and usable field. The plans included the trail along the north side, an elevated two-acre site in the northwest corner, a ten-acre field to be used for parking or activities, and a two-acre flat area under the trees where the building site was located. The old house and buildings were demolished and hauled away, but the rural water and electrical services were kept.

I came up with an idea to have a Dozer Day and invite local farmers and contractors to bring their dozers to town and level the property for the proposed plan. I called fourteen local farmers and contractors and got commitments for fifteen bulldozers and

Dozer Day and Picnic Area

a farm tractor with a dirt scoop to level the field. The only provisions on the equipment were that MCRF would fill the fuel tanks at the end of the day, a good lunch would be provided, there would be lots of drinks and snacks, and everybody would have fun. A date was selected, and the equipment started to move in. One dozer came from Hedrick, Iowa, and another came from Pella. DeLong Construction from Washington, who had done a lot of construction work for MCRF, donated a GPS dozer. You put in the specifications, and then that dozer would grade to the plan. The equipment was divided into four different areas of the field, and everybody was there early to get started. It was an extremely hot day, so a lot of water and soda was required to keep all the workers cool (although most of the equipment had air-conditioned cabs).

At lunchtime, everybody shut off their machines. Tables had been set up under the large oak and maple trees at the old building site, and Grate Expectations Catering made a great meal for all to enjoy. Martha and her friends served the lunch, with pie and ice cream for dessert. Joe and Jeanie Crookham came and ate with the volunteers and thanked them for all their help in leveling the field. After all the equipment went back to work, Joe and I talked about how this was a perfect spot for lunch, under the trees with a breeze blowing. We said that a picnic area should be developed under the trees, so the athletes and their families who came to activities or tournaments at the Lacey Recreation Complex could have a place to eat and relax and practice on the field. Work continued until about 4:30 in the afternoon; the field was leveled to the file in the GPS dozer, and the fuel truck came to the site to fill the equipment. The tanks took 946 gallons of fuel, and the equipment was loaded up and taken home. It was a great community volunteer event, and everybody had fun. Most wanted to know where the next project would be! The field was seeded to a bluegrass and rye mix by the volunteers.

Chisel Points in the Ground

All the donated equipment and the operators.
Photo taken by Musco Lighting photographer.

Dozer Day and Picnic Area

Only Joe and I knew about the discussion about the picnic area; but sometime later, Don Vos of the Mahaska County Farm Bureau approached me about the possibility of constructing a picnic area under the big trees at the Fallis property. Don explained that the local Farm Bureau was looking for a community project to do, and they would help fund a project like that. I explained to him about the discussion that had taken place earlier, and Don said it had to be a nice building—not a typical shelter. We received estimates for the concrete floor, concrete areas for four picnic tables under the trees, and the construction of a frame structure (twenty-four feet by forty feet, with a fifty-year steel shingle roof with an overhang and soffit). There would also be a metal ceiling so birds could not occupy the rafters. It was a $30,000.00 project; the Mahaska County Farm Bureau paid $20,000.00, and the picnic area was completed. The facility is used for starting points at cross country meets, marathons, and other events. The facility has also been the site of birthday parties and lunch breaks under the trees. It is a great place for visitors using the recreation trail to rest and relax, since the trail is directly in front of the shelter. It was a great project mostly funded by the community of volunteers!

Chapter 38

Brent Voss: A Lifetime of Memories

Martha and I met Brent Voss when our daughter, Judy, went to Whittier Elementary School in Oskaloosa. Brent was in the same kindergarten class. At the time, the Drosts attended the Nazarene Church in town. Occasionally, the church would have a Sunday school promotion and ask the children to bring visitors. Brent lived in the northwest corner of Oskaloosa, and we lived about one and a half miles farther northwest. When the promotions would come around, Judy would say, "Daddy, we gotta stop and pick up Brent this morning for Sunday school." Our car would stop at five-year-old Brent's house, and he would get in with our kids. Brent's father was a dirt contractor. He had a crawler loader and a dump truck and worked in the area.

When Brent was a sophomore in high school, he stopped at Drost Equipment to see about getting a job. I was president of the Oskaloosa School Board at the time, so I knew of the discipline referrals on Brent Voss (the president got a copy of them all). I also knew that Brent's father, Jerry "Whitey" Voss, had died five or six years earlier; that was not easy on a fifth grader.

The city was tearing down most of the downtown buildings west of South A Street to construct the Penn Central Mall. Wicker Construction was hauling the bricks and concrete to the east side of the highway at Drost Equipment. Brent wanted the after-school job of operating our old International Harvester dozer, which we were using to push the bricks flat every day. I really enjoyed operating the dozer and using it as "therapy," but I knew Brent could use some encouragement, so he got the job. Brent was very responsible and would always report in when he went to operate the dozer, then again when he had the work done for the day. He did very good work with the dozer.

Brent had a red Corvette, and he drove it carefully. One day, he came to report to me that he was ready to go to work, and he told me, "I got detention today, but I told the vice principal that I couldn't serve detention because I have a job for Mr. Drost, so I came to work!" (What I didn't know was that Mr. Baker, the vice principal, had then suspended Brent for three days because he would not stay for detention. I didn't know the trouble Brent was in!)

Now in life, there are times when you have ten seconds or less to do what is right. I responded with, "Well, Brent, have a seat." Brent wondered what this was all about. I told him, "As of now, you are fired! You need to learn that when you do something wrong in society, your world stops until society is repaid. Serve your detention."

Brent was quite shocked, and then I asked him if he wanted me to call Mr. Baker, who had the reputation of being the school's "junkyard dog" with the way he took care of discipline. No student wanted to make a visit to Mr. Doug Baker's office. I called Mr. Baker and told him that Brent was in my office and we were discussing Brent skipping detention. I asked Mr. Baker, "If Brent comes back to school and serves his detention, will you forget that Brent skipped?" We agreed that this was a last chance, and if Brent messed up again, he would just be kicked out of school. Brent went back and served the detention, then came back and reported to me to go to work. Brent said that he had served his detention and that I could call Mr. Baker and make sure he did. I responded, "If

Chisel Points in the Ground

I ever find out that you lied to me, I will **********, because somebody who lies is of no value." Brent went to the dozer and did his work. He was quite shocked by the events.

Later on, as president of the Oskaloosa School Board, I presented the graduation diplomas to both my daughter, Judy, and Brent Voss at the same ceremony. Time passed, and it was years before we would meet again.

A few years later, Brent came to Drost Equipment and introduced me to his girlfriend, Teresa. We talked for a little while, and then they left. Several months later, Brent and Teresa came to the store in Oskaloosa again carrying a baby boy named Brant. Brent said they were going to get married. About a year later, Teresa and Brent came in with Brant and a little girl, Victoria. (Another son, Bryton, was born to them soon after.) More discussion took place, and I learned what Brent was doing for a living: concrete. Sometime later, Brent stopped in the store again, but this time by himself. He wanted to see me.

Brent told me that the day he got in trouble at school and I explained life to him was the day he decided to turn his life around. At this point, we talked longer and I found out that Brent and Teresa had bought a little place north of Dexter, Iowa. He was trying to get started in the concrete business. One Sunday afternoon, Martha and I drove north of Dexter to the Voss residence. They had a dilapidated house with an outside door that had holes in it, and it was cold outside. Brent and Teresa were not home at the time of the visit. I found out that Brent was picking up discarded pallets at various locations and cutting them into form stakes, which he would sell to contractors. He and Teresa were doing that in an old chicken house with the kids in a buggy under a heat lamp.

At that time, Martha and I decided to "adopt" Brent and his family, for whatever that might entail. So, visits were arranged. It seemed Brent had gotten away from church and the religious meetings, so we encouraged him to get his family in a church. Down the road to the south about a mile was an elderly farm couple named Allen and Marie Atherton. They were regulars at the Dexter Assembly of God Church, and they invited Brent and his family to worship. They all went together. Brent really liked the pastor and his wife, so the family got involved with the church. Brent helped with the construction of an addition to the church and even taught Sunday school. The Athertons and the Voss family bonded as Christians. Allen was older and Brent was a helper to him when he could use assistance with his livestock.

Brent succeeded in getting an SBA loan to acquire one set of concrete forms and a truck so he could pour concrete foundations in Des Moines and the surrounding area. Brent always worked hard, and it was just a short period of time before he needed another set of concrete forms for the quantity of work available to him. Brent also wanted to farm his own little piece of land, so he bought a John Deere 4020 and a six-row John Deere planter from me.

The "adoption" was accepted well by all parties involved, and the Drosts invited Brent and Teresa to go on vacation with them to the Island of Kauai in Hawaii. Brent accepted quickly, but Teresa said they could only be away from the three kids for a week. The trip was planned. It was a great vacation for all, even though Martha and I were old enough to be the Vosses' parents. Brent and Teresa got up early to watch the sunrise over the ocean, and everybody was busy all the time. The first time that folks go to Hawaii, they try to do all the activities, so being tired at the end is common. Both Brent and I like to eat. Duke's is a great place, and the Bull Shed is good for steak, lobster, and prime rib. Then there are the seafood places. It was a memorable trip for everyone, and the Vosses didn't go off and do things by themselves because they said it was fun to be with the Drosts.

For me, this relationship has been very rewarding because Brent has accepted me as a mentor. He has always been open to asking questions, and he knows that he is going to get a truthful answer, even if he doesn't agree with the advice. Our discussions are often about business or agriculture, but often our questions are of a spiritual nature. The question could go, "Okay, Boss, I have a question. I just heard this radio preacher say . . . ? What do you think the answer is? What do you believe about that issue?" I know Brent has a Bible in his truck and reads from it every day.

As time went on, I found out that Brent is not afraid to plunge into a new business venture or expansion if it makes sense financially. I told Brent early on that he had to make a business plan for each entity he had, including the farm. It had to include a detailed budget of the income and the expenses. That shows the anticipated profit, and it is a very good method of doing an ongoing evaluation of your business during the year. It took me a few years to get Brent convinced, but once he got started, it became an annual practice. Having a very good accountant is important to any business, but with the multiple businesses Brent is involved in, it becomes even more important. I got Brent connected with Jerry Uitermarkt of Schuring and Uitermarkt in Pella. Brent and Jerry really hit it off, and that is a good working relationship. I take pride in being a mentor to a very successful, kind, Christian businessman and family man like Brent.

I don't know everything Brent and Teresa are involved in, but it is known that about nine months after the Hawaii vacation, a set of twin girls was born to them. A couple of years later, there was another little girl. Brent's farming operation has increased, and all the equipment is from the Oskaloosa Van Wall location (formerly Drost Equipment). The concrete foundation business is very successful, with more than one set of concrete forms. There are several other business entities that Brent and I discuss regularly.

I have taken Brant, Brent and Teresa's eldest son, under my wing and am a mentor to him and his wife, Kassidy.

When Brant and Kassidy were going to get married, the couple asked me to marry them. I told them no because they needed to start off their marriage right with a certified preacher doing the vows. For the wedding, Dick (a former pastor of Dexter Assembly of God) and I officiated the ceremony together. Dick did the formal part of the wedding, and I gave a short talk about how to treat each other as God intended. Both Dick and I wanted to announce the new couple to the world, so we decided to do it together. As if on cue, we said, "And now for the first time in history, we introduce to you Mr. and Mrs. Brant Voss!" And all the people present thought it was perfect.

Chapter 39

Our Travels

When one acquires a liberal arts education, the goal is to have a broad background in many subjects. It is the same way with traveling to the many regions of the United States and countries around the world. It provides a broader perspective on events and makes us better global citizens. When we travel, we must get out of our comfort zones and try to live as a native, trying the different foods, experiencing their lodging, spending time with the locals, and experiencing their culture. We should live as they live and not as a rich American. When we travel, we need to come home with a new view of the diversity of God's great creation.

This is a short synopsis of the many travels Martha and I have taken around the United States and to various parts of the world.

When Martha and I got married, our honeymoon took us to Cape Girardeau, Missouri. There was no direct route to this town on the Mississippi River in southern Missouri. During this short trip, we also went to the Meramec Caverns, which was our first time in a large cave. We stayed in the Cape three nights and drove home the day before Christmas.

I took the next trip, which involved living in El Paso, Texas, at Fort Bliss. I went to Fort Bliss in August, and Martha and Judy (six weeks old at the time) moved down in January. We left at the end of March. While at Fort Bliss, it was a whole new culture with desert all around. Juárez, Mexico, was across the Rio Grande River, and the family visited a few times. A visit to the Carlsbad Caverns in New Mexico took us on a road trip through the desert country.

Our Travels

Since I flew several times in the military, I had to learn about airline schedules and maneuvering through many different airports. Among them were Kansas City and St. Louis, Missouri; El Paso, Texas; Denver, Colorado (downtown Stapleton); Albuquerque, New Mexico; San Francisco and Los Angeles, California; Honolulu, Hawaii; and SeaTac in Seattle, Washington. The longest flight was from Oakland, California, to Anchorage, Alaska, then on to Yokota, Japan, and landing at Long Biên, Vietnam, just outside Saigon.

As a Ford tractor dealer, I earned a trip to London, England. The big city was a new experience for Martha and me and provided many sites. Some of the places we visited were the Tower of London and the Crown Jewels and Buckingham Palace, where we saw the changing of the guard. We went to Windsor Castle, took a small boat ride on the Thames River, went on a visit to Westminster Abbey, and had dinner in the catacombs under the streets of London.

Ford also provided Martha and me with a trip to the Canary Islands, which took us to an area of the world where the water was not safe to drink. Also, it was the first time we experienced bus drivers on curvy mountain roads, with what Martha thought was a "wild driver." This was in a location where English was not the language, and Martha had to get along with my limited knowledge of Spanish for a week. We made friends with Dennis Owens, a Ford dealer from Decatur, Illinois, and his wife, Peggy.

I traveled to Port Elizabeth, South Africa, with a mission group from the Nazarene Church in Oskaloosa. The airplane trip included a two-day layover in London; a stop in Nairobi, Kenya (where guards came on the plane with machine guns); a stop in Johannesburg, South Africa; and then to Port Elizabeth on the southern tip of Africa. It was on this trip, which took place in December 1977, that the apartheid problem of South Africa became obvious to me. South Africa had black beaches and restaurants, white beaches and restaurants, and then colored (a brown mix of cultures) beaches and restaurants. They did not associate with any group other than their own. It was in Port Elizabeth that we saw poverty similar to that in Vietnam. People were living in cardboard box homes in the city. The group and I observed young men in the bush who had been circumcised as a ritual at about age twenty.

On the trip home, we had a two-day stop in Amsterdam in the Netherlands, then back to the United States on a KLM DC10. I was invited to the cockpit and got to view the Atlantic Ocean from there, with all the maps and flight instruments. In Amsterdam, the group visited Anne Frank's apartment, where she hid from the Nazis in World War II. We also visited the Rembrandt Museum, and a smaller group went to observe the famous red-light district, where ladies sell their bodies in storefront windows. The days also included a train ride through the countryside to Rotterdam and back.

In 1981, Martha and I went on a mission trip to Guatemala City, Guatemala, to build a dormitory on a campus. It was just following a major earthquake, and we saw the devastation. We took a bus tour to the ancient capital of Antigua in Guatemala, where we saw the natives living in makeshift tin huts or worse. On a return trip with a cruise in 2009, we saw that the same tin huts were still occupied.

Martha and I have enjoyed visiting Hawaii on many occasions because of the beautiful weather, the beautiful scenery, and the solitude of (almost) being in a foreign country but still under the Stars and Stripes. We have visited the Island of Oahu and the Pearl Harbor Museum and surrounding area, as well as the Polynesian Cultural Center, the North Shore, Diamond Head Volcano Crater, and the zoo. We visited the Big Island of Hawaii, along with Volcano National Park, the town of Kona, the city of Hilo, and the Parker Ranch. We took a helicopter flight over the active volcano. In Maui, we watched the sunrise over the Mount Haleakala Volcano Crater and took the Road to Hana. We went on a whale watch on a glass-bottomed boat out of the old whaling town of Lahaina, and we took a ride on the Sugarland Train. We also visited Molokai and took the walking hike down the sea cliffs (with forty-two switchbacks) to the Father Damien Leper Colony. We went to the wild animal park and experienced a fast food restaurant where it took two hours to get a hamburger! Kauai is the Drosts' favorite Island, where we have visited the Fern Grotto, Waimea Canyon (the Grand Canyon of the Pacific, according to Mark Twain), numerous waterfalls, the Puff the Magic Dragon mountains, the Na Pali Sea Cliffs (the tallest in the world), and Hanalei. One night, we were invited to Violeta's home for dinner with their family. Violeta was the housekeeper at the Beachboy Hotel, where we stayed for several visits. We always asked to stay in Violeta's section because she took such good care of us. We have also had dinner served to us at sunset on the beach and have had a private chef prepare us an authentic Hawaiian meal in a condo we rented.

Martha and I got acquainted with Robert and Wendy Ruwoldt at Dan and Teresa Augustine's farm north of Rose Hill. The Ruwoldts live in Horsham, Australia. We took a trip to New Zealand to visit Selby Askin (who had bought a used self-propelled forage harvester from me). We went to the South Island of New Zealand, and Selby and his wife, Janelle, took us on a tour. We flew into Christchurch, saw the mountains of New Zealand, and visited a school near the top; we visited Milford Sound and Doubtful Sound and also went to the Glow Worm Caves. The number of sheep is amazing, as well as the number of deer being raised. From New Zealand, the Drosts flew to Melbourne, Australia, and the Ruwoldts picked us up and took us on a short drive—250 miles to their farm. They took us along South Shore Drive, and we saw the beautiful coastline and the Twelve Apostle sandstone projections in the ocean. Robert grilled fresh lamb on the "barbie."

Martha and I made a second trip to Australia to visit the Ruwoldts and the Schillings. Robert Ruwoldt had brought Graeme Schilling to Iowa for Graeme's fiftieth birthday because Graeme wanted to visit the John Deere tractor factory, which I arranged. I got the group a Gold Key Tour, where the farmer follows "his" tractor that is being

Chisel Points in the Ground

built on the assembly line. All our names were posted on the screens in the factory in Waterloo, Iowa. Graeme and his wife, Pets, treated Martha and me to a week of hospitality, which included Sunday morning at their Lutheran church in Pella (Australia), lunch at Graeme's brother's huge farm, and a kangaroo hunt. The hunt takes place at night with a huge spotlight, and I shot a kangaroo in wheat stubble. Martha rode in the cab of the truck to experience it. The tour also included going to the grape growing region along the Maury River, and we took a boat tour on the river.

Then, Robert and Wendy hosted us for another week, which included seeing the koala bears in the eucalyptus trees. Martha was hugged by a huge male kangaroo, and we went for a fly-about in a neighbor's 210 Cessna airplane. We again attended their Lutheran church. The last night was a party at the local restaurant, which started early and lasted to almost midnight. It included all the neighbors and even the local John Deere dealer! To rest, Martha and I spent a week on the Island of Fiji on the way home, where we learned "Bula!" (Which means "hello.") A ferry ride from the Regent of Fiji took us to several of the small islands in the South Pacific. The ride really showcased the beauty of the region (the most beautiful in the world!). We also rented a car for one day and took a drive. We found out that Fiji is a third-world country, and the main road to the capital had a one-lane bridge. The farmers were raising sugar cane with oxen and really small tractors.

I earned several cruises to Alaska in 1996, the year after our daughter, Judy, got married. Martha asked her new son-in-law, Eugene, if they would like to go along on the cruise with his in-laws, and they agreed. The cruise started in Vancouver, British Columbia, and sailed to Ketchikan and then to Juneau, the capital of Alaska (but no roads lead there). The cruise then went on to Skagway, the home of Sergeant Preston of the Royal Canadian Mounted Police from 1950s TV fame. It included a train ride up the White Horse Pass, which was part of the gold rush of 1900. The cruise then sailed on to Glacier Bay, and we watched glaciers calve (when ice walls fall into the ocean). The cruise ended back in Vancouver.

When Judy's son, Daniel, was eight years old, the Littles invited the Drosts to go to Alaska with them on a cruise and land excursion. (No, not free!) The cruise was very similar to the first time, but after the narrow-gauge train ride up the White Horse Pass, the tour group was put on a motor coach. We spent two days traveling across the Yukon on the Trans Alaska Highway, which was built by the United States Army in 1942 to get equipment to the Aleutian Islands to keep the Japanese from invading there. The cruise lines built a motel halfway to Fairbanks, and we spent the night there. It included a cookout, a fire ring, and a show. Daniel really liked the fire, and he ate ten smores! The scenery was very beautiful, and the trip took us through North Pole, Alaska. Daniel was not impressed with Santa Claus! We spent three days in Fairbanks and rode on a paddlewheel steamer, visited Susan Butcher's sled dog farm, panned gold, and had lunch at an abandoned gold dredge. Martha and I signed up for a shore excursion, which was a plane ride north of the Arctic Circle that started at 9:00 p.m. We landed at Fort Yukon on the Yukon River and saw a fish wheel in the river. The flight back was at 11:00 at night, but since it was one of the last days of June, the sun never set. One could see the sun on the other side of the earth. Photos could be taken without the use of a flash. In Fairbanks, the tour boarded the passenger train to go to Anchorage with a stop at Denali National Park about noon. The train travels generally along rivers, but it's always in the mountains and is very picturesque. The trip into Denali in an old bus yielded sights of wildlife at a great distance, including moose and caribou. Denali stayed hidden in the clouds and fog the whole time we were there. At noon the next day, the train trip continued into Anchorage, and we spent the night there. The flight for Minneapolis was at 6:00 in the morning.

As you read in Chapter 30, we took a Panama Canal cruise with Joe and Jeanie Crookham. The trip started with a plane flight to

Chisel Points in the Ground

Atlanta, Georgia, and then a nonstop flight to San Diego. From San Diego, the ship sailed to Cabo San Lucas. Jeanie drove our Jeep on a guided tour through the arid country, with a stop at a country school where native Mexicans prepared an authentic meal for us. The tour continued down a dried-up riverbed to the ocean, where humpback whales were for the winter. We made a stop in Huatulco, Mexico, which was just a tourist trap; the shops opened for the ship and closed as it sailed. We made a stop in Guatemala to visit an old coffee plantation, where everything was done by hand, including picking the coffee beans. The drive took us through the old historic capital of Antigua. We made a stop in Costa Rica to take an aerial tram ride through the rainforest, in the top canopy of the jungle. On the trip back to the ship, alligators could be seen in the river.

You'll remember that one evening, when the ship spent the day at sea, Joe and I arranged for a marriage vow renewal ceremony by the ship's captain. The ladies were totally surprised! The ceremony was held in a lounge, with the ship's orchestra and photographer present. The ship arrived at the southern end of the Panama Canal under the Bridge of the Americas early in the morning. Coffee and Panama rolls were served on the front end of the ship. The three Miraflores locks are on the south end, and the ship was pulled through with "donkeys" (or tugs on rails). Gatun Lake connects two sets of locks, and the ship exited the canal through the Gatun Locks late in the afternoon. What an engineering and construction feat for the time!

The ship sailed to Cartagena, Colombia, where you'll remember we were met by a contractor who installed Musco lights and his wife; they were to show us Cartagena. Cartagena was first constructed in the late 1500s, with seawall forts and other defenses. The troops were kept in bunkers under the wall. New Cartagena (with tall buildings) was built after 1960 and is very modern. Our guides took us for lunch in the old district, to that restaurant where the entry door was only four feet tall for protection from invaders;

we ate native food. From Colombia, the ship sailed to Fort Lauderdale, Florida, where we departed and flew to Minneapolis. The Musco jet met us there, and Martha flew the jet by sight to Cargill at Eddyville. The pilot landed in Oskaloosa.

As I wrote about in Chapter 30, we took another cruise with the Crookhams to the Baltic Sea, which is on the north side of Europe. The cruise was earned from John Deere, and you'll remember the Crookhams upgraded the flight to first class. We flew from Minneapolis to Copenhagen, Denmark, and then on to Stockholm, Sweden. We boarded the 175-cabin ship in Stockholm after touring the city. The tour included a visit to the National Lutheran Church, which was huge but only 125 attended per week. The next stop was Helsinki, Finland. The ice-breaker ships were in the port, even though we were there in late June. The tour also took us to the Church on the Rock (another Lutheran church). It was a dome church, and John Deere brought a famous musician in to sing for the tour. The ship then sailed into St. Petersburg, Russia, and we sailed past the mothballed Russian Navy. In St. Petersburg's harbor, the program included an authentic Russian meal with beef stroganoff and other food of the culture. A white night canal tour was scheduled; we left at 10:00 at night, and the tour on the canals of St. Petersburg started at 11:00 p.m. You'll remember that the tour guide was an electrical engineer, and Joe and I sat next to her on the outer deck of the boat. We questioned the lady about capitalism, and it was obvious that the Russian people only knew about "payoffs" to accomplish anything. We could take photos without a flash until 1:00 a.m., when the tour ended. The tour also included the Hermitage, a world-famous art museum, and the Peterhof, where all the dignitaries attend meetings. We also saw Catherine the Great's summer palace. The palaces were all covered with a lot of gold, which must have been fake. The trip from the Peterhof to the harbor was on a hovercraft boat. From St. Petersburg, the ship sailed back to Stockholm, and then we took the first-class flight back to Minneapolis.

Chisel Points in the Ground

In 2018, we planned to drive Route 66 from Rolla, Missouri, to Barstow, California. We obtained some books about Route 66, which showed old motels, restaurants, diners, points of interest, and other interesting spots like state and national parks. Along the way, we visited Jason and Sarah Vos on their ranch in southern Oklahoma. We also made a stop at the Blue Hole; took a trip down the Red Canyon Road out of Flagstaff, Arizona; and made a stop at the western rim of the Grand Canyon to see the Native American glass floor, which stretches 4,000 feet over the Grand Canyon's floor. A very small cup of coffee was nearly four dollars.

We also made a stop in Oatman, Arizona, where wild donkeys roam the streets and go into the stores (this stop was recommended by a customer). The most interesting hotel along the route was Hotel Parq Central in Albuquerque, New Mexico. It was in old downtown, and it was built as a railroad hospital in 1926. The Italian-inspired exteriors with granite stairways to the building and the warm, inviting décor remain faithful to the original construction, when the hotel served as the hospital for employees of the Atchison, Topeka, and Santa Fe Railway Company. The free breakfast was on fine china and served by hotel employees like a restaurant. We ended our Route 66 adventure in Barstow, California, where the old two-lane Route 66 turns into an eight-lane freeway.

In Barstow, the car headed north to the Grand Sequoias in Yosemite National Park, then across the mountains to the valley and south to Joshua Tree National Park. The trip also took us to Death Valley, where our highest elevation was over 7,000 feet and the lowest was close to 400 feet below sea level. Martha had not seen *20 Mule Team* on television during the 1950s, but it became real to me.

Our customer, Steve Roquet, was in Henderson, Nevada, at the time working on some of his properties. Steve showed us around Henderson, which is a suburb of Las Vegas. Steve got us a deal on the king room at a real Hilton. As I was going to check out, Mark Cady, the chief justice of the Iowa Supreme Court, was in the elevator. Mark was there for a meeting, and I found out that Randy DeGeest and David Dixon of Oskaloosa were his classmates in law school and that they were still friends. Hoover Dam is close, and we went across the dam and then headed for home. Wolf Creek Pass was on our selected route; C.W. McCall wrote a song about the pass. It tells the story of a semi driver who has a few problems when he loses brakes on his eighteen-wheeler going down the hill with a load of chickens. Martha had not heard of it before, but she found the words on an iPad. It was a great three-and-a-half-week trip, but Iowa still looked like a great place to live.

 Martha and I have traveled to most parts of the United States and over lots of the world, but the most memorable trip was a family vacation to celebrate our fiftieth wedding anniversary over Christmas 2018. The whole family—including our three children with their spouses and children (for a total of fourteen souls)—flew to Honolulu, Hawaii, for a cruise stopping at five ports. The stops were at Maui, Hilo, and Kona on the Big Island, then Kauai, and then back to Honolulu. Each family selected and paid for the shore excursions at each stop; the evenings were family time on the ship. On Christmas Day, Martha and I took a tour to the summit of Mount Mauna Kea (elevation 13,700 feet) on the Big Island out of Hilo. There is a ski slope at the summit, and the road to the top was closed that morning until the ice melted, but the ice was still on the guardrails. On Christmas night, there was a family dinner in the main ship dining room (so it was dress-up). Everyone came to our cabin later, where we read the Christmas story and sang carols off the deck on our rear corner of the ship. On the last night of the cruise (a Friday), I arranged a wedding vow renewal ceremony in the chapel (Martha didn't know). All the family was there. Our butler helped get the event organized, and the ship musicians were there along with the ship photographer. The hotel manager of the ship did the ceremony. I had requested a Christian service, and the crew did a great job. Our granddaughters, Abby and Ashley, served as attendants and held the flower lei for Martha and the nut lei for me. A family dinner was planned in the main dining room, and all the family dressed up for the celebration and enjoyed a delicious meal and a cake for dessert. During the meal, the male waiters serenaded Martha and me with the song "Let Me Call You Sweetheart." On Saturday, the last day of the family's trip, we all took the bus tour of downtown Honolulu and then spent the day at the Pearl Harbor Museum. When the tour ended at Pearl Harbor, the bus dropped the family off at the mainland terminal, and Martha and I went to the interisland terminal to fly to Kauai for another two weeks. You'll read a lot more about this fiftieth anniversary trip in Chapter 41.

With all of our travels, Martha and I have a good idea of how people live in the rest of the world and how fortunate we were to be born in the 3% of the world's population that is American. Being gone just makes home a very special place to come back to live.

Chapter 40

A Reward in Our Travels

During the planting season of about 2005, the Drost Equipment store received a postcard from "a lonely farm boy" serving in the United States Army in Baghdad, Iraq. He asked if the John Deere dealer would send him and his friends a couple of caps and tee shirts to remind them of home. That is a reasonable request, and in a few days, four very nice John Deere caps and two John Deere tee shirts were on the way to the APO (Army Post Office) address given to us. Any red-blooded American would do the same.

A couple of months later, we got a postcard in the mail with a photo of Sergeant Clay Conley and his buddy all dressed in their combat gear and armed with M4 assault rifles. It was a thank-you note for the caps and shirts. Shortly after that, on a Sunday afternoon, I took some lined paper and a pen and wrote a letter to my new friend in the Green Zone of Baghdad. In the letter, I wrote that the sergeant looked old enough to have children and that I was sent to Vietnam when I had a wife and baby girl at home, so I could understand what he was going through with the separation from his family. I also wrote in the letter that Martha and I try to go to Hawaii in February and other stuff; it was a four- or five-page letter. I always end my letters to servicemen by saying I am praying for God's protective hand to guard them and give them wisdom as they perform their duties. I put it in the mail and never expected to hear any more from it.

A Reward in Our Travels

It was before Christmas. One morning, after I'd come back from visiting farmers in the country, I received a phone call—it was Sergeant Clay Conley calling from Baghdad! I was surprised, but Clay was very thankful for the letter, which he had shared with members of his platoon and others. Clay said they were sitting, looking at the Drost Equipment website (our name was on the cap), and his friends had urged him to give me a call. Clay told me that he was actually a civil engineer with the water department in Honolulu, Hawaii—he was not a farm boy, but I forgave him for lying! During the conversation on the phone, Clay told me, "I would paddle my canoe to Kauai to meet you." And the conversation continued, with Clay inviting Martha and me to come to Honolulu where he would take us on a military tour like we had never seen before. Wishes of "Merry Christmas" were exchanged, and the call ended. After a short period of time, a card arrived at the store with Clay's phone numbers and again the offer of a military tour.

When Martha and I got to Kauai in February and got organized, we called Sergeant Conley because he was to be home by February. We left a message with the date and time that we could fly to Honolulu (an eighteen-minute flight). Sergeant Conley left a message for me that the date was fine and to meet him at the taxi stand of the interisland terminal of the Honolulu airport at 9:00 a.m. Martha and I flew there, and nobody came at 9:00, or 9:05, or 9:10, or 9:15, or 9:20. I told Martha we just might spend the day in Honolulu by ourselves. At about 9:30, a small car came in fast and out jumped Clay—he was known to us from the photo he'd sent, and he had found my picture on the web. It was an immediate friendship. Our first stop was at Ford Island, which was the first site destroyed by the Japanese on December 7, 1941. At the Ford Island base entry gate, Clay flipped an ID, and we got immediate entry. Clay showed the Drosts the airport tower and the mess hall that were strafed by the Japanese. The bullet holes and marks have been preserved for visitors to see. The next stop was Pearl Harbor (not the visitor

Chisel Points in the Ground

center, but the main naval yard). Clay drove to the gate again, flipped his ID, and all the guard said was, "Would the ma'am in the rear seat please fasten her seatbelt." "Bad" Martha did not have it hooked! Then we were on the Pearl Harbor base, and nobody had asked for an ID from either me or Martha. Clay drove around like he owned the place. There was a lot of chain link fencing for the protection of boats in case of terrorism. As we passed a couple of piers with lots of submarines, Clay asked, "Do you want to tour a sub today?" All I could say was, "Well . . . yeah."

Clay parked the car, and we went to the gate in the chain link fence next to the pier, which was guarded by two Navy guys with twelve-gauge pump shotguns. Clay asked if they were giving tours of boats that day, and the guard responded that he was not sure but to go check. Now we were behind the chain link fence and heading up the pier with at least eight big submarines. When we got to the first one, Clay flipped his ID again and asked the question of the posted guard, who also had a twelve-gauge pump shotgun. Clay was overheard by an officer having a smoke, and the officer went into the submarine and came back with a young sailor to give us a tour. Still, nobody had asked me or Martha for an ID, and now we were on top of the USS *Santa Fe*. We were soon to find out that it was an on-duty, nuclear-powered attack submarine that had just come back from a six-month patrol at sea. This is a list of the parts of the submarine that were shown to us:

- We walked across the top of the sub, past the "sail" to the rear, where we looked over the rear at the rudder.

- Then we went back up front on the top to the doors that they fire missiles through.

- We saw the navigation room with all the maps and charts for the Pacific and Indian Oceans. They showed us how to narrow the view down from all the oceans to just the pier in Pearl Harbor.

- Next, we saw the work area, the enlisted men's quarters (small bunks), the officers' quarters, the enlisted mess, the kitchen, the officers' mess, the captain's table, the food cooler, the food refrigerator, the food freezer, the doctor's office with an operating room if it was needed, and the white nuclear reactor (we got within three feet but were not allowed to go through the door). This was all on the top two decks.

- The guide then took us to the torpedo room on the lower deck. When the tour got to the torpedo room, it was loaded with torpedoes down the center, along the left side of the submarine, and also along the right side. I asked what the size the torpedoes were, and the guide said they were twenty-two feet long and twenty-two inches in diameter. The three stacks all had a different explosive head on them. The guide showed us how the torpedoes were loaded in the torpedo tubes. When we asked, we were told that the torpedo fits in the tube very tightly and that they are blown out of the tube by compressed air. I was asked if I would like to experience firing the tube with an air block. Of course, the answer was, "YES!" The guide said that after the air tank was pumped up (which took some time), and when the firing button was engaged, it would be loud and the ship would rock to the side. It made a very loud noise indeed, and the submarine shook! From the rear of the boat came an officer who was upset. No, really mad! He yelled, "Who gave you permission?" It was quite tense. I think the officer thought I had just blown up half of Honolulu!

Chisel Points in the Ground

The tour was over, but we had seen all of the USS *Santa Fe*, and the guide gave each of us a challenge coin from the submarine. Then we went to Clay's car. It was a tour we'll never forget.

After Pearl Harbor, Clay took us downtown to a rooftop restaurant, and we all had lunch. We were then given a tour of the government district of Honolulu, which included the Ileana Palace of the Kings and Queens, the State Capitol, and the Justice Building. Clay took us back to the airport, where Martha and I flew back to Kauai to finish the vacation.

When Martha and I got home and went back to the adult Sunday school class, Gerald Heslinga (a World War II veteran of the South Pacific) asked if we got together with the soldier from Iraq. We told Gerald that we did, and he was interested in the activities, especially the submarine tour. He said we got a tour that a senator of the United States would get, and the senator would never get the torpedo block experience! His other comment was, "And all because of four John Deere caps and two tee shirts! What a deal!"

Sometime later, I tried to contact Sergeant Clay Conley, but it was just as if he were gone. We have never met again.

Chapter 41

Our First Fifty Years

If you've been reading up until this point, many of the stories in this chapter will be familiar. But I want to take some time to look back on the first fifty years of my marriage to Martha.

When we got home from our honeymoon, Martha and I made our home in an upstairs apartment on Fourth Avenue East in Oskaloosa. I had one semester of college to finish, and she was employed in the registrar's office at Penn College making $1.75 per hour. We combined our checking accounts, and Martha put my name on her savings account. We only had combined accounts; never did we have separate money—it was always our money.

I decided I needed a part-time job, so I went to see Leland Van Gorp at Van Gorp Implement, the local John Deere store. He hired me on the spot. When I told my dad about it and said that I was going to work in the shop, he and I went to Big Bear on the west side of Oskaloosa. I think he paid for the set of tools. As I remember, it was a hip roof toolbox, a set of wrenches, a set of sockets (no metric then), screwdrivers, pliers, and a hammer (not Snap-on). In the late thirties, Dad had worked at Roy Lytle's, the Allis-Chalmers dealer, tearing engines down. I started working at the John Deere store on January 2, 1969; it was part-time, scheduled around my classes. My first job was to rebuild a John Deere 2010 tractor with a loader that had been through a fire.

We had one vehicle to drive, and I had morning classes until graduation. Our Ford Falcon did us good. We went to the First Christian Reformed Church in the morning. We also went to church at night, a lot of times to the Good News Chapel. Alvern Boetsma was the very young preacher (and he had short sermons).

Sometime in late March, teaching positions would open up. Tri-County in Thornburg advertised for an industrial arts teacher, and I applied, was interviewed, and got offered the job. I was about ready to accept the position when Jim Carrol, the superintendent of schools at Montezuma (where I had student taught in the fall of 1968) called and told me that Dave Beck (who had been my supervisory teacher) had resigned. Montezuma wanted to hire me as their new industrial arts teacher, and I told him yes. The contract was for $6,500.00, plus $100.00 for materials to keep up my skills. We both continued working as I finished school, but the one vehicle wasn't working out real well. We went to White's bicycle shop and purchased a three-speed Schwinn men's bicycle for me to ride to work. I rode it until we moved to Montezuma. Graduation day came, and I got the little piece of paper that nobody has ever asked to see. Then we tried to figure out what to do with the Montezuma job. I worked full-time for the summer at Van Gorp Implement in the shop, doing whatever Ray and Lee wanted done. My theory of work was that if they wanted the shop floor cleaned, all I needed to know was which broom they wanted me to use. It didn't matter whether they wanted me to use a thirty-inch floor broom or a toothbrush; I was theirs from the time I punched the clock in to the time I punched it out. And I rode my bike (J.D. Fleener will verify this FACT).

We talked to Dave Beck, and he wanted to rent us their home in Montezuma. We took him up on the offer. We had zero furniture and only the kitchen utensils that Martha had. We went to Western Auto, owned by Reynold Watts. He showed us some furniture, and from a catalog we ordered a sofa and chair with an end table, a bedroom suite of a regular-sized bed and a dresser, and a kitchen table and six chairs. It all came to a little less than $1,000.00. (Martha was rich since she had $3,000.00 in a savings account.) We paid cash, and Reynold delivered it to us in Montezuma.

Chisel Points in the Ground

When we got moved to Montezuma, I taught seventh graders all the way through seniors in the junior-senior high school. Martha drove to Oskaloosa and worked at Penn through the registration time. Then she got a job at Sutherland Printing in Montezuma (on the east side of the square). We only lived three blocks away. She was a proofreader for all their printing and also helped with layout. We got involved with the kids at school and were the junior class sponsors. We videotaped the football and basketball games, both home and away, and we had an HO-scale slot race car set in an upstairs room. Some of the kids would come over to race cars. It was fun quality time in Montezuma. Sandy Van Cleave was a junior at the time, and she was also the star forward for the Montezuma Bravettes. They played in the state tournament when the girls played six-on-six basketball. She still holds the record of the most points scored in a tournament game. I got a part-time job working for Lowell Ferguson on his farm just south of Montezuma on Highway 63 on Moon Creek. I also drove to Oskaloosa on Saturdays to work at Van Gorp. We drove to Oskaloosa every Sunday to go to the First Christian Reformed Church and spend the afternoon visiting family and friends.

In mid-December 1969, the first National Draft Lottery was televised on TV. All 366 birthdays were put in a fishbowl. The order they were drawn from the bowl was the order young men would be drafted into military service. I was in the age group for the first draft lottery. Martha and I sat on the couch, intently watching our ten-inch black-and-white TV as July 17 was drawn out as number ninety-eight. We had no idea at that time how our lives would change because of the drawing.

We had been married for a year. For our first anniversary on December 20, I took Martha to a very "romantic" restaurant on I-80 north of Montezuma. It was the Dickey truck stop, but it was good and neither of us knew any different. It sure was fancier than the Lil' Duffer. We also decided it was time to have a baby, even though my draft number was certain to be called. Even with the Army as a possibility, Vietnam never entered our minds. We were just naïve kids thinking the Army would value a smart, educated Iowa farm kid and that I would get "good duty." It happened; Martha was pregnant, and no sooner had that news come, but I also got a letter from the Mahaska County Draft Board saying that my friends and neighbors had decided I should go to the Army in mid-April. A lot of things had to happen quickly, but the Draft Board gave me an extension for reporting until the latter part of May. We had decided that the teaching career was not what I wanted to do the rest of my life; it was too much inside, and I wanted to be outside. The year of teaching was still very successful and loaded with very valuable lessons.

We went to tell my folks about both pieces of news (Martha's pregnancy and that I had been drafted). My mother simply said, "And Martha can move in with us." Very simple with no hoopla. She could have the basement, and they would get the rest of the upstairs finished. I resigned my position at Montezuma so they could hire a permanent replacement, as they would've had to guarantee my job back if I didn't. Principal Badger and I decided to shorten my student classes and close the school year, so I did the grades and finished things up. We loaded all our belongings on the red Chevy dual truck with the red livestock box and took our bedroom suite and living room set to my parents' basement. The rest we stored in a warehouse north across the road from Edmundson Park.

I had to report to Fort Des Moines, and my parents took Martha and me. As was always the case as long as I was in the Army, we would say goodbye, and then Martha and I were left alone for our own goodbye kiss and embrace. Vietnam was still not a thought (being naïve helps). I was only going to basic training, and then we could be together (or so we thought). Martha went home with my folks, and I was in the Army. The next day, I was inducted and taken to Fort Leonard Wood in Missouri for basic training. My folks and Martha came to pick me up for the Fourth of July holiday, and they also brought Martha down for my graduation at the end of July 1970. The day before, I had been told when I picked up my new orders that I was a very lucky draftee; I was going to Fort Bliss in Texas for radar and missile control training. In ninety days, I would be in Germany with my family. We were making plans that as soon as our baby "Jack" could travel, it would be to Germany. (You need to read the military chapters to find out what actually happened.)

Judy was born on November 11, 1970, and I did not get home to see her until Christmas leave, when I flew home. We had Judy baptized at the First Christian Reformed Church when I was home in my Army full dress uniform. Then, we loaded up our Mercury Comet and headed out to Fort Bliss, which is in West Texas by El Paso. We lived in a little house on Hope Street on the base. The Sundays I was off and not restricted, we went to the Brigade Chapel to the Protestant service. Uncle John and Aunt Bernice stopped by to see us after their farm closing-out sale. They were moving to Phoenix to start a new life. Aunt Bernice had polio in the fifties and needed a change in climate; they were the only visitors we had.

When I was finished with Bliss and the NCO Academy, I had orders to Nam, so we rented a U-Haul trailer and put it behind our Comet. We bought lots of Gerber's at the commissary, as well as diapers and baby stuff at the post exchange (PX). We headed to Iowa. I was going to do it nonstop until a little girl raised such a ruckus that we had to get a motel in Kansas for a few hours. I had thirty days in Iowa, and then I was off to the Des Moines airport for another goodbye. The family could go to the gate in 1970, and my folks said goodbye, and then just Martha, Judy, and me. Reality struck at that moment because I had a one-way ticket and the destination was Long Biên just outside Saigon, Vietnam. There was no guarantee we would see each other again this side of Heaven, but we both trusted that God would see us through no matter what happened.

I was in the transfer station in Oakland, California, on Mother's Day 1971. I went to chapel. Shortly after, I was on a bird for Nam. In the time I was gone, I called home two times to a ham radio operator in Illinois. There was a three-minute time limit, and you had to use the terms "over" and "out." But you could hear the voices. Martha wrote to me every day, and she sent an audio tape once in a while. I wrote as often as possible (my letters were free postage). I arranged to get an R&R so I could fly home for Judy's first birthday. I had only ten days from my arrival in Honolulu until I had to be back in Honolulu, so the time was short.

We did take a three- or four-day trip by ourselves with Judy. We went past the Little Brown Church in Nashua, Iowa. It was soon time for another goodbye at the Des Moines airport, but Martha knew I would be home for Christmas because of President Nixon's order that if a soldier had been in the military for eighteen months and had been in Vietnam for six months, they would be home for Christmas if they had a job. I had a job lined up at Van Gorp Implement.

Martha had started the process of buying six acres on Route 3—now Kirby Avenue—from Durant and Betty Barnard. My dad and Martha had gone to Oskaloosa Home Loan to get a GI-guaranteed loan. The agreed price to buy was $21,000.00, and the appraised value was also $21,000.00 for six acres with a house, barn, and other outbuildings. When Martha and my dad went to sign the closing papers, Robert DeCook, Sr., was the president of Oskaloosa Home Loan. He told Martha he needed the down payment of $1.00, and Martha told him she didn't have a dollar. My dad told me that Robert DeCook took his billfold out, got a dollar, and gave it to Martha for the down payment. The payment was $158.00 per month, which was a large percentage of our income. They signed the papers. Before they left, Robert DeCook said, "Martha, you take this dollar because you need it a lot more than I do!" My dad and brothers did some work in the house for us, like taking out the chimney and removing the wall between the kitchen and dining room.

I came home on December 16, 1971, on a flight to the Ottumwa airport. There was no ceremony, band, or speeches, but there was Martha, thirteen-month-old Judy with her arms out wide, and my mom and dad. We grabbed my duffel bag and went home to our place. It was about sixty hours since I had left the combat zone in Da Nang, Vietnam. I had not spoken to a counselor or minister or nobody, and I was in our home with my family. Captain Klus, my Vietnam leader, wrote Martha a really nice letter that spoke to what she might expect from me when I got home. She thought it was a funny joke.

On January 2, 1972, I started my job at Van Gorp Implement in Oskaloosa as a mechanic. They had given me a job as a requirement of the early out, and I was paid $1.75 per hour (we got fifty hours but no time and a half for overtime). We went to Mose Van Zee (the local Nash Rambler dealer) and bought an old green Ford pickup with a white utility box on it for $400.00. That would be my wheels until 1974. Martha had done such a good job taking care of "the no money" when I was gone that she retained possession of the family checkbook and still has it today. If I need a check to pay for something, I always tell the people that it might bounce because they rarely see my name on a check.

Leland Van Gorp and Raymond VerSteegh were the owners of Van Gorp. Lee ("Whispering Jack") ran the sales and parts. Raymond was in charge of the service, so I basically worked for Ray. I know Ray had told customers they had a college graduate coming to work for them. I learned a lot about what to do and what not to do, and I also learned to always take care of the customer.

Martha and I continued going to the First Christian Reformed Church, and we knew the right answers to the religious questions. We were putting an offering in the plate every Sunday, and we were paying a little more for what they called "the budget" (but not a lot—there wasn't much to begin with). One evening, a deacon my age from the church came to our door and asked, "When are you going to start paying your share of the budget?" Little did he know that he could have brought us some food or money from the deacons, as we had so little money. But he had gotten married, joined the National Guard, and had been farming with his father. The seventies were a great boom period for agriculture, so he was living the "good life." I didn't realize that God was using this time in our lives to prepare us for what He really had in store for us.

Our son, Bob, arrived on January 21, 1973. I left work to take Martha to the hospital to have a baby, and then I went back to work. I left work three days later to take them home, and then I went back to work. Our house had been built in 1918, and until we moved in the same couple had lived there since it was built. They had no children, and they had done very little to the inside except put in electricity and a bathroom. We remodeled a room a year until every room in the house and the electric wiring, plumbing, and roof were updated. We did most of the work ourselves. Somebody asked us once why it took us twelve years to get the house fixed up. The simple answer is that we could hardly find the money for one room, and we would never have been able to do it all at once; we couldn't have made the payment. We had no extra money for anything, so we put our fifty-cent artificial Christmas tree in the kids' playpen beside the ten-inch black-and-white TV. At Christmas, all that was under the tree was clothes and necessities. We called it a night out if we could go to McDonald's or the Lil' Duffer. I tried to make a little extra money with some calves in our pasture, but it was not a lot. We had some pigs for a while, and that was lots of work. We sure had no money to go on a vacation or trip. Martha kept a big garden, and she would sell strawberries, tomatoes, and anything else we had extra of after canning and freezing our stuff. My folks raised a lot of chickens for eggs, so Mom would order 125

Chisel Points in the Ground

rooster chicks for eating. When they got to four pounds, she would have Martha and our sister-in-law, Faye, come over and she'd try to teach them how to butcher a chicken. We would get twenty chickens in our freezer.

And then in June 1974, Ford Tractor representative Dick Allen came to Van Gorp Implement and our life changed. God was indeed watching over His sparrows. Life would never be the same (you can read all about that in another chapter).

Martha has always lived as the Bible says in Ephesians 5:22–24: "Wives, submit yourselves to your own husbands as you do to the Lord. For the husband is the head of the wife as Christ is the head of the church, his body, of which he is the Savior. Now as the church submits to Christ, so also wives should submit to their husbands in everything." I know that means to obey the husband, but it puts a lot of responsibility on the husband as well to treat the wife as an equal and take care of her. Look it up—the Bible gives very clear instructions for the husband to love his wife as Christ loves the church.

Martha was always very supportive of our business, and she did a great job of raising the family and taking care of me. We lived within our means, which means if we couldn't pay for it, we didn't buy it. We went many years before we got a charge card, and then only for the convenience when we would go to a meeting or on a trip. Some places you cannot check into a motel without a charge card, no matter how much cash you have in your pocket. When we started our business, Drost Equipment paid me a salary of $1,000.00 per month, and I had a company vehicle. Martha knew that every week she would get a paycheck and she could take care of the bills. The first years of business, I didn't know how to manage a business or people, but I did know how to work. So, I spent a lot of time at the store. Martha never complained about it. If I needed her to do it, she would bring supper to the store, and we would eat together. She also came to the store every Saturday at noon and brought us lunch. Then she (or we) would clean the front end of the store and mop or vacuum the floor. Then she would clean the restrooms. She did that until December 31, 2013 (when we sold the business). After that date, she said, "They are not our toilets, and I am not cleaning them!"

We were very fortunate that the farmers came and bought things from us, and the business grew. Ford Tractor, New Idea, and Lindsay Brothers offered incentive trips to various places when you met the established sales goal or level. We earned lots of trips in the seventies and early eighties. We traveled with Ford to the Canary Islands off the west coast of Africa, to London, and to Hawaii. They would do an all-inclusive trip, so the only money needed was for gifts. The New Idea Company awarded us trips for selling Uni-Harvesters and manure spreaders, and we went to Acapulco, Mexico, and San Diego and other places with them; they were also pretty much expense-free. The Lindsay Brothers trips were different. The company paid for the plane fare and hotel, and they provided breakfast every morning, but the activities and other two meals a day were on us. We earned lots of trips from Lindsay Brothers to Hawaii, but we had so little money we couldn't rent a car or eat anything other than fast food. We got a lot of walking miles in to get around and see anything. We shared the trips with our employees over the years. When we became John Deere dealers, we got more trips. We went to Hawaii at least ten times on incentive trips. Our employees, Dean and Carol Hoksbergen, accompanied us to Maui and we took a trip to the top of Mount Haleakala to see the sunrise over the volcano. Verlan "Fish" Eveland and his new wife, Debbie, went with us to Honolulu. David DeJong and his wife, Barb, also went with us to Honolulu. I know Tom Evans and his wife, Agnes, and Glenn and Susan Knox went with Dave and Barb to Jamaica. John Schippers and his wife, Cindy, went with Dave and Barb to Ireland, while Randy and Rochelle Roose went to the Big Island of Hawaii. I know we earned cruises to the

Mexican Riviera, the Alaska Inland Waterway, and the Baltic Sea, which took us to St. Petersburg, Russia, for an overnight stay.

It was time for another baby, so on December 25, 1976, I took Martha to the hospital, and she had a baby boy just before noon. The doctors had told us that because of the heartbeat, it was a girl, so we only had girl names picked out. The baby had extra parts, so it was a boy. We asked the nurses what we should name him, and they all said, "It is Christmas . . . name him Nicholas." So that was his name. I fed Martha dinner at noon in the hospital, then went to my folks' house and had my dinner with the kids. We remodeled the upstairs into two bedrooms with closet space. Then Bob went upstairs, and Nick did too when he was old enough.

For our tenth anniversary, I took Martha away for the night so we could celebrate our marriage. We continued to do that for the rest of our married life. My folks were always happy to keep the kids. The first time we went to Ken Iburg's motel in Oskaloosa. Other times, we went to pretty fancy places (usually someplace in the state of Iowa). I usually made the reservations and the plans, but one year Martha was going to do it. She drove because I always tried to keep the destination a secret, and we went to a nice place in Fort Dodge. It had a very nice pool, so swimsuits were packed. Surprise! Our anniversary is December 20, and the pool was outdoors!

We tried to take a family vacation every summer. We went to the World's Fair in Knoxville, Tennessee, with the Ken Rexroth family and stopped at Mammoth Cave National Park in Kentucky. We also went to the Wisconsin Dells with the Bob Waal family, and we rode the "ducks" in the lake. I got my head stuck in the drain in the waterslide, and it was funny to everybody but me. We also drove to Yellowstone National Park. We left on Monday morning and were back Saturday evening. That was when we thought it was wrong (morally opposed to God) to travel on Sundays. The kids used little bottles for the restroom, so we didn't have to stop. There was never enough money to eat any place other than fast food.

We won enough trips from Lindsay Brothers that we took the kids to Honolulu, Hawaii, with us twice. We also took Martha's mother, Wilma Vernooy, along with us. Like I said, the plane tickets, hotel, and breakfast were included, but from there we were on our own. We always had fun, but it sure wasn't from the expensive activities that we did. Our kids asked us a few times about why we couldn't do the activities and sports like their friends' families. I simply told them what my dad had told us: "Don't look at what you see on the outside. Look at what you can't see like bills, credit card debt, liens, and mortgages." It seemed to work until they got older, when Nick started saying when we told them we were out of money, "Yeah, okay, but you know where to get it!" I might have, but I didn't go get it.

Martha was driving by our store one summer, taking her mother to Ottumwa to shop, when Mrs. Vernooy remarked, "I sure hope that you and Carl amount to something someday. You drive the oldest car of any of my kids, and you live in the oldest house." I asked Martha how she responded, and she told me that she was speechless and had no response. It happened to be the summer before we started building our new home. We paid the workers every Friday morning, and we never went to the bank and borrowed any money. We had one of the finest John Deere stores in North America, but the "poor soul" just had no clue. We had people who actually went to the courthouse to check the mortgage records to find out how large our mortgage was. I am sure they were disappointed that they couldn't find out how much the house cost or how much we owed.

When the kids were in high school, I insisted that mechanical drafting was in the class schedule for them all, including Judy. The class teaches students to see an image in three dimensions. Bob and Nick took architectural drafting, and they were given the task of drawing the plans for our new home. The plans would be coming along really good, and then the boys would decide to change them to the way they would like the house to look. The requirements were not that extensive, but the roof had to be designed with no valleys. It had to be a walk-out basement, and there needed to be an art room upstairs with indirect light. I wanted an office, and two bedrooms would be enough. When it appeared there would be enough money in the bank to pay for the house, I searched for an architect that Martha could work with. Mike Stodala from Des Moines was hired. He was working on a guaranteed maximum fee. After the original planning, he had intended to turn it over to a draftsman, but he was having so much fun with our home that he did all the plans and specifications himself (and he did it with a pencil instead of a computer program!). We were planning on having the house face toward the road. Mike told us that in this part of Iowa, we should have the house face the southeast at a six-degree angle to get the most good out of the sun in the winter and have the least effect of the sun during the summer. The house is set at six degrees, and it faces the country instead of the road.

When we finally had enough money to pay for the house and were ready to dig the hole, Calvin Rexroth was asked to come and help set the top height of the foundation. He had built hundreds of homes, and the homes always looked good. So, Calvin told the contractor what the top height of the foundation wall should be. It is several feet above the country road in front. Voss Concrete from Dexter did all the footing and foundation work. (Remember, Brent Voss is one of the "adopted" young people who have accepted my tutelage over the years. There's more about that story in another chapter.) The only contracts written on the whole house were for the elevator and the laying of the bricks. When the framing was to start, I took a week off work. I had invited my brothers, Dick and Tom; my son, Nick; and my nephew, Jackson, to come and help frame the house. Hawkeye Lumber brought us piles of wood, and the whole house was framed in a week. The black paper was on the roof by Saturday night, and it never sprinkled on the framing.

The house was all closed in with paper over the windows. All the rest of the house was done by time and material. Each contractor was told to bring their weekly bill on Friday morning. Martha would be down at 9:00 in the morning to pay everybody for their week's work. There was money in the house savings fund to pay for the house. It is hard to beat building with cash, and there certainly is satisfaction in building a house and having saved over several years to get it done. It took a year to the day to complete the house, and the move from our original home to the new house took place on day 366.

We had built a house, but only love can make it a home. It was really nice to have a new house, but with all the new appliances, furniture, and decorations, there is a real danger of being so protective that people won't feel comfortable and won't come. Martha and I had a long discussion that it would be up to us if the grandchildren came to our home or not. If all our responses were "NO," or "DON'T DO THAT," or "DON'T TOUCH THAT," the grandchildren would not want to come, and we did not want that. Our home was for everybody to enjoy, and the grandkids came and ate and played games and we all had a great time. We had one requirement: The kids could not drink in the living rooms out of a glass until they could handle it, but they could use sippy cups. It was strange to have a ten-year-old choose a sippy cup because they didn't want to spill. We had a basement full of games, including a pool table that I traded for a lawn mower, plus a ping pong table and an air hockey table that we earned for selling stuff. There were also lots of ride-on toys. The room is large enough to play big.

After a few years of living in the house, Martha had gathered up enough money to finish up the basement. A full kitchen was included, with a dish washer, a range refrigerator, and a full set of cupboards. A full set of dishes and silverware was also included. We could have a party and not have to transport dishes to the basement. Mom Drost always had the Drost family dinners at her home. When she got up in years, Martha took over the responsibility for the Thanksgiving dinner. It is held in the basement, and everybody on the Drost side is invited to be there for noon dinner. It has worked out well with the large room to set up tables to serve and eat at. After dinner, the tables and chairs are put away, and the kids have room to play. If the weather permits, the playground is just outside the door, with a fenced concrete basketball court, swings, slide, and wooden train for all to enjoy. And the older folk can have room for separate discussions and table games. It works well for other parties, such as Sunday school class parties and even an all-church party when we attended the Pella Nazarene Church.

Mom Drost came to her last Drost Thanksgiving in 2010. I went and picked her up because she wouldn't drive. She always wanted to be the first at the party, and she was told that when she wanted to go home, she just had to tell us and home she would go. We had the usual Thanksgiving dinner. With Mom, there had to be turkey, mashed potatoes and gravy, and a little cranberry something. There is always a mountain of food because Jim brings the turkey and ham; Martha fixes the potatoes, hot rolls, and the drinks; and then everybody else brings what they want to fill in. (And then there is dessert.) Mom was always a great cook and a good eater, so she always enjoyed the food. It was a beautiful afternoon, and the kids were outside playing. The adults were having a great time, and Mom Drost was really enjoying herself. Mid-afternoon, I went and brought up the Drost Railway train—which is a steam engine built on a lawn mower with five barrel cars behind it—to give rides to the kids. The train would pull up on the concrete outside the east basement door, then we'd take the train tour around the yard and go back for more. Mom Drost was out enjoying it all. The neighbor kids were even out, and they got a ride as well.

The family started to leave, and Mom was still there. She had been asked several times if she wanted to go home, and her answer was that she was having a lot of fun. After everybody else had left, she said she was ready to go, so I loaded her up and headed to her house. On the short two-mile trip, she told me, "I don't think I could stand another war. First Dad in World War II, then you in Vietnam, and now Captain Dan flying helicopters in Afghanistan." Then she said, "You are going to make such a great grandpa. I could just tell by the way you took care of all the little kids. You never knew my dad, and Grandpa Drost was just nothing but mean, so you showed me you can do it." And that was the last conversation I had with Mom. On Saturday evening, she had a stroke, and she died in the hospital in Des Moines on Tuesday morning.

You'll recall that on December 20, 2018, Martha and I celebrated our fiftieth wedding anniversary with a trip to Hawaii with the whole family (fourteen people total). The whole family flew to Hawaii on the day of our anniversary, which was a Thursday. We went to Honolulu by way of Phoenix on American Airlines, and we had a lei greeting at the airport before going to the Embassy Suites on Waikiki. We arrived late in the afternoon. On Saturday at noon, we were transferred to the ship, which was called *The Pride of America*. It was a ship of the Norwegian Cruise Lines. Martha and I had gotten a suite on the rear corner of the ship. It was large, with a normal room with a pull-out couch, another bedroom with a regular bed, and then our bedroom, which had a king bed in it. It also included an L-shaped deck that our whole family could be on at one time. Our room was decorated with a cake and "HAPPY ANNIVERSARY" spelled out in silver letters over the deck door. There were also balloons hanging from the ceiling, and above our bed was an eight-foot heart made of six-inch bells cut from paper. It was beautiful. The suite also came with bowls of fruit and a butler named Gulsen. She told us her job was to pamper us, and she would get us whatever we wanted.

We were supposed to sail on Saturday evening, but due to some maintenance, we sailed on Sunday evening and arrived in Maui on Monday morning. Our son, Bob, and his family had asked us to go to the Brazilian restaurant on the ship on Sunday evening, so we were eating as the ship departed. The Aloha Tower in the bay was lit up in red and green colors, and it looked very festive for the Christmas season. On Maui, Martha and I took a cab tour from the ship. The cabby took us to a botanical garden with very beautiful flowers, and then on to the old seaport town of Lahaina. It has a huge banyan tree and an old narrow-gauge sugar plantation train. The cabby took us to the beach resort, with all the hotels and golf courses. It is very beautiful. He took us back to the ship, and it was Christmas Eve.

The ship was decorated very beautifully for Christmas. The schedule showed a veterans appreciation event in the wine bar, so Martha and I went. There was only one other vet there, but they had another cake and champagne. All three of us preferred and drank ginger ale, and it was a nice event. On Christmas morning, we were at Hilo on the Big Island. Martha and I took a shore excursion to the top of the inactive volcano Mauna Kea, with an elevation of 13,742 feet. The tour was in a four-wheel-drive, twelve-passenger van. It stopped first at Rainbow Falls, which was very pretty. The driver took us to the summit of Mauna Kea. It was twenty-six degrees in Hawaii on Christmas Day. I was expecting snow, but we only found ice from a nighttime rain. We also got to see one of the huge telescopes on the top.

That night, the whole family dressed up and went to the fancy restaurant on the ship for our Christmas dinner. Everybody could order what they wanted, and the price was all included in the fare. After dinner, everybody came to our suite, and Martha read the Christmas story in the Bible from the shepherd's perspective. Then we all sang "Silent Night" as the ship cruised toward Kona, the next stop. Martha also led us all in playing Christmas bingo. The prizes were my extra change, but it was a fun party away from home.

The next morning in Kona on the Big Island, we had scheduled a submarine trip on the *Atlantis* to the see the reef, fish, and ocean bottom. There is no pier for the cruise ship to tie up to, so they lowered some of the lifeboats and used them to tender the passengers to shore; it was a unique experience. The submarine held about forty people and went down to a maximum depth of 107 feet. It was a new experience, and we saw the fish in a totally different perspective because at that depth the colors are not nearly as pronounced. When we got to shore, we ate lunch and walked around Kona and visited the old church from Captain Cook's time. We had been to Kona thirty-five years ago with Glen and Betty Veldhuizen, when they celebrated their twenty-fifth wedding anniversary. We saw the King Kamehameha Hotel, where we'd stayed with them. We kept our grandkids, Ashley, Taylor, and Abby, overnight and went to the magic show in the theater. It was good, and the kids really enjoyed it. I had told our butler, Gulsen, that we were having our grandkids for the night and asked if she could bring us extra fruit. She did, and we had two bowls of fruit, a big plate of grapes, and a plate of chocolate chip cookies that we all enjoyed.

On Thursday morning, we arrived at Nawiliwili Harbor on Kauai. (Kauai is where Martha and I always go.) We had hired a small bus to show our family the Kauai we know. The kids had designed and printed a blue tee shirt for each of us that said, "Carl and Martha's Anniversary Cruise—50 Years of Smooth Sailing." There was also a ship printed on it. Fourteen people with the same blue shirts drew attention. Our driver was John, and I told him he was a Drost for the day. He was a nice man and did a very good job of taking us to places on our itinerary. He told us about the island for the duration. The tour included going to the Outrigger Waipouli, where we always stay so our family could meet the staff and see the pool and the area of our room (to see how much we suffer there).

The Waimea Canyon is a must-see. Mark Twain called it the Grand Canyon of the Pacific. The elevation changes from sea level to about 4,000 feet in about forty minutes. At the bottom of the canyon is the town of Waimea, where Captain Cook first landed in the islands. We ate lunch at Chicken in a Barrel, and everybody enjoyed their order. The next stop was the Kauai Coffee Plantation and Visitor's Center. They have at least fifty different coffees that one can sample. They explain how coffee is grown and processed, and you are given the opportunity to buy lots of stuff.

John then took us to Poipu and Spouting Horn, which is a hole in the lava on the shore. The waves force water up through the hole, which makes a spout that is very unique when the waves are rolling. Poipu is the touristy section of Kauai. The sun shines there more, and it is a great place to snorkel and hang out. Brennecke's is a world-famous beach restaurant in Poipu, but we did not stop there. Then we were taken back to the ship by way of the eucalyptus tree tunnel, which covers about a mile of the road. It was planted a long time ago to keep oxen cool when they pulled sugar cane carts.

We got back to the ship in time to get changed to go to the luau at the Kilohana Plantation. We all had reserved seating, so we were all next to the stage. The food was good, and Martha and our daughter-in-law, Jennie, went up onstage and did the hula (wiggle a little to the left and a little to the right). Our grandson, Daniel, stayed with us after the luau and we enjoyed the fruit. Friday was supposed to be on Kauai, but it had stormed during the night, so the shore excursions were canceled; everybody did what they could. Daniel came and found Grandpa, and we spent the day at shuffleboard and dinking around. The ship sailed around 2:00 in the afternoon to the north side of Kauai to see the Na Pali Cliffs, which are 4,500-foot-tall sea cliffs. Since there is no road there, the only way to see them is from the ocean, and they are beautiful.

The last family activity planned was at 6:30 on Friday evening. You'll remember that it was a marriage vow renewal ceremony that everybody knew about except Martha (including the family, the butler, Gulsen, the ship activity director, and others). All Martha knew was that we had to dress up for a family dinner at 6:30 in the fancy dining room. I took Martha, both of us dressed up, to the dining room by way of the chapel. When we went by the chapel sign, Martha started singing "Chapel of Love," but she had no clue what was just around the corner.

The ship's officer was all dressed up with fancy leis, the butler was in her uniform, and the ship's cruise director was in her snow-white uniform. All the family was seated in the chapel, all dressed up. Martha was really shocked, as the aisle had rose pedals all the way up and flower bouquets. I asked if she would marry me again, and she said yes. The ship's officer did Christian vows of renewal in Hawaiian style, and we exchanged leis instead of rings. It was special with all the family present. It was the highlight of our trip. After the ceremony, we went to the fancy dining room for dinner all together. After our meal, Gulsen had arranged for another anniversary cake. The crew brought fourteen clean plates and forks. We cut the cake, and then four male servers came over and serenaded our table with "Let Me Call You Sweetheart." The whole restaurant got quiet, and they all applauded and enjoyed the serenade. And the cake was good! I think Daniel got four pieces.

It was a memorable night, but we had to have our packed bags in the hall before we went to bed. On Saturday morning, all fourteen of us left the ship, claimed our bags, and loaded on a bus. The driver gave us a tour of Punchbowl National Cemetery (the Arlington of the Pacific), which is located in a volcano crater above Honolulu. The tour then continued through downtown Honolulu, past the State Capitol (which is a building surrounded by water), the Iliani Palace (which is where the last monarch lived), and the old churches and other attractions before we arrived at Pearl Harbor. Pearl Harbor closes at 4:00, so we had the rest of the day to tour the USS *Missouri* on Ford Island. We had to take a shuttle to get there, and we had lunch there. The USS *Arizona* Memorial includes a video about the events leading to and the day of the attack on December 7, 1941. It also gives a little history of the rest of the war in the

Pacific. Then it is a boat ride around the actual USS *Arizona* Memorial. The memorial was closed because of structural issues, and we did not disembark. The museum takes a long time to go through with all the signs to read and the interactive displays.

The bus left around 4:00, and we went to the international airport in Honolulu and dropped twelve family members off at the American Airlines mainland terminal. Then the bus took Martha and me to the interisland terminal. The family flew back to Iowa, and we flew to Lihue Airport on Kauai and checked into the Outrigger Waipouli in Kapa'a for about two more weeks.

Chapter 42

Troubled Young People

In 2003, Martha and I were attending the Nazarene Church in Pella. Martha went to the restroom at church one day when a young lady, Jennifer, came up to her. We knew her name, but we didn't really know who Jennifer was. She told Martha that she and her husband, Dustin, had been married for six months and were ready to "split the sheets" (divorce). Her mother had told her maybe they should talk to Carl and Martha for advice and help, since they had no money for a counselor. Martha told me about it on the way home, and I asked, "So what did you tell her?" Her answer was, "I said I would tell you."

How can you tell somebody no when they are broke and need help? We told Jennifer we would see what we could do for them.

The following Sunday evening after church, we met the couple at Arby's in Pella to talk and get acquainted. It was obvious that living together before they got married hadn't made a lot of difference, and they sure didn't know what caring for each other meant or showing love for one another. Jennifer had been raised in the church, but I wondered if Christ meant a lot to them. It has always been said that absence makes the heart grow fonder, and they had never really been separated for a period of time like Martha and I had when I was in the Army and then in Vietnam. We told them we had never been involved with helping people with their marriages, but if they wanted to meet regularly, we were willing to try.

At the time, Jennifer was working as a bartender on the south side of Pella, and Dustin was driving semitrucks all over the United

States. We agreed to meet on Sunday evenings after church, and we found out early in the talks that they were being very honest with us, which made our task easier. Martha and I told them that whatever they told us would stay between us and that their parents or relatives would never hear it from us, which made it easier for them to tell us lots of stuff. (We asked and received their blessing to include this chapter in this book.)

We told Jennifer and Dustin that we had a strong faith in our Lord and Savior Jesus Christ and that we knew Jesus had carried us through the tough times. We shared with them our example of getting married when we had no money, me getting drafted while Martha was pregnant, and then getting sent to Vietnam with a little daughter at home. We had nothing when I got home, but we never doubted Jesus' love for us and the promise that He would take care of us. Jesus promises that He will be with us always, and that means through everything. They needed to get their relationship right with Jesus. We also asked about their friends, and we found out that their friends were having a bad influence on them. Some of these friends were daring Jennifer and Dustin to try things, and some of the parties they were attending were awful. We told them they needed to totally redo their social life and get better friends. The best part of their relationship was that they did love and care for each other, but they really needed to show it and express appreciation for each other.

One of the other major problems is that they had no money, and they had the "sins" of the past to deal with. Judgments were on file against both of them, and as soon as either of them got a better job, a creditor would file and have their paycheck garnished for the maximum allowable, so they would actually have less cash. We advised them to get rid of the credit cards and get out of the 22% interest as soon as possible. They set up payment plans at the credit bureau and the hospital. When it really got hard, Martha and I would loan them some money, and we would keep track of the amount, but we never counted on getting anything back. Again, we were thankful God had blessed our lives to the point that we could maybe influence Jennifer and Dustin's lives, so they could see the benefits of a relationship with Jesus Christ.

One particular evening, we were at the Pizza Hut in Pella, and Jennifer and Dustin told us some of the things that had happened that week and the way they had each reacted. That is the way we started each session, with them telling us about the week or the time period since we'd last met. It was an absolutely ridiculous report; they had really acted like kindergarteners! I'd had my fill and told them they were acting like little kids. If we weren't in Pizza Hut and they weren't supposed to be adults, I would have spanked them for acting that way to each other. They didn't know what to say, but I could tell they already knew they had messed it up.

That sets the stage for where Jennifer and Dustin came from. On May 10, my phone rang, and it was Jennifer. "Carl, do you know what day it is?" she asked. "No," I responded. Jennifer told me it was their first anniversary, and they were still together. But Dustin had lost his job driving trucks because he'd been caught too many times with a suspended license. I offered him a very dirty job of cleaning up farm equipment at our store. Jennifer had to drive him to work and pick him up, and he certainly couldn't drive any company vehicles with no license.

Dustin told me one night that he had to go to court in Jasper County. I asked what for, and he said it was for driving several times with a suspended license. We talked about it, and the next day, I called my attorney to ask if he would call the county attorney to see if Dustin could plead to something different. The answer from Jasper County was, "This man is going to jail!"

I found out when the case was, and I went to the hearing. There must have been ten people on trial that day, all for driving with suspended licenses. The county attorney took his time presenting the case on each one, and then it was Dustin's turn. The attorney showed a rap sheet of three full pages on record for Dustin, who had no attorney or former employers or family members there except Jennifer. When it was time for sentencing, every person there got ten days in jail. Then it was Dustin's time. The judge read the charge and asked if there was anybody to speak for Dustin. I raised my hand, and the judge recognized me. I told the judge who I was and that we owned Drost Equipment, where Dustin was employed. I told the judge that Dustin needed a second chance and that I'd had a heart-to-heart talk with him. I wanted to be part of the solution to get Dustin to be a productive citizen. The judge ordered that Dustin serve forty-eight hours. Dustin and Jennifer had it all figured out that if he got jail time, he would be able to serve it over the weekend. When everybody was sentenced, the judge ordered the bailiff to take all of them into custody, so they handcuffed Dustin and hauled him to jail. Jennifer and I went to the jail and filed for work release, but that did not take effect until the next day, so he would spend nineteen hours in jail before Jennifer could pick him up to bring him to work. These were the rules: No stopping between the jail and the worksite for anything, including fuel or food. His forty-eight hours expired at 11:00 on his second day. Dustin will tell you that when the jail cell door slammed shut, he decided he must do something with his life.

Dustin continued working at Drost Equipment doing menial tasks. He couldn't drive company vehicles because we couldn't get him insured. The good news is Dustin did get his driver's license back, and he got off the state insurance and was a very good employee. Everybody liked him because he always had a smile on his face. Our semitruck driver moved on, and Drost Equipment needed a new driver. I talked to Dustin and asked, "If you could have any job at the store, what would it be?" Dustin responded, "Drive the semi, but I know that won't happen."

I called my insurance company and asked the underwriter if he would insure Dustin to drive our semi. The underwriter asked if I was feeling okay with the record Dustin had. I told him I was okay and to look at Dustin's record; there were no speeding tickets, no moving violations, and no reckless driving. All the charges were for overweight violations on the truck or negligence for not taking care of the fines. Dustn's former employer had not helped on anything. I told the underwriter that I would put Dustin on a very short chain; one violation, and he would be back to washing dirty manure spreaders. But I believed Dustin deserved a second chance! The underwriter said that if I believed that much in the young man, he would go along with the second chance.

What a story of mixed-up young lives, but there is great news! Jennifer and Dustin worked at their relationship, changed almost all of their friends, got into a relationship with Jesus Christ, got into small groups at a different church, and had two very energetic young boys (like Dustin was at their age). They have paid us back every cent they ever borrowed from us. Dustin drove for us until we sold the company plus a year after that without a single violation. Every May 10, I get a call from Jennifer or both of them, wanting to know if I know what day it is. Our joke now is that Martha and I never expected them to see their first anniversary, let alone their twentieth. We still go out to eat occasionally, but we don't go to Arby's and we can talk about successes in their relationship.

I got a call from Dustin a few years ago where he told me that on his weekly trip to New York, he had heard Dave Ramsey speak about financial money management, and he had been listening to him daily. I had taught the Dave Ramsey financial course to a high school Sunday school class, so I knew and respected Ramsey's teaching. Dustin told me about what he had heard, and he had told Jennifer about it too. Now they were starting Ramsey's way. The big thing when you follow these teachings is to start with the largest bill with the highest interest rate and put all available money toward it. When it is paid off, you go to the next one until all the bills are paid. The other plan Ramsey has is to make a budget and put the money for each item in an envelope. Don't spend more than what is in the envelope. Then anything left over is put against the largest bill. You don't spend more than you take in.

Now, Dustin is driving over the road to New York and back every week. Jennifer is working two jobs at a daycare in Lynnville and at a barbecue place one night a week. They are not spending more than they are bringing home. The great news is they are debt free, have an emergency fund, and can go on dates and enjoy themselves! They especially enjoy spending the full ten days at the Iowa State Fair. We are so proud of Dustin and Jennifer and are amazed to see how lives can be changed when Jesus Christ enters in and they attempt to follow Him. We are convinced they know what LOVE is in their lives!

Chapter 43

Sunday Scholars

I don't know how many times I have read in church bulletins or newsletters: "Wanted: Sunday school teacher for third grade or high school." I have read them and said, "Oh, yeah." Such was the announcement in the Sunday bulletin and monthly newsletter of the First Presbyterian Church one morning in Oskaloosa.

Now, on my spiritual journey, I have tried to be responsive to the Holy Spirit in the things I do, but especially if I KNOW God is speaking to me! I woke up one morning in May or June of 2011, and I knew I was supposed to teach the high school Sunday school class. Now, one might ask how I knew . . . but it was as clear as a sunshiny day! That evening over supper, I said to Martha, "I think I am supposed to teach that high school Sunday school class." She immediately responded with, "I think you should too. You would be good at it."

Now, my degree is in secondary education, but I was sixty-five years old. The young generation was different. Would they like me? Still, I knew I was supposed to teach the class. I went to church the very next Sunday morning. Before church, Joan Boer, the Christian education director, sat behind us. She asked if she and I could have coffee and cookies together at coffee time after church, and I simply said, "Sure." We got our coffee and cookies and sat and spoke about small things. Then Joan said, "You know, we are looking for a high school Sunday school teacher We had the teens vote, and it was unanimous that they wanted you. The preacher was kinda upset because he didn't get a vote! Would you pray about teaching the class?" I told her, "NO!" She looked at me almost in shock when I told her, "I won't pray about it because I already know I am supposed to teach it." I told her the story and none of us could believe it.

The class started at the end of August. It was a fairly large group, with most of them being sophomores at Oskaloosa High. It took a little while for them to get used to me (an old guy), and I had to learn all about the new generation. I really didn't care if they were Millennials or Generation X, Y, or Z. The good part about the class was that Amy McGriff headed a youth program called Zero Gravity, and they met every Sunday evening for social time. So, I tried to teach a class centered on the Bible and how it applied to the life we live. I searched for appropriate material. It was difficult, but the group seemed to like what I found. Time marched on, and I found Dave Ramsey's financial material for teens. I ordered the video series and workbooks for the group. I paid for all of the material because God had blessed Martha and me so much that we could afford it. It really made it much easier to get the material approved by the Christian Education Committee and the Church Session. The teens really went after the financial information, which was all Bible-based. I was very honest with the group that I didn't agree with everything he said. (I think that really gave me credibility.) I told them that Martha and I had credit cards, but we had never paid interest on any of them. If you had one, you had to be responsible. (Ramsey said to cut them all up and never use one.) He also said that you should never take out a loan, and I had to tell the group that I would never have succeeded in business if I had not borrowed money. One of the most important lessons was that you should never spend more than you make or bring in. We had as many as twenty-seven students present on a Sunday morning. My two grandsons who do not attend church came to almost all the sessions, and there were even some parents who came to learn.

I searched for a long time for a Bible-based book about common issues all teens face in school and society. A book was finally found:

Critical Issues, Absolute Answers. It had twelve chapters with eighty-five different lessons. We used one of the lessons each week; the subjects were emotions, teen pregnancy and premarital sex, suicide, homosexuality, and the list goes on. I had to be very honest with what the Bible says about the issues, but each student had a book with all the Scriptures in it. The teens really got into that book, and each one of them got a copy that Martha and I paid for. We felt it was important for each to have. We also gave a copy to each of our grandchildren and passed out or recommended the book to other teen leaders. Our class in 2014 had settled in at about eleven or twelve young people, but they would never stay to attend church.

An adult Sunday school class was studying a book titled *Why Young People Leave the Church*, and they asked me if they could come on a Sunday and interview the class and ask appropriate questions. I told my class ahead of time and told them to be honest with the adults or it would be meaningless. They needed to speak up if they wanted anything to change around the church. The adults came one Sunday, and the discussion was very good. The adults asked if they could come back the next week, and the teens agreed. I again told them to be brutally honest. When the adults came back, the first question out of their mouths was, "We know you come to Sunday school regularly, but it is rare that you stay for church. Why do you come to Sunday school and then leave?"

The group was really interesting. If it was a difficult question, they would think about an answer, and then they would look around the room and as if silently deciding who would answer. But this time they all pointed directly at me. The next question was, "Why?" Again, the group looked around, and finally one of them spoke: "Carl will let us ask any question. He will be nonjudgmental with his answer, and he will not be critical of us. The answer will be what the Bible says, then he will tell us what he believes, and then he lives what he tells us." I have never been so proud of a group of young people! They were telling adults that most adults think teens like them need to be as spiritually mature as a fifty- or sixty-year-old person; they forget what they were like as teens. Most adults are very judgmental of teens and make comments like, "Did you see them on the phone in church?" or, "Those young people talk all the time," or, "Did you see how short that skirt was and how holey those jeans were?"

Toward the end of May 2014, I told the class that the following Sunday was graduation from Oskaloosa High School, and I would be giving each of them their diploma. They wondered why, and I told them that as president of the School Board, it was my honor. I also told them I knew it was not a very popular thing for high school graduates to come to Sunday school, and they all agreed. Then I said that the Sunday morning after graduation, I would be at McDonald's at 9:00 with money on the table to buy them a drink or breakfast—just whatever they wanted. (And again, I was able to do it with the blessings that God had given Martha and me.) They were quite shocked and had to ask if I was serious. Would I really? I assured them that I would be there. All summer long, I had the class at McDonald's. At least one came each time, and the most was eleven. We would be overheard by the adults, and some of them asked if they could come and join us, but none ever did! I never asked the Church Session whether we could go to McDonald's (their answer wouldn't have mattered). But on Sunday morning, when I would get to church from McDonald's, several people would ask how many came and what we talked about. I would give them the number, but my answer to what we talked about was always the same: "Life issues."

The last Sunday before they all went off to college, we were at McDonald's, and they decided their group name would be the Sunday Scholars! The church service afterward was to be Camp Sunday, where all the children who had been to Camp Wyoming were recognized. When that was ending, three of the teen group went up on the platform. I could hardly believe my ears, "Would

Chisel Points in the Ground

Carl please come up here?" They said I had been their teacher in Sunday school for the last three years, that we had spent the summer at McDonald's, and that they were now going off to college. They said they got together and thought about the best lesson I'd taught them (out of approximately 150 lessons). Then they taught the lesson to the whole church that morning.

The lesson began at the whiteboard, where a stick man was drawn hanging underneath a parachute. The chute was divided into panels. The story goes that an American pilot was shot down over North Vietnam, and he parachuted down and was captured by the North Vietnamese Army. He spent seven years in the Hanoi Hilton as a POW. His name was Charles Plumb. When Charlie got released from Hanoi and was having dinner in a nice restaurant in Kansas City, a young man came up and asked, "Are you Plumb?"

"Yes."

"Charles J. Plumb?"

"Yes."

"And you flew off the *Kitty Hawk* and got shot down?"

"Yes, why do you ask?"

The man replied that he had packed Charlie's parachute, and he wanted to know if all the panels had been in place, if it had opened properly, and all about it! When Charlie tells the story, he goes on to say that up until that night, the parachute packers were in the belly of the aircraft carrier. Nobody hardly noticed them, but that day when he needed his parachute, that insignificant young man became very important. In Charlie's book, *I'm No Hero*, his point is that as we go through life, we are supported by a parachute that has been packed—one panel by your mom, another by your dad, another by your Sunday school teacher, your Scoutmaster, your pastor, and the list goes on. It creates a parachute that God puts together for each person to support us as we go through life. I trust that I put a panel or two in each of their parachutes, for their teen years and adult lives. Then the teens gave me a parachute with a soldier hanging underneath, a set of dog tags with scripture on them, an ink pen, and a notebook. I was so honored, and the audience was in awe that THOSE TEENS would do such a nice thing. The teens also asked if I would meet them at McDonald's when they came home on break, and for sure I would and did. Martha and I made it a practice to visit each one on their campus and see the college and where they lived, then take them out to dinner wherever they chose. It was a wonderful experience. We also had a Christmas dinner each year at our house, and they picked the menu: Grandma's corn, Grandma's beans, Grandma's hot rolls (our grandkids had told the group about these when they went with me to Sunday school), and Martha's mashed potatoes. Martha could pick the meat, but it was pie for dessert. What a party it was!

Now, years later, we still get together. Our favorite place has become Samari's Sushi and Hibachi Grill at Jordan Creek in West Des Moines. We always pray before we eat. One of the waiters asked Martha if I was a preacher, and she got the chance to tell him about the group. Another time, we were at the restaurant, and Claire Carmichael had come back that day from Brazil. She had brought me back a very beautiful mahogany wood carving of the Christ the Redeemer statue overlooking Guanabara Bay, and she gave it to me there. One of the waiters saw me admiring it, and he went and got a small wooden carving of an Asian person on a keychain and gave it to me. It is hanging on the mirror in our car as a constant reminder of the Sunday Scholars. The Christ carving is in our curio cabinet, along with a few other prize possessions. The Sunday Scholars who now come to the gatherings are Grace Vavra; Courtney Fiechtner; Hannah Hurl and her friend, Cole; Samantha (Stearns) and her husband, Jordan Fash; Samantha Braundmeier; Claire Carmichael; Jeremy Hartl; Andrew Brouwer; and Logan Lundsford.

Just so you know how great the group was and their intellect—they are all college graduates, and among their ranks are an electrical engineer working at Collins Avionics in Cedar Rapids; a fourth-year medical student at Carver College of Medicine in Iowa City; a Drake University Law School graduate; a secondary Spanish teacher in Earlham, Iowa, with special education and English as a second language endorsements; a church administrator and clerk to an Iowa state representative; a neuroscience graduate working in a home for troubled teens; an archeologist now in Tempe, Arizona (formerly in South Korea teaching students English because that was her dream); a financial adviser; and a person working in the insurance industry. What a group we have! Time keeps marching on. There have been weddings, law school graduations, medical school graduations, and more. Our last dinner meeting was at the Bravo Italian Kitchen at Jordan Creek.

The Sunday Scholars has been a very amazing activity and experience for me that only God could have put together. It has also been extremely rewarding. If God is in it, we can't go wrong. We must be willing to follow His leading! We will never know where He will take us if we don't sign up for the trip.

Chapter 44

Momma Margaret White

In 2007, our youngest son, Nick, and his first wife, Kara, decided that they couldn't live together any longer and got a divorce. They had a three-year-old daughter, Abigale ("Abby"), and she was and still is a precious girl. Martha was all distraught with the situation, and I said to her, "Pull yourself together, get your lip off the ground, and remember that Abby needs a solid relationship where she will feel safe and secure. It just might be you!" Abby came to our home quite a bit. If Abby was there on a Sunday, she would go with us to the Presbyterian Church. Floyd and Margaret White always sat in front of us. They were in their upper eighties, and they were *always* friendly. One Sunday during church, Abby colored a picture out of the children's bag. At the end of church, I told Abby that she should give it to Margaret and Floyd. The next time Abby was in church, the Whites told Abby that they had hung the picture on their refrigerator and that we should stop and see it (which we did at some time). That began our friendship with the Whites—a three-year-old little girl and an old couple in their upper eighties.

As time went by, Martha and I found out that all the White children lived away from Oskaloosa. So, the Drosts would take the Whites out for dinner or lunch or would just stop by to visit (and maybe take Abby along). Floyd got older and his health failed, and then he died and left Margaret alone at their home across from Edmundson Park in Oskaloosa. When we would have Abby in church with us, we would take her and Margaret out for lunch afterward. Their favorite place to eat was Applebee's in Pella. The two of them would ride in the back seat. It was amazing to watch the five- or six-year-old girl riding next to a ninety-year-old lady, chattering away and oblivious to anybody else in the car. They really bonded. Margaret had no grandchildren or great-grandchildren living close, so Abby became her Oskaloosa granddaughter.

As time moved on and Abby got older, she started to play the trumpet. We took Abby with her trumpet to Margaret's house on her birthday, and Abby played "Happy Birthday" just outside the front door so the whole neighborhood could hear. When Abby would have a birthday party, we always had to pick up Margaret to attend. One year, the party was held at The Peppertree Restaurant north of Oskaloosa. Grandpa Drost usually got seated next to Abby. This year, the party room was all decorated with nametags by the plates, and Abby showed Margaret her seat next to Abby. Grandpa had been replaced! We continued to go to Applebee's occasionally for a meal, and they were always great friends.

I don't know if anybody can tell when it happened, but Martha and I adopted Margaret as "Momma," and Margaret adopted us as her Oskaloosa kids. Most everybody does what needs to be done for their parents, so we helped Margaret when she needed help. When her children and their spouses would come, they helped too. Martha and I would take Margaret to church and other places. As Margaret got into her upper nineties, she was still living alone in her home across from Edmundson Park, and she was still driving where she wanted to go. We would talk about going to assisted living and other options with her and her family. I kept telling Margaret she would know when it was time to move. Margaret told us in early 2018 that she'd had a near accident driving her car, and she didn't know if she wanted to drive anymore. So, we started talking about assisted living again.

Margaret's daughter, Carolyn (who was Martha's classmate in high school), would come and stay the summer, and they went and looked at Homestead Assisted Living in Oskaloosa. They put Margaret's name on the list. It was decided that Margaret would move to Homestead in September, when Carolyn was in Oskaloosa. Margaret fell and broke her hip at age ninety-nine (not good at that age), and she went to the hospital and had surgery. Then she went to Northern Mahaska Rehabilitation and was there quite some time, including through September and October. She got well enough to go to Homestead, and a room was available. My son, Nick, and I moved the bed, dresser, couch, lamps, and some of Floyd's stained glass into Margaret's new home. At noon on November 7, 2019, while Margaret ate her lunch, Nick and I went to Northern Mahaska with a pickup and loaded up all of Margaret's belongings, including her recliner lift chair, and took them to her room at Homestead. After Margaret's lunch, Martha picked her up and took her to her new home.

Margaret had a very good friend at Homestead named Betty Stanley. Betty's room was across the hall from Margaret's. Betty showed her around and took her to the dining room and other places there; they got together a lot and they told each other good night every evening.

Then in March 2020, COVID-19 struck the country, and all the care facilities were shut down to visitors. The only way to visit Margaret was to look through her window and talk to her on the cell phone—not very convenient. Everybody who has a one hundredth birthday deserves a party, but it is hard to have a party for someone who is quarantined and locked up in a facility. Still, I planned a party with the assistance of Kandis at Homestead. We decided to have the party in the yard in front of Margaret's room and invite people to come. Kandis told me that they would open the window and leave the screen in place if we could keep four feet of distance. We planned to place a table in front of the open window. Margaret had a favorite nurse named Jessica Strasser. I asked Jessica if we could hire her to be with Margaret during the party in case Margaret needed something. Jessica said, "Yes, I would love to do that, but you can't pay me." Sixty people were invited, and the one-hundred-year banner was put in place in front of her window. We ordered cupcakes, and Margaret had a party. Jessica did Margaret's hair, and Margaret looked like a queen through the screen. Just about everybody came to the party. The mayor even came and read a proclamation that it was Margaret White Day. There was a certificate in a frame. It was a great day for Margaret!

Carolyn came for the summer, but she could only visit her mom through the window or take her to a doctor's appointment. It was in October that Homestead finally opened up for visitors, but it was difficult to get in because of all their protocols. Margaret did well in the quarantine, and the whole facility did well in keeping COVID-19 out or to a minimum. In the spring of 2021, Homestead allowed residents to leave the facility for family events or places they wanted to go without having to be restricted to their rooms for ten days.

Margaret's birthday was on May 24. In 2021, when Margaret turned 101, the family planned to take her to her old home across from Edmundson Park for a family birthday party. The Drosts were invited as part of the family. It was a great party with lots of food and talking and catching up on old times. At 3:00, Margaret was worn out and asked to be taken back home. Carolyn was not there for the May party, so I decided Margaret should have another party on July 24, which is the same month as my birthday and Martha's. That way, Carolyn could be there. Margaret has some favorite foods, which we made sure were at the party: Abby's sweet corn on the cob, Casey's cheese pizza, Wendy's chili, Frosty Udder vanilla ice cream, and Jaarsma cherry pie. Of course, Abby was there, but she couldn't play her trumpet because of a shoulder injury, so she and Margaret sat and talked and just ignored everybody else. It was quite the party. Carolyn picked Margaret up and took her home again.

As I mentioned, during the COVID-19 time, people could go visit through the windows (if they had a window). Martha and I would do that, but a couple of times a week, I would drop off a manila envelope with a "love note" written on the outside and photos of things that Margaret would enjoy enclosed. At least twice a week, at 7:00 in the evening, Margaret and the Drosts would talk on the phone. Margaret always enjoyed hearing Martha play the accordion. So in November, when Martha played in church, she took her accordion to Margaret's room and played the same songs with the door open. The Drosts found out later that the Thanksgiving and Christmas music Martha played was heard through most of the facility.

Margaret turned 102 and celebrated with a birthday party on May 24, 2022. The party was attended by her family in the meeting room at Homestead Assisted Living. They served her favorite meal of burgers and baked beans, and she wore the birthday girl hat. It was a fun time. On July 24, Carolyn picked up Margaret and took her to her old home across from Edmundson Park, and we had the July birthday party. Abby was there and played "Happy Birthday" a couple of times, and we had Casey's pizza, Frosty Udder ice cream, and cherry pie. Of course, we had Abby's sweet corn too, and Margaret ate every kernel off a big ear with her own teeth. ("It ain't sweet corn if you cut it off!")

A couple of weeks later, there was an outbreak of COVID-19 at Homestead, and Margaret got it. She passed on to be with Jesus just three weeks after such a great party.

Momma Margaret White

Momma Margaret with Abby (her Oskaloosa granddaughter).

Chapter 45

Public Service: Bringing the Vietnam Wall to Oskaloosa

I trust that as you have read this book you've seen that I have never felt like it was unfair for me to have been drafted into the Army and taken a trip for a few months to the Republic of Vietnam. I was naïve, yes. I have told lots of folks that I was fortunate to have gone to Nam as a sergeant and served there, and I was able to come home healthy and "halfway normal." I was twenty-three years old when I got to Nam, and I had my twenty-fourth birthday there, so I was older than most (statistics show that the average age of servicemen in Nam was around twenty). It was obvious that the older personnel got along better with the separation and the stress; a lot of the younger soldiers got hooked on alcohol or drugs. As an information tidbit, one could buy a cap of H (heroin) just outside the compound for fifty cents, and the beer was free when you were in a rear area. A lot of soldiers came home with some real problems, such as being young and having emotional issues, being alcoholic, or being addicted to drugs at the worst.

In Washington, D.C., there is the Vietnam War Memorial, which is a granite wall with all the names of those who died in Vietnam during the war. The names are arranged on the wall starting in the center top panel, where you'll find the names of the first who died. From there, the names move outward by the time of death. To follow

Public Service: Bringing the Vietnam Wall to Oskaloosa

the sequence, you must go down the center top panel to the bottom, then move to the right panels all the way to the end of the wall, and then start at the left end and come back to the center. There are 58,318 names, and it is called "The Wall That Heals."

The Vietnam Veterans Memorial Fund has a half-size traveling wall that can be brought to local venues. Martha and I helped our local American Legion post and Veterans of Foreign Wars post bring the traveling "Wall That Heals" to Oskaloosa. The wall travels in a fifty-three-foot semitrailer. When it's in location, the sides open up to a small Vietnam War museum. All 58,318 names are on the wall in the same order as the wall in Washington. A computer is provided to find the name of a relative or a friend who died in Vietnam. The location is open to the public twenty-four hours a day from the time the wall is set up to the time it's taken down. The organization has found that a lot of troubled vets come during the night when there is nobody around, and we found this to be true.

The display was set up at the Southern Iowa Fairgrounds from July 8–11, 2010. We decided to put a wreath in front of the twelve panels where there are names of the twelve soldiers from Mahaska County who died in Vietnam. Mulch walkways were constructed fifteen feet in front of the panels, so mourners could be left alone by the wall as others passed by. I was in charge of the setup and teardown. There was never a project that was easier to get helpers with than this one (there was too much help!). Martha and I had provided some funds, but there was a lot of work to make this project a success. One always asks, "Was it worth all the time, energy, and money?"

About an hour before the opening ceremony, I went out to check the display and make sure the area was prepared. There was a lady kneeling in front of one of the panels by a wreath. I went over and spoke to the lady and said something to the effect of, "There has to be someone special on the wall." And the lady responded, "Yes, my son." During the ensuing conversation, the lady said her son went missing in action in 1968 as a helicopter pilot with the rank of warrant officer. His body wasn't recovered until around 2005. The lady asked if I would like to see some photos, so we walked to her car and she showed me pictures that had been developed from the film in her son's recovered camera. The photos showed her son at the controls of the helicopter he was piloting at the time. She also had photos of her son's burial in Arlington National Cemetery, with the flag-draped coffin on the horse-drawn caisson.

So yes, all the hard work, time, and dollars were paid in full before the event even started. It never got better than that. Her son had paid the ultimate sacrifice, but this lady paid the full price as well. After the event, several Vietnam vets came and expressed appreciation for being able to visit the wall in Oskaloosa. It really did provide healing for them.

Here are my closing remarks from the Vietnam Memorial Wall ceremony in Oskaloosa:

"Good evening, I am Carl Drost and a Vietnam veteran.

"I have lived the American Dream. So, what is that? The American Dream is a little boy (or girl) born to parents who care for them—who don't have much money, but it doesn't matter. It is having parents who see that their children are educated: a rural country school, a public junior high and senior high, and a college education. You work and you graduate debt-free with a knowledge that God had a plan for your life.

"It is marrying a young lady, and together you have dreams and aspirations of a life together. It is moving to a new town and starting a teaching career and loving young people. It is being the junior class sponsor and setting up for the prom and not knowing that a young lady is pushing a darning needle into your rump (or hanky), and not feeling pain, then getting a pair of red socks before you leave. It is sitting in front of the TV watching the first National Draft Lottery and seeing your birthday get drawn out as number ninety-eight. It is having to decide with your wife if you should continue teaching school (and be inside the rest of your life) or get drafted. They call them 'open doors,' I guess. It is being convinced that the Army will find real value in your education and abilities, and then finding out they don't care since you are a draftee. It is having KP (or kitchen patrol) duty on graduation day. It is being sent to Vietnam with a six-month-old daughter left at home. In General Tom Franks' museum in Hobart, Oklahoma, a plaque says: 'We went to Vietnam as boys, we came home as men!'

"The American Dream is to believe that God has a plan for you and that God will provide open doors and opportunities for you. The American Dream is to live your life so one day a total stranger comes to see you at your place of employment and tells you that his company wants you to be their dealer. It is the American Dream that a young Vietnam veteran who has no money can find a person with money who believes in him. Then the veteran and a friendly banker become partners and open a business. It is the American Dream that the business becomes successful and grows and expands. The American Dream. Part of the American Dream is the RESPONSIBILITY part. They say, 'Where much is given, much is expected.' That requires that we give back to the community and the area. I think part of the dream is Little League, soccer, basketball, the school board, the recreation board, and the list goes on.

"This is what makes America great—when people decide we are responsible to make our place a better place. I am getting to be an old guy, and I guess we begin to philosophize, but the veterans who served went willingly to defend our right to the American Dream. We have the freedom to go out and do about anything our hearts and minds want to do. The veterans preserved that right for us. Again, thanks for serving and thanks for visiting the wall."

I have always been very thankful that the Vietnam experience had no lasting emotional effects on me, but I have always had sympathy for those who did have lasting effects on their lives. I am thankful to God for being with me through it all and for all the opportunities given to me after my return from across the pond.

Conclusion

I hope you have enjoyed reading this book about the events of a life well-lived and that you have learned some lessons that somebody else (meaning me) learned the hard way. I hope you have seen how God has led me in life and that it is not what is on the outside that counts in the long run, but what we can instill on the inside of others. The Bible tells us that what we give to God and to others will be returned to us many times over—maybe not in money but in other blessings that only God can give.

Here are some Bible verses I'd like to leave you with:

- **Psalm 112:5**: "Good will come to those who are generous and lend freely, who conduct their affairs with justice."

- **Acts 20:35:** "In everything I did, I showed you that by this kind of hard work we must help the weak, remembering the words the Lord Jesus himself said: 'It is more blessed to give than to receive.'"

- **Luke 6:38:** "Give, and it will be given to you. A good measure, pressed down, shaken together and running over, will be poured into your lap. For with the measure you use, it will be measured to you."

And so I say to give back. My accountant told me several years ago in one of our discussions at tax time, "Generous people always get ahead!"

Thanks for reading my book. My prayer is that it will help you live for Christ in a corrupt world.

www.ingramcontent.com/pod-product-compliance
Lightning Source LLC
Chambersburg PA
CBHW041312240426
43669CB00023B/2961